WE
SURVIVED
GENOCIDE IN RWANDA

WE
SURVIVED

GENOCIDE IN RWANDA

kigali
GENOCIDE MEMORIAL

in association with

AEGIS
THE GENOCIDE PREVENTION ORGANISATION

WE SURVIVED
GENOCIDE IN RWANDA

Edited by Wendy Whitworth

Published in Great Britain by
Quill Press
in association with The Aegis Trust
The Exchange, 38 Water Lane, Newark
Nottinghamshire, UK. NG24 1HA

British Library Catalogue in Publication Data
A catalogue record for this book is available from the British Library

ISBN   0-9543001-7-3
       978-0-9543001-7-3

Design and artwork by Glen Powell Graphic Design
Printed and bound by Jellyfish Print Solutions, Swanmore

Dedicated to the million men, women and children of Rwanda

whose stories are not told,

because they did not survive to testify

what they saw and suffered.

CONTENTS

Contents

Contents

Foreword

This book is not an easy read. But there are times when we should listen to the hard truth because it forms the start of understanding.

For those who were not there, it is near impossible to comprehend the enormity and brutality of what happens during genocide. The stories in this book bring us a little closer, providing a glimpse into a period in Rwanda when, for three months, values most people take for granted – such as the respect for human life – were crushed as the Government lifted moral constraints and made killing an obligation, mobilising the population to destroy all Tutsis and any Hutus who did not share the genocidal ideas.

These stories remind us that the cost of genocide is, above all, a human one. Those who share their painful stories with us in these pages are some of the few who slipped through the net of total destruction in Rwanda. They are not statistics. They have names – as did their families who did not survive. They had hopes and dreams that were shattered.

They were ordinary people, caught up in extraordinary circumstances. Their loved ones were taken from them in a cruel manner. Years later, the void of loss is not filled. Yet a huge burden is placed on them – for the sake of the future, there must be unity and reconciliation.

From a distance, it is sometimes easy to form quick judgements about the need for reconciliation, unity and peace. The survivors in this book express mixed feelings about the future. They all know it is important to look ahead and to strive towards unity. But reading this book, we begin to appreciate that this is no simple task.

For example, how does a nine-year-old, who finds her parents' bloated bodies in the living room after their execution, stay sane, when every day during her teenage years she is reminded that she does not have parents as she struggles her way through school? (Manzi Gaudence Uwera, pp. 256-262).

That these survivors are able to hope for the future and look to building a new Rwanda must command the respect of everyone.

Finally, each of these stories is an indictment of the international community for its failure to stop mass murder. They are a reminder of the consequences when world leaders do not uphold moral and international obligations to protect those at risk of genocide.

James M. Smith
Chief Executive, Aegis Trust

ACKNOWLEDGEMENTS

We Survived: Genocide in Rwanda could not have been compiled without the effective collaboration and cooperation of a great many people, both in Rwanda and the UK.

Warm thanks go firstly to Rwandan genocide survivor Beata Uwazaninka, who selected and compiled the testimonies; to Wendy Whitworth, Publishing Manager of the Aegis Trust, who shaped and edited them; and to Glen Powell, who designed the final volume.

Many thanks also go to the members of the documentation team in Kigali, who all played an important role in creating this book of testimonies and without whose fundamental work it could not have been produced. Thanks to Isaac Mugabe, interviewer; to the transcribing team: Martin Niwenshuti, Seleman Karangwa, Augustin Uwamahoro, Yves Rudasingwa, Arthur Uwisabo, Valentine Mukarwego, Claudine Nzirabatinyi, Immaculee Mukandori and Vestine Mukansanga; to the team of translators: Coco Rulinda, Avit Kayumba, Doreen Kamikazi, Richard Mutabazi, Liban Mugabo, Olivier Muhikira, Cassius Muhikira, Lyse Nyirarukundo, Nicole Mihayo, Joan Uwimana, Cathy Murore, Donat Byarugaga, Dany Mbesherubusa and Eric Ngangare; to the acquisition coordinator, Manu Kabahizi; assistant coordinator, Liliane Rutera; cameraman, Potin Kabahizi; and photographers, Nathanael Boarer and Yves Kamuronsi.

Finally – and most importantly – heartfelt thanks go to all the survivors of the genocide in Rwanda who have trusted us with their stories.

James M. Smith

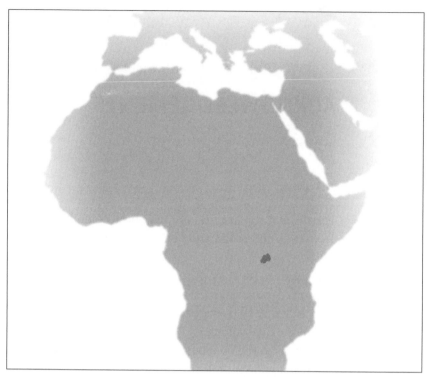

Rwanda, Africa

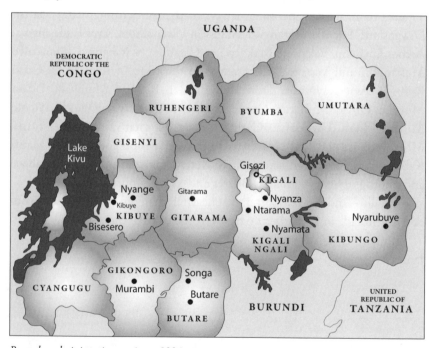

Rwanda, administrative provinces, 1994

Kigali districts, 1994

Glossary

AERG	*Association des Etudiants et Elèves Rescapés du Génocide*, Association of Student Survivors of the Genocide.
APROSOMA	political party: *Association pour la Promotion Sociale des Masses*
AVEGA	Association of Genocide Widows in Rwanda
CDR	political party: *Coalition pour la Défense de la République*
CND	*Conseil National pour le Développement*, parliament building
CPR	*Conseil Protestant au Rwanda*
ETO	school: *Ecole Technique Officielle*
FARG	*Fonds d'Assistance aux Rescapés du Génocide*, fund for the victims of genocide
Gacaca	'judgement on the grass', traditional Rwandan local courts used to try some of those accused of crimes in the genocide.
Ibuka	Rwandan survivors' association
Inkotanyi	'fierce warriors'; the Rwandan Patriotic Front Tutsi soldiers
Interahamwe	'those who stand or fight together', Hutu militia group
Inyenzi	cockroaches, derogatory term for the Tutsis

MDR	political party: *Mouvement Démocratique Républicain*
MRND	political party: *Mouvement Révolutionnaire National pour le Développement*
Opération Turquoise	French-led operation to establish a 'safe zone' in the prefectures of Gikongoro, Cyangugu and Kibuye
Parmehutu	political party: *Parti du mouvement de l'émancipation des Bahutu*
PL	political party: *Parti Libéral*
RADER	political party: *Rassemblement Démocratique Rwandais*
RPF	Rwandan Patriotic Front
RTLM	*Radio-Télévision Libre des Mille Collines*, used for Hutu extremist propaganda
UNAMIR	United Nations Assistance Mission for Rwanda
UNAR	political party: *Union Nationale Rwandaise*

Charred remains of a Rwandan identity card, 2004 © Aegis Trust

Historical Background

Roots

By the time of the genocide in 1994, the media in the West often portrayed Rwanda as a land of warring tribes. But this was not so. Indeed, the extreme ethnic division is a relatively recent development. The Hutus, Tutsis and smaller Twa minority had lived in Rwanda for many centuries. The Hutus were largely agricultural people, the Tutsis were predominantly cattle-herders and the Twa hunter-gatherers. Over the centuries, much intermarriage had occurred and the ethnic groups were no longer completely distinct. All Rwandans spoke the same language, Kinyarwanda, and there was no significant difference in religion or culture.

Ethnic differences were apparent in the late 1800s, during the reign of King Kigeri IV Rwabugiri. He centralised power and developed structures that allowed a Tutsi elite to govern. There was a social and class framework akin to Europe's medieval feudal structures, though arguably more complex.

All the small differences were magnified and exploited during the colonial era.

Before 1959, no massacres took place between the Hutus and Tutsis. In fact, hostility over territory was more likely to occur within competing factions or clans of the same group than between the Hutus and Tutsis.

Rwanda became a German colony in 1895 and remained so until the First World War. The Germans retreated in 1916, leaving Rwanda and neighbouring Burundi under Belgian control. The relative harmony that had existed between Hutus and Tutsis was soon eroded after the European colonists arrived.

As elsewhere in the colonies, early explorers and anthropologists developed ideas in Rwanda that would promote racism and discrimination. Because the Tutsis were generally taller and thinner than many Hutus, they suggested that the Tutsis originated from a superior race in the Nile valley, who were more like the European whites. Compared to the 'Bantu' Hutu majority, the Tutsis were considered more intelligent and hard-working.

It served the colonisers' purpose to maintain a Tutsi King and create a ruling class. Although only a minority derived benefit from this elevated status, it was generally the Tutsis, not the Hutus, who were given privileged positions. The Belgian authorities formalised division between the ethnic groups, introducing identity cards to Rwanda in 1932. When the cards were issued, 15 per cent were identified as Tutsis, 84 per cent as Hutus and 1 per cent Twa.

In years to come, this ethnic identity determined much of an individual's opportunity in Belgian-run Rwanda. By 1957, most of the school places, the posts in the country's civil service and nearly all chiefs and sub-chiefs were Tutsis.

The Church, politics and race

During the 1920s, the Church became the dominant institution in Rwanda. Initially, the Church endorsed the official racism favouring the Tutsis.

Towards the end of colonial rule, however, the Church reversed its position to favour the Hutus. Mgr. Perraudin, Apostolic Vicar of Kabgayi, was strongly pro-Hutu and encouraged the drafting of the 'Hutu Manifesto' by Grégoire Kayibanda in 1957. This document demanded that political authority should be transferred to the Hutu majority.

Political landscape

Following the death in 1959 of the Tutsi ruler King Rudahigwa, there was a violent uprising of radical Hutus, who killed thousands of Tutsis. Many Tutsis fled to neighbouring states for refuge, especially to Uganda.

Three years later, in 1962, Rwanda gained independence from its Belgian rulers. Its first Government (The First Republic) was led by Hutu extremist Grégoire Kayibanda, founder of the Parmehutu, a "movement for emancipation of the Hutu ethnic group". Democratically elected in 1961, Kayibanda promoted Hutu consciousness and unity.

Rwanda became a highly centralised state with a single-party system. During the 1960s, Tutsis in exile attempted to regain power or overthrow the Hutu Government, and in response massacres of Tutsis were once more carried out. Again, thousands of Tutsis fled Rwanda in order to escape death. The notion of an 'internal enemy' developed during this period and the word *Inyenzi*, (cockroach) was coined to identify the Tutsi population.

Against a background of further discrimination against the Tutsis, the Hutu General Juvénal Habyarimana seized power in a *coup d'état* in July 1973 and restored a degree of order. Rwanda was again a one-party state, with Habyarimana legitimising only his own party, the *Mouvement Révolutionnaire National pour le Développement* (MRND). He declared that all Rwandans were members of his party.

The regime's stability attracted development aid from the West and the general environment was relatively free of unrest or state-sponsored persecution. Then, in 1986, coffee prices collapsed. As the economy deteriorated, the ruling Hutu elite – the *Akazu* – tightened its grip on available wealth and political power.

At the same time, international donors began demanding financial and democratic accountability. In June 1990, following a meeting with President François Mitterrand of France, Habyarimana declared that a multi-party system would be established.

In 1991 several new political parties were formed, including the *Mouvement Démocratique Républicain* (MDR), a party containing both extremist and moderate Hutu elements; the *Parti Social Démocrate* (PSD), a consistently moderate Hutu party; and the *Coalition pour la Défense de la République* (CDR), formed by Hutu radicals linked with death squads who had begun to train for, and carry out, massacres of Tutsi civilians.

Habyarimana's MRND was responsible for establishing the *Interahamwe*, a flamboyant Hutu youth militia that gained enormous popularity. Advocating 'Hutu Power' and 'Hutuness' at the expense of Tutsi lives, their message was reinforced and spread by an extremist media.

RPF invasion, 1990

Seven hundred thousand Tutsis were exiled between 1959 and 1973 in neighbouring countries. These Tutsi refugees had children who were largely educated in English and fully integrated into Ugandan society, with many joining Museveni's army fighting to end the tyranny of the Obote II Government. Despite negotiations, they were prevented from returning to Rwanda. They formed the Rwandan Patriotic Front (RPF) in 1987. Although Tutsi refugees were naturally attracted to the RPF, it was not founded on an ethnic basis. It was an opposition movement and rebel army that included any Rwandan who wanted to remove the extremist Government from power and restore equality. Many moderate Hutus in exile also joined the RPF's struggle.

On 1 October 1990, the RPF invaded northern Rwanda. This civil war resulted in the internal displacement of 300,000 people, both Hutus and Tutsis, many of whom were held in internal refugee camps. Habyarimana used the country's right to self-defence from an 'invading army' and consolidated his diminishing support internally and externally in his bid to fight the war.

Every Tutsi civilian in Rwanda was branded a member of the RPF's 'fifth column', as the Rwandan Government's talk of Tutsi conspiracies deepened ethnic divisions. French forces were sent to support the Rwandan army's defence of Kigali. The French military assisted in training paramilitary groups, which later carried out Habyarimana's genocidal policy.

Massacres of Tutsis were carried out regularly from October 1990 to February 1994. None of these were spontaneous outbreaks of violence; no one was brought to account for them. Death squads such as the 'Zero Network' were formed in 1991 with the close cooperation of Habyarimana.

Peace process

After the RPF invasion in 1990, efforts were made to resolve the civil war. Belgium and France, in particular, pressured President Habyarimana to negotiate with his opponents. Reluctantly, he joined with opposition parties to form a coalition Government in April 1992. The coalition then agreed to start talks with the RPF in Arusha, facilitated by Tanzania's President Julius Nyerere.

The Arusha talks were thorough in addressing the issues of the civil war. It was hoped that power-sharing, ethnic integration of the armed forces, resettlement of displaced persons and arrangements for elections would lead to peace and stability. A ceasefire, agreed in August 1992, collapsed two months later. It was then strengthened and signed again in August 1993.

The peace agreements worked on the premise that once the civil war between the Government and RPF was resolved, then the conflict between Hutus and Tutsis would also end. They did not take into account that the greatest threat was the growing ethnic division, not the war. Solutions to this underlying problem were more difficult to find. Hutu radicals increasingly hardened their resolve against the peace process. Concerned that the Arusha Accords would lead to true power-sharing, 'Hutu Power' groups continued to massacre Tutsi civilians.

Although Arusha was a well thought-out initiative with short-term success, its consequences were in fact the opposite of what was intended. In their quest for democracy and ethnic equity, the negotiations persuaded the Hutu ruling elite (*Akazu*) that unless it took decisive action, its days in power would be numbered.

Certain Hutu Power factions found any loss of power unacceptable. The conclusion the *Akazu* reached led to the planning of the all-out extermination of the Tutsis and other opponents. Within this fertile ground, the Hutu movement used the well-intentioned peace process to deepen the furrow of ethnic division, in which they rapidly sowed the seeds of mass murder.

Propaganda

Propaganda became an important tool in conditioning the Hutu majority to accept and participate in atrocities against the Tutsis. *Radio Télévision Libre des Mille Collines* (RTLM) was a popular radio station, initiated by members of the Government to spread hate propaganda. Its popular tone masked its highly inflammatory message. When the genocide was underway, RTLM was used to incite hatred, give instructions and justify the killings.

More than 20 newspapers and journals incited hatred towards the Tutsis. *Kangura*, one of the leading propaganda papers, suggested that the Hutus needed to prepare themselves because the Tutsis were planning a war that would "leave no survivors". As early as December 1990, *Kangura* had published the "Hutu Ten Commandments," which stated that any Hutu interacting with Tutsi neighbours and friends was a traitor.

Early warning on the eve of genocide

A sequence of events took place prior to the genocide, which demonstrates the process underway:

1993

21 October   The Hutu president of neighbouring Burundi, Melchior Ndadaye, was assassinated in October 1993 in an attempted *coup*. In the resulting bloodbath, around 50,000 Hutus and Tutsis were murdered in tit-for-tat reprisal massacres. Thousands of Hutu refugees fled to Rwanda, Zaire and Tanzania; and Tutsis congregated in towns and camps where they could be protected by the army. President Habyarimana of Rwanda used the event to demonstrate that the Tutsis could not be trusted. Whatever action was to be taken against the Tutsis would be disguised as an act of pre-emptive self-defence.

3 December Rwandan army officers informed the United Nations (UN) of a "Machiavellian Plan" to orchestrate massacres throughout Rwanda.

27 December A Belgian intelligence report stated that "the *Interahamwe* are armed to the teeth... waiting for the right moment to act."

1994

11 January General Roméo Dallaire, Commander of UN forces in Rwanda, faxed UN headquarters with information provided by a Hutu Power informer, who disagreed with the planned anti-Tutsi extermination and the registration of all Tutsis living in Kigali. The informer reported that there were 1,700 trained men in Kigali, all armed. They could kill 1,000 people in 20 minutes. Dallaire's request for permission to take immediate preventative action was denied.

17 January The UN Special Representative reported special training camps for militia.

27 January *Radio Mille Collines* broadcast a call for the Hutu to "defend themselves".

January Human Rights Watch published information on arms entering the country, directly and indirectly, from France.

February The Papal Nuncio gave the Italian Ambassador two lists showing the Tutsis who were to be killed.

2 March A ruling party official disclosed that "if things go badly, the Hutus will massacre them [the Tutsis] without pity."

March Belgian military intelligence was informed by the Rwandan military that if the Arusha Peace Accords were implemented, they were ready to liquidate the Tutsis.

4 April Hutu Power leader Théoneste Bagasora informed UN officials that "the only plausible solution for Rwanda would be the elimination of the Tutsis."

These early warnings were clear, but the international community either had a problem comprehending the scale of what was planned, or lacked the political will to protect those under threat of their existence.

President Habyarimana was in further discussions about the Arusha Accords with neighbouring heads of state. Returning to Kigali airport on 6 April 1994, his plane was hit by ground-to-air missiles, killing all on board, including Burundi's President Cyprien Ntaryamira.

Genocide

President Habyarimana's plane was shot down on 6 April at 8.30 p.m. Kigali time. Prime Minister Agathe Uwilingiyimana and other moderate ministers were immediately barricaded in their homes. Within an hour of the plane crash, Hutu militia had set up hundreds of roadblocks around the capital city to stop Tutsis or moderate Hutus escaping. Prominent Tutsis who had been on death lists were killed immediately by some 1,500 elite members of the Rwandan Armed Forces.

Moderate Hutus were the first to be targeted because the Government intended to remove all opposition in order to proceed with the genocide without hindrance. On 7 April, Prime Minister Uwilingiyimana sought protection with the UN. The Prime Minister and her husband were found by the Presidential Guard and both were murdered. The ten Belgian UN peacekeepers protecting her were removed, tortured and shot. This led Belgium to recall the rest of its troops, leaving the remaining UN force pitifully weak.

In parallel with the radical Hutu leaders' primary objective – the extermination of all Tutsis – the first wave of killing was instigated to secure their power base. They took only a few days to make their position safe and their targets included:

1. Moderate Government members and opposition party leaders;

2. Moderate Hutus of significance;

3. Critical voices within Rwandan society, including journalists, jurists and human rights activists.

Théodore Sindikubwabo became President. Jean Kambanda was appointed Prime Minister. From then on, Kambanda effectively took control of the genocide.

By 11 April – five days after Habyarimana's death – 20,000 Tutsi and moderate Hutus had already been killed in Kigali. From 12 April, the focus of killing was on the Tutsis. Large-scale massacres took place in churches, hospitals, schools and village streets. The Tutsis were made to dig large graves and were buried alive. Many sought shelter in churches. Grenades were thrown in; then the killers would walk in and shoot or hack the wounded.

Machetes, clubs with nails, axes, knives, poles, grenades and guns were used. Achilles tendons were cut to leave victims writhing in agony, awaiting their fate, immobilised. Guns were available but rarely used, as they were considered a painless means of killing.

The genocide was to be complete; no survivors were to remain. Fields, forests, swamps and hills were all searched for escapees and survivors. The genocide started in Kigali, but quickly spread through the network of Prefects, Burgomasters and local administrators. The efficient system of local government and the chain of command from central government worked effectively. Threats were issued to all non-compliant Hutus, followed by the killing of a number of Prefects, Burgomasters, priests, nuns, professionals and officials who disobeyed the instructions.

Most Rwandans were members of the Catholic Church or other Christian denominations. The spiritual and moral leadership of the clergy was important in conditioning the response of Christian people to the incitement to kill. There were a small number of clergy who carried out heroic acts of goodness. However, the Christian leadership failed even to make a clear denunciation of the genocide until it was too late.

Teachers betrayed their own students and in some cases even murdered them. Doctors often refused to treat wounded Tutsis or dismissed them prematurely. Hospitals were known hunting grounds for the killers, who knew that injured escapees were likely to go there.

The world stands by
International community

The reaction of the international community was typified by its evacuation of foreign nationals at the beginning of the genocide, the evacuation of Belgian UN peacekeepers and the reluctance of national governments and international bodies to commit resources to relieve the suffering of the victims. General Roméo Dallaire, head of the UN Assistance Mission in Rwanda (UNAMIR), cabled New York shortly after the plane crash and said, "Give me the means and I can do more."

Dallaire calculated that he needed 5,000 troops to contain the potential violence that could erupt. At that time, he had 1,260 troops under his command. On 21 April, the UN Security Council passed a Resolution stating that it was appalled at the ensuing large scale of violence in Rwanda, which had resulted in the deaths of thousands of innocent civilians, including women and children. However, the same meeting voted to reduce the UNAMIR force to 270 personnel and to limit its mandate.

Two weeks into the conflict, the Red Cross identified it as a tragedy on a scale rarely witnessed. At this time, Rwanda had a seat on the UN Security Council and was even able to vote on issues pertaining to Rwanda, while its own Government was carrying out the genocide. Secretary-General Boutros-Ghali realised a week after the decision to scale down forces that the focus had to be on stopping massacres, not brokering a ceasefire.

On 17 May, the Security Council agreed to establish UNAMIR II with 5,500 men and the mandate to use all necessary force. It also imposed an arms embargo on Rwanda. A critical feature of UNAMIR II was the provision by the United States of armoured personnel carriers (APCs). The transfer of the 50 vehicles became bogged down in leasing, shipping, painting and sticker arrangements, to the extent that it took more than one month for them to arrive in Uganda, which had the nearest large airport. By the time the UN reinforcements arrived in Rwanda to stop the genocide, it was already over. The Rwandan Patriotic Army had liberated Kigali on 4 July 1994 and halted the systematic killings.

The only international soldiers who did arrive in Rwanda before the genocide ended were French military carrying out 'Opération Turquoise', ostensibly to create a 'safe area' between the conflicting sides. France had played an active role in arming and training the Rwandan armed forces during the civil war, and many members of the Hutu militia saw the French as allies. Initially introduced to stop the killing, 'Opération Turquoise' provided a gateway into Zaire for the Hutus – including killers – who were fleeing the advancing RPF.

Awareness of this failure to stop the genocide resulted in the strong, if sometimes uncoordinated, response from international aid agencies to cholera epidemics that hit Hutu refugee camps in Zaire immediately afterwards. The convention of providing relief for refugees (among them killers in the genocide) served to salve a Western conscience that was troubled by the absence of political response.

War or genocide?

Many analysts, journalists and policy-makers saw the killings as the result of a civil war between the Rwandan Government and the RPF. In reality, when the genocide began in the early hours of 7 April, there had been no military engagement. The RPF resumed fighting in order to stop the massacres. The move by Hutu leaders to kill a million unarmed civilians was a conscious decision distinct from – and preceding – subsequent military engagement.

The Organisation for African Unity (OAU) report on the Rwandan genocide states: "Instinctively it was taken for granted that the killings were the by-product of the war. Let a neutral UN help stop the fighting and the massacres of innocents would stop. Those closest to the scene understood and tried to convey a different reality: an outright genocide had been launched that was quite independent of the war."

War is always dreadful and tragic; and the war in Rwanda was no different. Rwanda has orphans, widows, bereaved parents and spouses on all sides. Much innocent life was lost and many people – including Hutus who fled after the genocide – perished in the camps in the D.R.Congo. They are also remembered as part of the tragedy of this period. However, because it was the confusion between war and genocide that misled commentators and policy-makers in the international community, a distinction is made today between remembering the victims of genocide and the victims of war. This does not lessen individual loss and suffering; many live with sorrow for different reasons and it is they who have the almost impossible task of rebuilding their lives and country at the same time. This is one of Rwanda's challenges today. It is a testament to Rwandan determination to live once again as a nation.

Women and children

Women and children were a specified target of the *genocidaires* for murder, rape and mutilation, so as to ensure that a new generation of Tutsis would not emerge. Tutsi women were systematically raped, frequently by known HIV-infected males, and either killed or spared to suffer on another occasion. Hutu women in mixed marriages were raped as a punishment.

Women and children were not only victims of the genocide, but also perpetrators. Children were frequently forced to participate, often by killing their friends or neighbours. Hutu and Tutsi women were also forced to kill their Tutsi children.

Heroes and friends

Despite overwhelming terror, fear, mass murder and unimaginable horror, some people were a ray of light in the darkness. When it seemed that all sense of humanity was lost, a great many Rwandans showed extraordinary courage. These are the heroes of the genocide – those who showed some humanity and consideration for their neighbours while looking death in the face.

Gisimba, for example, who saved over 100 people in his father's orphanage; Yahaya and his daughters who confronted the *Interahamwe* to save a little girl's life and allowed his yard to be used as an escape route; and Gitabita Nyirantaba, a nurse who saved a boy who had dragged himself to Kibuye hospital. Stories like these will form a volume of their own in this series of testimonies by the people who were there during the genocide.

All around Rwanda there were people who tried to defend themselves, most notably in the hills of Bisesero, where the men organised themselves and fought back with sticks and spears against guns. While they were fighting in the hills, their women and children were raped and killed in the villages. Few of the men in Bisesero survived, but they resisted for weeks and died with honour.

While most of the international community left the country, there were a few who stayed. There was little they could do without support, but their solidarity and heroism made a difference. The UN soldiers who stayed behind under Lt. General Roméo Dallaire's command and Philippe Gaillard and his staff on the International Committee of the Red Cross were unable to stop the tide, but nonetheless tried to do what they could. The rest of the world abandoned them.

James M. Smith

Anne-Marie, 2004 © Aegis Trust

ANNE-MARIE

A sword in my heart

Before the genocide

Born in 1967, I grew up in a loving home with my parents, two brothers and five sisters. In 1990, I married a man named Jean-Marie Vianey Bucyana. We had our first child in Kicukiro, a boy we named Patrick. After his birth, the authorities started persecuting the Tutsis. They arrested my husband, accusing him of being an RPF [Rwandan Patriotic Front] accomplice. He was jailed for two weeks and after his release was put under tight surveillance. This troubled him greatly, so he left us and fled to Kibuye. The authorities used to come looking for him at our house, but he was never there.

One day in 1993, the *Interahamwe* [Hutu militia] came and knocked on my door, demanding to know his whereabouts. I told them I didn't know where he was. They searched the whole house and when they couldn't find him, they began looting our possessions. One of the men said he wanted to rape me, but I screamed. The others said, "That's not what we came for." So they beat me up and left. Though I had shouted for help, in those days nobody would come. Even when people were being hacked by machetes in their homes, no one would intervene.

After this incident, I called my husband and he told me I had to leave, but said I had to make it look as though I was only going on a short trip. Leaving our possessions and livestock with our maid, I took my son Patrick and went to live with him in Kibuye. Later, in 1993, I gave birth to my second child, a boy we named Iradukunda, meaning 'God loves us.' My husband and I opened a small restaurant. Then we closed the restaurant and sold wholesale beer and sacks of beans. My husband also worked as a construction contractor. This was where we were in April 1994 when Habyarimana's plane was shot down.

The genocide

Immediately after hearing the news, soldiers surrounded our home; we lived close to a military camp. We thought they just wanted money. My husband tried to get us a room in the Eden Lodge [a hotel], but the soldiers would not allow us to leave. When the killings began, they came and took my husband away. Shortly after, I could hear those who took him away singing that they had killed a 'cockroach', and I knew he was dead. One soldier came up to the house. I was sitting with my baby boy on my lap. He grabbed the child and threw him against the wall. He died from the impact. I ran to pick up my baby's body, but the soldier threatened me and told me to lie down. And there he raped me. I don't really have the words to explain all that he did to me. At some point he heard a commotion and ran off.

One of our neighbours was a Tutsi woman, married to a Hutu. (I knew her as 'Mama Diane', the mother of Diane.) Her husband was away, but his Hutu friends took her to a parked bus where they used to gather, and they took me as well. Once on the bus, they realized that it would probably be searched by the authorities and decided to take her back home, saying that nobody would widow a 'Hutu Power' member. At that time, nobody was killing the wives of Hutu men. They took her back and left me alone on the bus.

When night came it was raining heavily. The watchman guarding the bus, a man named Nyandwi, told me that he wanted to have sex with me. He said that I was to give birth to his child, to be named Iyandengeye Nyandwi (Nyandwi the protector). I didn't care if he killed me or not. I asked him, "So is this your way of helping me?" Then there was shouting from looters and he ran off. After he left, I got off the bus and slept beneath a car.

At about three in the morning, I walked to a neighbour's home, but she told me to leave, saying my presence would get her killed. Closer to my house, I saw a small bush. I thought it would be a good place to hide. I struggled to get into the bush, but it was so hard. Then I thought, "Even the bush will not accept me." I found one spot on the side that was hollow. I was wearing a red T-shirt, so I covered myself with leaves and brush.

I had left my son Patrick with the maid at my Tutsi neighbour's house (the woman who had gone on the bus with me). When my son cried in the middle of the night, the maid complained, "Other 'snakes' have been killed, why do I have to look after this one? I am going to give it away." When I heard that, I wondered why I was hiding anyway. My husband was gone, my baby was gone, why should my eldest be killed all alone? It would be better to die with him than to leave him lonely in death. So I went to knock at the woman's door. A man named Sediri saw me and yelled that of all the people they were looking for, I was the only one missing. My Hutu neighbour begged him to pardon me. She gave him money and a radio. The man said that even if he didn't get to kill me, someone else would.

When Zacharya, a colleague of my husband's, heard that I was still alive, he came on a motorbike to take me away. I didn't know that he had been involved in my husband's murder and thought I would be safe with him. People were telling the maid to keep my son, so that if I died, maybe he would live. But she refused, saying that everyone knew my son, because his father had been popular in the neighbourhood. So I had to take him with me.

Zacharya had taken many houses from Tutsis and he took us to one of them in Safi Cyumbati. There were three separate units in the house, with three separate doors. In one there was a girl, in another there were *Interahamwe* and he lived in the third. He put me in the unit with the *Interahamwe* and then he locked his room, where he kept all the machines and equipment he had looted. Then he left, telling the Chairman (head of the local administrative cell), "I would like to come back when you have cleared away the rubbish" – meaning that he would like to return when they had killed me and my son. The Chairman demanded that I give him money – or else. He said he knew that I had given money to other people. I told him that I had money at the post office and would get it for him later. He accepted that and left. I remained at this house for six days and was raped every night. At any time one of the *Interahamwe* wanted me, he took me – even in front of my son, who was with me.

At dusk on the sixth day, a group of *Interahamwe* came to the house and told me to follow them. They had clubs, machetes, grenades and other weapons. They told me that they wanted 'Hutu Power', not 'snakes'. Then they all took turns raping me. I can't say if it was one, two or...

Then they left and another gang of *Interahamwe* came. The new gang took me to a home that they had destroyed and the same thing happened there. Then, later that night, a third group came. They took me to a school where they had a meeting. Everyone followed us carrying machetes, clubs and even guns, although guns were not being used at the time. They gave me a hoe and ordered me to dig my grave; they couldn't be bothered to do it themselves. I was naked; they had already taken my sarong. I started pleading with them to shoot me with a gun, and not to kill me with a spiked club. They asked me if I knew the price of a bullet. While they were deliberating, another gang of *Interahamwe* came. The leader of the fourth gang, a man named Banyaga Barayata, asked why they hadn't killed me yet. Because I was claiming to be a Hutu, he ordered the group to take me back to the house, and then take me to the Commune in the morning to check my tribe. He said that if they found I was a Hutu, they were to kill my son – and if they found I was a Tutsi, they were to kill both of us.

As they were taking me back to the house, someone went and told an old lady whom I had helped in the past that a poor, naked Tutsi woman and her child were going to be killed. The old lady joined the group as we headed back to the house. I didn't notice her then, but later that night she stole me away to her house and worked hard to hide me.

Soldiers would often come around the house. Even the old woman's daughters were *Interahamwe*. Sometimes they threatened to turn us in, but the old woman would plead and eventually she bribed them with alcohol. However, it got really bad and they started hunting for me. The old lady would carry my son on her back, saying that he was her grandson. People believed the lie.

Then we started hearing rumours that the RPF were advancing and killing. We heard propaganda that they were grinding children up in blenders and forcing Hutus to eat them. Everyone started fleeing. I was still staying with the old woman. When the time came for them to go, I asked myself, why leave? But I had no reason to stay; there was nothing for me there. So I decided to leave with them. We went to a place called Rubengera. Tutsis were still being hunted there and the old woman was worried about my presence, so I had to stay in hiding. After Rubengera we found a house in Cyangugu and I became their maid. My child was the only reason I stayed and worked for them. I am very lucky that my child survived.

Then they decided that they had to leave Rwanda. They told me to go with them, but once we reached the Rusizi River, where we would cross into Zaire, I thought about how I would survive there. I felt as if I was already dead and going to Zaire would not change that. All I had was my child; I had nothing else. Even the clothes on my back did not belong to me. At that river, I decided to stay in Rwanda.

After the genocide

I went back to the house in Cyangugu and spent the night with a woman whom I had met there before. The new Government had arranged for buses to take people back to their homes. After several days, I took a bus back to Kibuye, where I lived with the sister of the old lady I had been living with before. It was a very hard life there and my child was not doing well. The woman we were staying with had no children of her own and was not concerned about our well-being. But I was determined to do anything for the sake of my son. There were many orphans in the area where we lived and fortunately an orphanage opened. I spent five months at the orphanage, where we stayed for my child's sake.

Then I met someone who was from Kicukiro (formerly Kanombe), who had news for me from home. They told me about the deaths of my family and also that my older sister was still alive. That made me very happy. I decided to come back here, to Kicukiro. Life was hard here, too. I had to start all over again. The house had been razed to the ground and I had nothing to sleep on, only dried banana leaves covered with mats. But I kept on thinking that maybe life would get better.

When I came back, I lived on someone else's property near my land. As the years passed, I felt worse and worse. I began thinking more and more about the many women who were raped. Those thoughts make me very sad. Even today that sadness does not end. The thought that someone came, raped you, destroyed you and killed your child... It is an extreme strain on my heart that will never end.

I told a woman friend about being raped. Before that I was lonely and could not find anyone to tell my story to. She advised me to go and have a medical check in Muhima with ARBEF (the *Association Rwandaise pour le Bien-Etre Familial*: Rwandan Association for Family Well-Being). I went there and they took a blood sample.

Living with AIDS

Around two o'clock in the afternoon, they gave me my results. They told me I was infected with HIV/AIDS. I immediately fainted. I was shocked, confused, in denial. On my way home I took the wrong bus. When I finally reached home, I felt like I had gone mad. I felt worthless; I felt I was finished. That's when I started to feel the trauma. I looked for something with which to commit suicide, but I couldn't find anything. My poverty made it worse, intensifying the emotional suffering. After I got AIDS, I used to look in the mirror every day. I would see myself already a skeleton; already dead. Ever since I found out I was ill, I have never received any medication for my illness, not once.

I had no place to live until Ibuka (Rwanda's national survivors' association) came looking for survivors who were badly off. They built houses for us, although the houses have started to deteriorate, and when you are outside, you can see inside.

I only half survived. I am still carrying death in me; not only the death that AIDS will bring. Others say they escaped from the sword, but the sword is still in my heart; and even in death, I do not believe I will find rest.

Only my son gives me the strength to live. It is a miracle that I am still alive. If I can survive a few more years, he will be a little older, and maybe he will have a chance in life; maybe he will not become a street child.

Anne-Marie, 2004 © Aegis Trust

Veneranda, 2006 © Aegis Trust

VENERANDA

He made me do what he wanted

Before the genocide

My name is Veneranda and I was 26 years old at the time of the genocide. I have two sons, one called Thierry Gakwaya and the other one Serge Gakwaya.

Before the genocide, my life was good. I had a husband to whom I was legally married and we had children. We were separated in the 1994 war when the *Interahamwe* [Hutu militia] killed.

The genocide

During the genocide, they wanted to kill people from the Tutsi ethnic group. My husband was a Tutsi and so was my Dad. My mother is Hutu. There was no way my husband could have escaped. They came and killed him and I remained with the children. I never saw him again after that; people told me that he had been killed.

I could have chosen to be on my mother's side and be called a Hutu since the Hutus were not threatened. I chose instead to remain with my children because I couldn't imagine life without them afterwards.

My husband's entire family – his mother, brothers and sisters – were all killed. Nobody survived in his family. I was one of a family of five and today only my older sister and I survive from my Dad's family. My mother is also still alive, but we have no one else left.

About five minutes after my husband was taken away, a young man called John came. He found me crying. He told me he had heard that they were going to come and kill the children and me. He said they wanted to wipe out my husband's entire family and he wanted to protect us. I left with him.

It was getting dark when we got to his house. He hid me in the bedroom so that no one could see me. He left for a while, but then came back at around seven in the evening. He told me that I was going to agree to anything he asked me to do, since he had agreed to hide me. I asked him what I might be able to do since I was hiding at his place.

He replied that there was something he wanted me to do and I would just have to agree. I was scared. As an adult, I was starting to understand what he meant. He told me to lie down on the bed. I refused and said that I wasn't going to, that he could kill me just as they had killed my husband. He had a knife and he threw it at me, here on the knee, where I have a scar. He said he was going to do what he wanted to do – with or without my permission – since he was stronger than me. And that's when he made me do everything he wanted.

For three weeks, he used to come and rape me as he wished. He told me I shouldn't try leaving the house because there was a roadblock outside his gate. If I tried to leave, they would kill me very painfully. He said that he'd kill me himself if I tried to escape. He used to stand with other people at that roadblock and said I shouldn't make the mistake of trying to run away. The people outside would kill me.

Today, 12 years later, I haven't told my sons my whole story, but one day, when they are old enough to understand, I will discuss it with them. I hope that in the future they will be able to study and have good lives.

Veneranda, 2006 © Aegis Trust

Athanase, 2006 © Aegis Trust

ATHANASE BUGIRIMFURA

People should not be divided

Before the genocide

My name is Athanase and I was 18 years old during the genocide. I was born in 1976 in Kamegeri, in Kirehe cell.

Before the genocide, I didn't know my ethnic group at all. I found out I was a Tutsi when the war started. I heard about it when people were being killed because they were Tutsis. That's how I came to know about it.

Before the genocide started, I had no problems. We lived normally before they started burning houses. We lived in peace with our neighbours; there were no problems among us. I was still young then and didn't pay much attention to what was happening. I never saw any meetings, but I did see them persecuting people. For example, we had a neighbour called Mungerimana and they always attacked him with grenades. They did it because he was a Tutsi. The people behind those attacks aren't here any more; some have fled and others are in prison. But they were ordinary people and some were thugs from around town. I didn't see the authorities do anything about it. They never imprisoned or prosecuted them. But, as I said, I was young then so I didn't think much about it. The older people seemed to know what was going on. They were scared.

By the time I left home, the perpetrators had started to burn things. We saw them burning houses without knowing why. We could see them selecting some houses to burn, but leaving others, so we started wondering why. Someone said, "I heard they're looking for Tutsis." That's when we escaped and came here to Murambi. The attackers came, telling us that we were Tutsis. I'd never heard any of my parents or family members talk about it before.

The genocide

I don't remember the night the President died in the plane crash. But when

26

the actions began, I fled here to Murambi. When they burnt our house, it was around two o'clock in the afternoon. By that time, some people had already fled, but we had stayed at home. We couldn't get here before nightfall. We spent the night in the forests nearby, then woke up early and came here.

We reached a place over there called Gatyazo and found a roadblock. They stopped us, made us sit down and asked us for our identity cards. Those who didn't have them were asked to sit down. We begged for mercy. There was a man there in Gatyazo who knew us. He told us to go, that it was OK. "Whenever we want you, we'll find you – you can't just vanish."

We came to Murambi and sat here. Even when we arrived, no one could go to get firewood or water. If you did that, you got killed. So we locked ourselves in here. When we were just starving, some people brought us rice. They said the provincial mayor had sent it. It was delivered by car but I don't know who delivered it. I didn't manage to find out the names. Everybody thought the mayor had sent it.

By then we'd already been here around five days. I don't remember the date we arrived in Murambi. During that time, we ate the small amounts of food we had managed to bring from home before they started burning our houses. Plus some other food that our parents had managed to bring because we found them here as well.

After they brought the rice, they also brought soldiers to protect us. There were very few of them – two over there, another two here and two on the other side. I remember Tutsis kept coming for three days, but later they put roadblocks up. Anyone who went there got killed. Most of my family members were killed somewhere over there near those houses. I never saw those soldiers protecting us. If someone could be tortured and killed when the soldiers were watching, and they didn't say anything, how can I judge if they had really come to protect us?

They brought us rice just once and it was uncooked. We were starving, so in order to cook it, we destroyed the fencing round there. That's how we found a way to cook the rice – using the wood from the fence.

The attackers only came once. They came and killed everyone – except those who ran off and escaped. I can't remember the dates. I guess it was around three o'clock in the morning when that group came. We heard people throwing grenades, so people started saying, "Wake up, wake up, we're being attacked." We got up and saw a group of people over there – where that building is now. Then we collected stones and threw them at the attackers. But they had guns and grenades. We carried on fighting until the skies cleared and we could see, but then we admitted we were defeated. Those who could ran away and the attackers killed the others. Those who couldn't run, they lay there until they were found and killed.

We fought until morning. I must have left this place around 6.30 a.m. I ran away and went down into the valley. I reached a place called Ntyazo. The people I was with were killed one by one. Only one boy survived with me; he's in Kigali now.

As we fled, we found roadblocks. The *Interahamwe* [Hutu militia] stopped us and asked to see our identity cards. But they could see I wasn't old enough to have one. So they made me sit there while they killed some people or let others go. That time they let me go as well. I had to go through a lot of roadblocks because you couldn't walk a kilometre without coming to one.

I went to Rusatira where my aunt had got married. The war hadn't reached that area then. But after I spent just one night there, the war started there as well. People suggested that we should flee, so we asked "Where to?" They replied that it was better to die running than sitting there. So then we left Rusatira.

We reached a place called ISAR Rubona [*Institut Supérieur d'Agronomie au Rwanda*] – that was where my aunt's cattle used to graze. We stopped there and sat on the hill – there were a lot of people with us. But after a few days, the perpetrators followed us and started throwing grenades at us. We ran away and people got scattered again; some were killed and others carried on running.

We walked that whole night until we reached Ntyazo, where we found another roadblock at a small bridge. They stopped us and asked us where we were coming from and where we were going. We told them we were fleeing and they asked us why. "From the war," we told them. They asked us if we had identity cards. Some said they did. Others knew why they wanted to see them – they wanted to see the ethnic groups – and so they threw them away.

They made us sit on that bridge and then called the brigadier. When he came, he said, "These people are to be shot." Then he realised it would involve using a lot of bullets, so he ordered them to use machetes and clubs instead. When I heard that, I immediately jumped into the river. I expected it to be deep, but it was shallow. Another boy and I jumped into the river. We hid under the pipes that support the bridge.

The other people on the bridge were killed and then they came to us.

They surrounded us and started stoning us inside the pipes where we were hiding. I still have the scars on my head. We saw that there was no way to escape, so we came out. They killed the boy I was with.

I asked them to forgive me and said that I wasn't a Tutsi. They asked me where I had come from and I told them that I had come all the way from home to graze someone's cattle. I knew one person's name and I lied that I had spent a night at my aunt's. I told them that everyone had been killed – the people they had just killed were the only ones left. I carried on lying to them, saying that I was fleeing with the people they had just killed. They believed me and handed me over to the brigadier. They said he would give me a letter to allow me to pass through the roadblocks.

When I got to the brigadier's office, I found other boys who had done the same as me. They had already been given the letter and were leaving. The brigadier wouldn't keep on writing the same letter all the time, so he asked me to run after the others and go with them. I followed them, but I didn't know which way they had gone. I carried on walking and reached a place – I don't know its name. I was stopped there again. "You, intruder, where are you coming from and where are you going?" they asked me. "Look, this one's escaped," they said. "Look at that blood. They killed 'it' and 'it' refused to die. Let's get him." They started beating me up so that my arm and leg were weakened.

I managed to get away from them. When I reached Kinyamakara, in a place called Kamwambi, I met a man who lived in my home village, Kirehe. He didn't know me well, but found me when they sat me down at the roadblock in Kamwambi. He heard me saying that I came from Kirehe. So he came and asked me, "You say you come from Kirehe. Who is your family there? I know every family in Kirehe." I thought that if I said my father's name, he would hand me over to the perpetrators to kill me. We had a neighbour at home called Frederick, so I lied and said I was from Frederick's family. And he replied, "If you're from Frederick's family, they should let you go." He ordered them to leave me alone. "I know that boy. I'll take him up to his home. I know they're still alive there." So we set off back home.

When we reached Mpungu, he was going to visit his relatives and he said, "It's okay now, you're almost home. You can go now and I'll come later to see if you got there safely." As soon as we parted, I thought about the option of going back home. Our family was very well known in Kirehe, so I thought that if I went there, they would kill me.

By then it was getting towards evening. I looked for a bush near there and hid, waiting for darkness to fall so I could walk away. I sat there until I couldn't stand up. I tried to stand up, but I couldn't. I eventually left the place around four o'clock in the morning. I went home then, but when I got there, there was nobody left – not even houses. They'd burnt them all. So I went to hide in the forest on the hill near our home.

I knew a man nearby – I had once lived in his home. I decided to go and ask him for food because I felt very hungry. He was a family friend. In my heart I said, "If he refuses to give me food, I will just leave. And if he decides to kill me, then I'll let him kill me himself." So I went and found him there and he roasted some sweet potatoes and gave them to me. Then he told me, "Even though I've given you this food, you can't spend the night here because every night they come to look for Tutsis in my house."

He told me about Simarinka, another neighbour of ours, who had been killed in his house. The perpetrators had come for him the previous night and would maybe come back. He asked me to find another place to hide. He put the roasted potatoes in a paper bag and I went back to the forest where I had been hiding.

That night I remembered another family friend who lived in the same area, where my grandparents were born. So I went there and when he saw me he said, "Why are you coming here when things are so bad? What can I really do for you? It's okay now because it's night. You can spend a night here, then in the morning I'll take you to Mugomba, to my sister's house. I think it will be OK for you to stay with her since the situation is really bad for you." He took me to Mugomba very early next morning and his sister agreed to let me stay with her. But as soon as he left, she chased me away, saying that her kids were dying in Kigali and I was sitting there. "Get out of here," she said.

So I left her place and fortunately that day no one beat me or even insulted me. I carried on and reached CPR [*Conseil Protestant au Rwanda*], where I found refugees from Bugesera. I joined them and then I saw another young man from Isunga. I asked him if he could give me a job grazing his cattle and pay me with food and clothes. I told him I had just come from Bugesera and had lost sight of my parents. He said that was no problem and we could go home together. He was very kind to me. Then he gave me food in the morning and permission to graze the cattle.

He showed me where to graze them and I worked there for three months. By then the war was declining after the French had left. But some people stole a cow from the cattle I was grazing, so I left the job and joined other refugees. Things were somehow getting better. Then I went back to Nzega and stayed at our neighbour's.

After the genocide

During the genocide, I felt as though I had lost my mind. I felt useless and could do nothing for myself. I didn't have any hopes about surviving. I thought it was only God's will. I could see all those who had been killed and I felt I wasn't any better than them.

In my immediate family two people were killed, plus my parents – in total four. Only one young brother and I survived. But in my extended family many more were killed, because my grandfather had three wives – not less than fifteen people.

Can there be any justice? For me, those who committed crimes should be punished in the way they punished and killed other people. Because when you kill with a sword, you die by a sword, too. Because I gain nothing if they're in prison. They're there in prison eating food, yet all my people have been killed. I've got no one to depend on, no one to share my problems with, but they are there.

As for unity and reconciliation, normally one person unites with another after sorting out their problems. If someone has wronged you, he has to come to you and apologize. He should come to you so you can unite and be friends again. But up to now, so many people who participated in the genocide are free, not in prison. And they don't come to you and say, "You've had problems, let me help you in such and such way, or give you advice about some issue." Instead, whenever they see you, they face the other way or mock you.

No one has been to apologize to me. But if someone came and apologized and told me what had made him wrong me, I could forgive him. Even if I refused to forgive him, it wouldn't kill him. I think unity and reconciliation would be possible if those who committed the crimes approached you and told you why they had committed them. Then you would have opened up a dialogue. But I haven't seen anything like this in my commune yet, although I hear the words 'unity and reconciliation' on the radio.

Some of those who wronged my family are in prison. Some were released because the accusation wasn't genuine. I'm the only one following the case. The others who used to live in our village were all killed and those who are left are relatives of the perpetrators. They're the ones I would have given as witnesses, but it was impossible. So only one *Interahamwe* has remained in jail. *Gacaca* hasn't started in my area yet, but I think I might benefit from it.

The future

As for the future, I have no hopes. I can't believe that it won't happen again because you still find your neighbour saying that the Tutsis are imprisoning them. You find people whispering to each other everywhere in bars. Can you be hopeful that it won't happen again?

I think the Government should take care that what happened isn't repeated. We should become as one. People should not be divided.

I hope that Murambi is never forgotten in history. The building should be well constructed so that those who lost their loved ones can come and pray here. I think a school here that teaches about genocide would be fine. Survivors could play a role there: I could tell the young generation that what happened was very bad, that they should never do this again. We have to teach them. You can see that these young kids will grow up hearing that in 1994 there was genocide – just like we used to hear that there was a war in the 1950s. I think we should teach them about it so they don't think that blood has to be shed.

Emmanuel, 2006 © Aegis Trust

EMMANUEL GASANA

Unity is crucial

Before the genocide

My name is Emmanuel and I was born in 1979 in Kibungo province. My father's name was André Kalisa and my mother's Flavienne Mukagombaniro. I was 15 years old at the time of the genocide.

My parents were separated so I lived just with my Mum, who was an accountant in a restaurant. I had two younger sisters, Betty born in 1983, and Aimée Umukazana, born in 1985, and a little brother, Soso, born in 1981. I was the eldest child of the family.

Life was fine before the genocide. My Mum was very kind and would let me go and spend the holidays with my Grandmas on each side of the family. My Grandmas always took good care of me. At Christmas or other feasts like New Year and Easter, we used to go to Grandma's and we would eat, share and socialize with neighbours. We had a lot of fun.

Life wasn't too bad – except that some neighbours used to tell their kids we were *Inyenzi* ['cockroaches', meaning Tutsis] and incite them to hate us. But in general, people were good; no one would harvest or make banana wine without calling their neighbours in to share. People shared everything before the genocide.

Another example of how people cared for each other: if a woman saw a kid out late on the street, she would always tell him or her to hurry home – even though the kid wasn't hers. I remember that my Mum took in a boy who came to our house one day. He was from Kivuye [a war zone under RPF control in 1992]. He stayed with us and was treated like one of the family, although later on, he became a bad boy and started stealing and fighting other kids....

I really used to love school when I was young. It was fun because I met lots of different children and learned a lot about them. I never minded about the ethnic groups. I didn't even know about mine, so I played with any kids I wanted. I only came to realize about my ethnic group when I was in Primary Three, when the teacher called pupils of one ethnic group to stand up. Hutu pupils would stand proudly, but when it was the Tutsis' turn, other kids would yell at you and humiliate you... I remember that the first time, I stood with the Tutsi pupils, but when I realized that being a Tutsi was shameful, the following day I stood up with the Hutus. But then the teacher shouted at me and ordered me to sit down at once. I felt so ashamed that I never liked going to school after that.

My family never used to discuss ethnic groups. All I knew was that my grandfather had died in exile in Uganda.

In 1990, when the RPF [Rwandan Patriotic Front] troops invaded Rwanda, local authorities incited kids to hatred by teaching them songs that referred to *Inyenzi*. They were described as very thin people with big ears and big tails; and the kids were scared that these creatures would come and eat them. The authorities extended their teachings by telling people that these *Inyenzi* were within Rwandan society. This word *Inyenzi* really marked me. I was shocked!

Another thing that marked me was the time of the multi-party system. People had no strong position at all; they would join whatever political party emerged. For example, some people used to change from party to party until they belonged to the most powerful and pitiless party – so as not to be attacked themselves. In the end, there was no virtue at all.

I felt lost during this time... I didn't know where to be; I didn't like home any more. Then there was jealousy between the political parties and people started killing each other without remorse. Our neighbour David was a PL [*Parti Libéral*] member and was killed by members of CDR [*Coalition pour la Défense de la République*] and MRND [*Mouvement Révolutionnaire National pour le Développement*]. Before this period, people used to be confident and united, but suddenly we were thrown into an era of terror and hatred.

The genocide

I was at home when the genocide started. I remember that my Mum came home from work with a very different expression on her face. She was angry and upset at the same time. I didn't want to talk to her straightaway, but then I said to Soso, my younger brother, "Don't you think Mum looks strange today?" And Soso told me he had noticed it as well. When Mum had arrived home, she had dropped her things and gone to see a Hutu neighbour, Zitoni, to ask him what was happening. Zitoni brought her back home and told her to calm down.

The following morning, 7 April 1994, Mum didn't go to work and when we asked her why not, she said, "My dears, we're in trouble. The President has been assassinated and we, the Tutsis, are soon going to be killed. So don't tell anyone you are a Tutsi. Is that clear?" In fact, Mum had already managed to get a Hutu identity card. The street was really quiet that day and only *Interahamwe* [Hutu militia] were to be seen, wearing their uniforms and holding their machetes or sticks.

On 8 April, Mashanyarazi came to our house. He worked at the same place as my Mum and came boasting that he had killed 14 Tutsis in a place called Rwinkwavu; then he had thrown the corpses into a big pit. This really scared Mum, so we went to seek refuge in the house of Gatete, a Hutu neighbour. He hid us underneath his bed – along with another woman. I was only 15, but I was so scared when I realized I was amongst the many people who were going to be killed...

We stayed under Gatete's bed until we heard gunshots nearby. In fact, the mayor of Kabarondo had encouraged Tutsis living in Kabarondo who were hiding in their homes to come to the church. He said they would be sheltered there, but once they were all in the church, he called the police and soldiers from Huye barracks to come to Kabarondo church. About five o'clock in the morning, they started shooting people and throwing grenades at the Tutsis in the church. But these people didn't just allow themselves to be slaughtered. Some of them resisted, using traditional weapons, but because the soldiers had guns, they were never able to resist for long. People not killed by bullets or grenades were killed with the machetes and clubs of the *Interahamwe*, who went in to finish them off.

From five in the morning to four in the afternoon, we heard gunshots and people screaming in agony. The street was chaotic with the *Interahamwe* looting and killing people anyhow... That day, I saw a girl from my school. She was covered in blood, her legs had been blown off by a grenade and she couldn't walk, so she just pulled her body along the ground till she reached Gatete's house. I saw her and I heard her crying out for help, but as soon as the *Interahamwe* saw her, they just put her in a blanket and threw her into a deep pit nearby. She was still alive, but dying in agony.

The following morning, a lady came to the house where we were hiding. She was calling for help and Mum went to see who it was. It was

Nyaguheka, one of Mum's friends, and her legs were in pieces, blown off by a grenade. When Mum saw her in that state, she told me to take her to the nearest medical centre. Lundi, Gatete's houseboy, helped me to take her in a wheelbarrow, but the problem was that there were lots of *Interahamwe* in the street. We waited a bit and when they started looting a shop, we crossed the street carrying Nyaguheka. Just after crossing the road, I saw a lot of corpses and a dead body that was mutilated. It was horrible! It was the first time I'd seen a corpse.

When we got to the medical centre, the nurses told us to leave Nyaguheka there on the floor; they didn't care at all. When Lundi saw this, he told me, "If we stay here, we might get killed. Let's go!" So we left the wheelbarrow there and went back. But just a few metres from Gatete's house, at a turning, we saw hundreds of *Interahamwe* wandering around and killing people... Lundi said, "If they see us, they'll kill us. Let's lift a corpse like them and carry it over to that side, then we'll be able to escape and go back home." I was wearing a big coat and hoped no one would notice me.

We took a dead body and dragged it along... All the way, I saw the most horrible scenes of my life – people stoning their victims, others stabbing and hacking them... It was awful! When we got to the other side, I saw a man who was originally from my Grandma's sector. He was standing on a pile of corpses, holding a big nailed club. He was searching the victims' pockets, stripping them of anything he thought was valuable. And he used his club to kill anyone who was still breathing. In the time we crossed the street, he had clubbed three people to death.

We went back to Gatete's house and stayed there. But when Zitoni heard that the *Interahamwe* had been looking for Mum, he came and took her to another hiding place. (After the genocide, people told me that he hid her in the toilet... but I also heard that he used to rape her.)

A few days later, when the *Inkotanyi* [RPF soldiers] were advancing, people came and told us, "The *Inkotanyi* are taking over. They're killing people, so if you don't manage to flee with the others, you'll be killed." When Mum heard this, she came to pick us up and we fled amongst the big crowd of people leaving places near those under RPF control. There were hundreds of people fleeing. Our aim was to go to where Grandma lived.

Those days of fleeing were really hard for me – sleeping on the floor, outside, starving... It was really hard. One day, the *Interahamwe* among the crowd asked Mum for her ID card because they suspected she was a Tutsi.

She showed it and they said, "What? Are you a Hutu? You can't be a Hutu!" So they took us aside and told us to sit down at the roadside. We watched hundreds of refugees passing by until some people came yelling, "The *Inkotanyi* are close." At this, the *Interahamwe* told us roughly, "Get up and go!"

We carried on walking... but still it wasn't over. The same thing happened again when we stopped at a place for the night. But once again, we were lucky and were released. The *Interahamwe* who arrested us quarrelled a bit about my Mum because her ID was marked Hutu, although she looked like a Tutsi. But in the end, they let us go.

We walked for about five days from Gatete's house to Grandma's. When we got there, we realized that Grandma and all the extended family were also targeted by the killers, so they immediately hid us with them.

A few days later, a neighbour came to warn us about a group of attackers who were coming to kill us. He suggested that some of us should hide in his house – he hid me, three other kids and Grandma in the roof. Other members of the family were hidden with other neighbours.

Three days later, we knew that the *Interahamwe* had started to suspect we were hiding in those houses, so Grandma took us to another place. We walked for days, hiding in bushes and banana plantations... I remember that on the way, Grandma took us to an old Hutu friend of hers. He sheltered us and gave us food, but a few minutes later, he disappeared – he had gone to call for the *Interahamwe* to kill us... His wife told us he was involved in the killings, so we left the house straightaway and moved to another place.

My Mum had a younger sister who was married to a Hutu, and Grandma said we would be safe if those in-laws took us in. We kept on walking until we reached the house of a member of that family – he was the uncle of Grandma's son-in-law. We got there at about three o'clock in the morning. He welcomed us and hid us in the barn where the goats were kept. He sheltered us, fed us and did all he could to help us.

I wasn't with my Mum then. We had got separated when Grandma's neighbours tried to hide us and Mum had gone to hide at her uncle's place a few miles away. When she got there, the whole family had been killed; the only person who survived was her uncle's daughter, who was married to a Hutu. Mum stayed with them, but then she got terribly ill. Towards the end of May, her health was getting worse... Then the time came when her uncle's daughter and her husband decided to flee because they heard that the *Inkotanyi* were getting closer. My Mum couldn't walk by then; she was very weak. So they took her and put her in the banana plantation. She stayed there in the cold, in the rain; she was starving and ill and had no treatment... She got weaker and weaker until dogs started coming around her, pulling her clothes till they ate her... That's how she died.

At the beginning of June, my uncle's friend who had joined the RPF troops came to where we were hiding and said he was looking for us. Then we came out and the *Inkotanyi* took us to a camp established at ETO Kibungo [*Ecole Technique Officielle*]. I was with my Grandma, my brother Soso and some other cousins. My sister Aimée wasn't with us because Mum had asked someone to look after her when she was trying to find hiding places.

After the genocide

Life after the genocide wasn't easy at all. It had nothing in common with our life before the genocide. We were confronted with many problems – we had lost parents and relatives, we were poor... Life was so tough and different. I used to have a family that was always there for me, but then I had to take on responsibility...

After the genocide, Soso and my other cousins went back to the village with Grandma. At first, Aimée was adopted by a senior RPF officer when he heard what she had gone through. But later on, my uncle, who was also an RPF officer, found out about Aimée and then wasted no time. He went straightaway and took her into his home.

I stayed in the camp alone, but then I decided to join the army. In 1996, I went to school but it was too hard ... I was living at an RPF officer's, but I couldn't ask him for whatever I needed because he wasn't my parent. When I got to Senior Three, this officer was arrested and so my life was turned upside down again. I started visiting members of my family so they could help me... and, thank God, I managed to finish my secondary education.

Fortunately, I got a job straightaway and became a teacher. But the beginning was once again very hard – I had no shoes, no clothes, nothing!

Another problem came when my two sisters were thrown out of where they were being sheltered. Their guardians told them, "Your brother has finished school; he's working now so you can join him. Go now!" They came home and I tried to help them and pay school fees for one sister on the modest wage I was earning... It was hard, but I struggled on. Then when life was getting a little bit better, one of my sisters got pregnant, so I had to look after everything.

Later on, I tried to focus on my future by doing further studies at university, but I couldn't make it with all the responsibilities I had on my shoulders...

Today

I'm currently working as a guide at Kigali Memorial Centre and this work has helped me a lot. I don't have to ask anyone for help now; I do my best to clear my bills and it's okay. Before working with Aegis Trust, genocide was a taboo subject for me. I wasn't able to stand where people were discussing it, but today I feel free to tell my story. It really relieves me.

Unity is a crucial feature for our society. Without unity, people would slaughter one another all over again. But reconciliation? First of all, it cannot be an obligation; it must be something that comes from the heart. People have set up a kind of orientation to lead to reconciliation, but I don't think they are right. It's something without structure; it's natural!

At present, there is nothing to suggest that I will have a better future. But I do believe that God led me to this stage and He will make a way.

On the other hand, I would like to ask all those who have it within their power – the Government and teachers – to promote unity and reconciliation by all possible means. I also have a message for the international community: "Don't pretend any more that you aren't involved." If you do this, you'll be able to react to all kinds of conflicts that can lead to genocide; and therefore you will save lives.

People should support charity organizations like Aegis Trust that struggle to prevent genocide. And above all, they should help survivors who are confronted with the physical and psychological scars of genocide.

Emmanuel at the Kigali Memorial Centre, 2006
© Aegis Trust

Innocent, 2004 © Karen Kessi-Williams

Innocent Ndamyina Gisanura

We chose to fight back

Before the genocide

My name is Innocent and I was born in the Gitezi district of Kibuye, on the outskirts of the town. My family consisted of Mum and Dad and eight children, and I was the fourth born. The genocide began when I was 14 years old and in high school at the *Groupe Scolaire Nyamasheke* in Cyangugu. My entire family was killed, including Mum and Dad; I'm now the only one left.

The genocide didn't exactly start in 1994 – we could see signs of it earlier at my primary and high schools. At the time, there were car bombings, students were beaten up; there was a bad atmosphere and it seemed as if something was being planned. But 1994 was the grand finale, when I witnessed horrific, animalistic behaviour far worse than I could ever have imagined.

The genocide

It began when the President's aeroplane crashed and, on the orders of murderous soldiers and others who had planned the genocide, permission was given to kill Tutsis. The next day, they started attacking homes and killing people. In our area some people were killed. They came to remove us from our homes, burning them and taking our animals.

When the attacks started, my family decided to leave home and we went to my old primary school in Kirambo. There was a Presbyterian church and a hospital, and I remember that about 10,000 people took shelter there. But we were attacked by a group of soldiers, gendarmes, prison guards and people from the local authorities. They came in official cars to take us to the stadium in Kibuye, where they planned to kill us. But along with my father and some other men, I didn't follow their orders. Instead we escaped to the mountains of Bisesero and Kirongi where we could fight back.

Resistance

Bisesero and Kirongi are two high mountains facing each other. There are some forests but they are not dense, so we could see any attack coming and either defend ourselves or escape, depending on the number of attackers. From the mountains, we watched the killing of the people taken to the stadium. That night some people managed to escape and join us in the mountains. My mother was taken to the stadium, but later escaped to Bisesero with a few other survivors. I had six sisters and three of them were killed in the stadium.

In Bisesero we managed to defend ourselves day after day and we were starting to hope to make it through another week. But that's not how it happened – power lay in the hands of soldiers planning the extermination of the Tutsis. We resisted against the militia, the police and prison guards, and so in the end they sent a force of presidential guards from Kigali who eventually defeated us. We had been in Bisesero for a week when they came, a week when we hadn't rested at all; we were constantly fighting. It didn't stop us fighting back because we had no other choice. We continued fighting day after day. The fierce attacks began around 17 April and included presidential guards, gendarmes, and commandos from the Mukamira and Bigogwe camps, and others from Cyangugu. We had only one choice – to fight with will and commitment with our limited strength, to die fighting or give up. We chose to fight back.

Life in Bisesero was hard; they were overwhelmingly bad times and it's hard to explain. From the first day I arrived, I saw people dying bad deaths for no reason. It's made a mark on my life. Even though I was lucky to survive, it's still a problem because I cannot forget it. Those scenes frequently replay in my head like a film, even though it was reality. It's all kept somewhere in my head. It was hard, but we were really motivated to resist, hoping that some of us might survive. We continued fighting. They no longer used ordinary guns, but heavy ammunition, grenade launchers, rockets, anti-tanks, and so on. We had no other solution – we used stones and arrows for the elders and those who could shoot them. I was too young to have used such traditional weapons, so it was stones, beating with sticks, making noise as a group to help push them back maybe a metre. That killing continued day after day for almost the entire month of April. I can't forget the terrible day when they killed my older brother.

On 14 April they killed lots of men, including my father and others of his age group. These strong men had given us guidance, they had urged us to make a stand and fight back. We obeyed them day after day. But the goal of the *Interahamwe* [Hutu militia] and presidential guards was to eliminate all these strong men. My older brother was killed in their first attack and that's how I also lost my father and my uncle.

We were fighting against a recognised military force, and one of our strategies for defence was to move in a big group – separating would have made it easy for them to kill us. Their plan was to force us out of the mountains so they could kill us easily. Our goal was to stay there so we could defend ourselves and survive the longest possible time. So we stayed in a group and moved as a mass. Even though I was young, I'd go with the other men and fight. We used to run among the attackers so they couldn't shoot. We'd mix with them, hit them with rocks and tackle them with their guns. Then they would be ordered to move back to re-organise. They would sometimes bring their speakerphones and tell us that we should go to the stadium, that they wouldn't kill us. But those were lies; there was no way we would give up our positions, so at times we'd start the fight because we didn't want to move an inch backwards from where we were. We'd mix with them and fight.

I spent almost two months in Bisesero. I got there on 8 April and left on 23 May. But by the end there were only a few of us and we had a shortage of food and water. Fighting hungry against armed men is a problem. We were weak. Official figures say that 85,000 people were killed there, but I think there were more. I think there were around 160,000 or 175,000. Very many people were killed – in my family all my siblings, my father, uncles. I come from a big family – 188 people descended from my grandfather – but by the time the French arrived, they had all been killed except me and my uncle.

I was injured in the fighting – I was hacked on the head and also have a shot wound. That happened in the last days when the French came to create the *Zone Turquoise*. They came with their helicopters saying they had come to save us, that it was over and no more people were going to be killed. We could also see that the killings had ended. We came out of the forests and bushes where we were hiding, out into the open towards them. But they had trucks full of *Interahamwe* and they had made us believe they were full of food and clothes. It wasn't true.

When we came out of hiding, they immediately attacked us and that was when my uncle got killed. That day, I managed to escape even though I had been shot. We were surrounded by *Interahamwe* and they sent them in to finish us off. They killed nearly everybody, but they didn't get me.

When I got shot, I was leading a group of about 300-500 kids aged between 12 and 16 whose job was to alert people when there was an attack coming. We'd go to the mountains near ETO [*Ecole Technique Officielle*] Kibuye and scream, bang drums, jerry-cans and any other noisy object we could find. That way we let the people in Kirongi know, and those in Bisesero would come and give them a hand. And when Bisesero was attacked, we'd go and give them reinforcements.

On 19 April, when I got shot, my brother was also killed at the same time. There was an attack of presidential guards with their fast jeeps and they shot me as I was running to our positions. The people I was with rescued me by dragging me into our positions. They shot me in the leg near my foot, but I managed to escape. I ran with my uncle, but they shot him and when I stayed with him, he ordered me to run on. He told me that his time had come and I had a better chance of surviving to the next day and maybe the day after. I obeyed him and left, even though I didn't want to leave him to die alone. But he made me leave.

I escaped and returned to my neighbourhood in the valley of the Kirongi mountain. I managed to spend a week there, hiding from 23-28 April in a cave without food or water. I was desperately thirsty. I could no longer even speak or swallow saliva – I didn't have any. It felt as if my throat was about to close. Although I was in a place controlled by the French, militias and presidential guards, I thought I might as well take the risk of going to drink water because otherwise I would die of thirst. But I had no way of moving safely and when I went to a waterhole where cows drank, an attack group found me. I wasn't scared because it was my second month of witnessing killings. I asked them to let me finish drinking water first, and they did. Then they walked me with my bullet wound to the hole where they threw people after they had killed them.

I asked them why they were doing this. I knew already but just wanted to hear them say it. In my area, they had a registration book which was used to record all those killed. My family made up most of the population of the area and I was the only one missing in their book. They showed me the book and said they had been looking for me; now they had found me, they wanted to kill me. I asked if they would answer one question. They agreed, and I asked them why they wanted to kill me. They told me it was because I was a Tutsi, a 'cockroach', that Rwanda was not our country and so we must be exterminated. By killing me, they added, they were doing me a favour because my entire family and all the Tutsis had been killed, so living for me would be useless. I asked them why they were going to kill me when I had never wronged them, when in fact I had lived in harmony with them and their children. They told me to ask God because He was the one who created Tutsis and had abandoned them. I heard that and figured I couldn't add anything.

Even though they were angry, I asked them for one more thing. I didn't care because I knew they were going to kill me anyway. I had seen death and was no longer scared. I asked them to let me pray and they agreed. While I was praying, they started complaining that my prayer was too long. I begged them to let me finish and they did. I continued. They started complaining again, saying that my prayer was taking too long and they needed to go somewhere else to find people to kill. They let me pray for the third time, but this time they didn't let me finish. They hit me on the head with a club. I fell down unconscious and don't know when they hacked me. But I have four machete scars on my head, as well as the bullet wound in my leg.

From 28 April-2 May I lay there unconscious. I woke up after a dream about being killed and found myself in a hole. I crawled out with some difficulty. I thought about what to do next and decided to go to Kibuye town. I would go to the hospital and they would either kill me or treat me. That's what I did. I was really looking for a place for a nicer death. From where I was to Kibuye, it took me two days, walking and hiding. I got there on 4 May. One thing I remember is that I heard on the *Interahamwe's* radio that the RPF [Rwandan Patriotic Front] had captured Kabgayi and managed to rescue people who had fled there.

I reached the roadblock at the roundabout in Kibuye and people came to look. There were soldiers and one wanted to shoot me, saying that I was a 'cockroach'. I told him that I came from Bisesero and was not a cockroach. He replied by asking what the difference was between the RPF 'cockroach' and the Bisesero *inyenzi*. I kept quiet. When he was going to shoot me, his partner told him to leave me alone because I was dying anyway from my wounds. He said that killing me would bring him bad luck.

By then I didn't care. I just had one goal – to get to the hospital where I'd be healed or killed. When I got there, a crowd came to watch me and they started to beat me. They asked me why I had come there and I said, "To be healed or killed, one of the two." One woman stood out and shielded me. She told them they had killed enough people and if anyone killed me, they would be looking for trouble from her. She took me inside the hospital and treated me. But people aren't all the same. When this nurse had stitched me up, her colleague came and undid the stitches. It happened again and again, and eventually she asked her what she was doing. Her colleague eventually agreed she could treat me as long as she didn't use stitches; she could give me tablets and everything else, but not stitches. Perhaps the colleague thought that would impede my recovery.

The nurse obeyed and told me that she would do her best without stitches. She gave me antibiotics, washed me, fed me and even gave me clothes because what I was wearing was very dirty. I'd been wearing those clothes since 8 April when we ran away. She also hired *Interahamwe* to protect me. She paid them not to kill me. She assured me that she was going to do her best and if I died, it would be because she couldn't do any more.

I spent the entire month of June in the hospital. I left on 2 July and went to the *Zone Turquoise*, to the French military camp situated in the girls' high school. Even then, I couldn't go there by myself; I would have been killed on the way, so the nurse gave me those *Interahamwe* to protect me. They walked me up to the gate of the French military base and then left. I only managed to spend that month in hospital because of the nurse who treated me, fed me, clothed me and even paid for my protection. When the *Interahamwe* went out to kill elsewhere, they used to leave a notice saying that if they found me dead when they came back, it would be best if my killer was dead as well before they got there. Those were the terms on which I survived, while other people at the hospital were being killed on a daily basis, especially the many girls who had survived at the stadium and were kept to be raped. The militias would kill whichever of the girls they got tired of raping. When I got to the hospital, there were a few left but they were also gradually killed.

The nurse who saved me is still alive today. Her name is Gitabita Nyirantaba; she's between 45-50 years old and has a husband and four kids. She lives in Kibuye and still works at the hospital. Whenever I go to Kibuye for holidays, I stay at her place. Sometimes I just go and visit her. I feel overwhelmed by all she did for me. I have nothing to give her in return. She didn't even know me when she saved me. She just saw people gathering around me and torturing me and made a decision on her own to rescue me. I think that was God's will. So I put that lady in a category of humane people with a true human heart.

I got to the French zone and they received me. I remember the first thing they asked was whether I was Hutu or Tutsi. They asked me in French and I responded even though my French was not that good. I answered their question but they could already see I was a Tutsi because of the wounds. They let me in and I lived there with many other people.

After the genocide

On 17 July, the French took 50 of us to Congo [DRC]. We were separated into two groups, one that went to Nyarushishi, Cyangugu and the other to Goma. The group to Goma consisted mostly of injured or ill people whose recovery needed to be followed up. I don't know exactly why they moved us, but I think it was because the French zone shared borders with RPF territory and they might have been scared that the RPF would attack us and free us.

While I was with the French, I found out that one of my sisters was alive and was being kept as a wife by an *Interahamwe*. The French were going around retrieving people, so I told them about her and they went to find her. They spoke to the *Interahamwe* and they came back and told me that she was his wife and didn't need to be rescued. They refused to bring her to live with us and that's how she was killed in October 1994. When the French left Kibuye, the *Interahamwe* fled as the RPF was taking over. The *Interahamwe* killed whoever was left, including my sister.

I was about two months in DRC, then we came home to Rwanda. We didn't know that all the *Interahamwe* from Kigali and all over the country would come and live in the camp where the French took us, near Mugunga. They tried to kill us. The Red Cross and some other human rights organisations worked together and brought us home, all 50 of us. They took us to Goma; we crossed the border and eventually came to Ruhengeri where the Red Cross had a station. That was our destination because they had arranged a place for us in a home for genocide orphans. We lived there from January 1995. It was hard to get back home and I don't know how the Red Cross managed it.

In Ruhengeri, I lived in the orphanage and studied. I felt obliged to start a new life because orphanage life didn't offer me much future. By luck, some distant relatives in Gisenyi found me and took me in to live with them. I started a family life and I was like their adopted child.

I returned to Kibuye for the first time in May 1995. I go as a visitor now but don't live there. First of all, there's no place for me to live. There's no house – all our houses were destroyed. During the holidays, I go either to Gisenyi or to Kibuye and visit the remains of my home. I also visit the nurse who saved me and I go to see the mountains. When the holiday is over, I come back either to Gisenyi or to Kigali where I am boarding and studying at the Kigali Institute of Science, Technology and Management.

When I'm in Kibuye, I feel very sad; it's immeasurable. I cannot forget about Kibuye just because I had bad times there. It is my home. Wherever I go in this world, I will not forget that I was born in Kibuye. Most importantly, I cannot forget that I had a good life there in a tranquil family, being raised by my parents, living with my siblings, with all I needed – the affection of my parents, my siblings, my entire family... even of all Tutsis. We lived well and I can't forget Kibuye. I had a good life and a bad life there; I lost all those people, but it still remains my home. I can spend half an hour at the roundabout remembering when they wanted to shoot me. I can't forget the hospital where I lived for a month without any right to be there. Kibuye is a marked place inside of me. I have to visit it and if possible walk all the paths we walked during the genocide as we tried to save our own lives.

Innocent with Gitabita Nyirantaba, the nurse who saved him, 2004 © Karen Kessi-Williams

Yves, 2006 © Aegis Trust

Yves Kamuronsi

People are still hurting

Before the genocide

My name is Yves and I will be 23 years old in August. Before the genocide we were a family of six people living here in Kicuciro. There were four children and my Dad and Mum. At the time of the genocide, I was 13 years old. Only three of us were left; both my parents and my older brother were killed.

My earliest memories are of when we were all together, chatting. My father used to make us laugh a lot; he was very funny. He used to take us for a ride in the car. When we children were on our own, my big brother used to make us laugh a lot as well.

My mother was a very loving person. She loved talking and giving advice to people. Even at her place of work, people loved her a lot and they would always come and seek her advice. Family members – like her younger sisters or people from my Dad's family – felt so close to her. Nobody was afraid of her because she was very easy-going. She treated everyone as if they were family. She would give them all she had, only refusing what she didn't have. She really did her best to help people.

She used to take me aside and give me plenty of advice about life in general. Even before the genocide, she used to tell us that anything could happen. We could find ourselves orphans; they could both die in a car accident or something could happen to them. So she would tell us that we needed to stop being childish and grow up. We had to be hardworking and able to take care of ourselves – just in case we were forced to do it. She gave me advice to help me become a man.

My father was very talkative. Wherever he was, maybe in bars with his friends, they were always making jokes and he would come home and make us laugh as well. The one thing I remember is that we used to wait for him to come home every evening, even when it was very late, because he amused us a lot. He used to promise to take us for a ride or give us gifts or money to buy sweets on our way to church. We always waited for him to come home before we went to bed. If we went to sleep without seeing him, we used to go and find him in his bedroom very early next morning.

My older brother was very quiet. Some people didn't even believe he could talk! He never talked when Dad or Mum were there because he was afraid of them. In their presence he acted like a very quiet person or a grown-up. But whenever we children were on our own or with other children from the neighbourhood or school, he was so funny. He loved funky music, dancing and films. He was popular at school because he was calm and loved people. He used to tell me what was in fashion. He loved reading and listening to the radio. He used to teach me to dance in the bedroom.

One thing I particularly remember is the time we all went to see a Burundian musician at "Chez Lando" [a restaurant in Kigali]. We looked forward to it so much. It was very nice because we were all together and we had a lot of fun.

My strongest memory of my mother is of a time before the genocide. She took me aside and told me that there was a war going on, that no one knew what was going to happen. She told me that she and my father might die, that anything could happen to them, and we had to be strong. It was as though she knew she was going to die. She used to tell me, "You're the oldest" – even though I wasn't because I had an older brother. She always wanted to talk to me, to advise me how to behave and to love people.

I remember how my father used to take me out with the other men and buy me *brochettes* [kebabs]. My mother even used to get angry with him about it and ask why he was taking her child out at night. I really liked being with my father; it made me feel invincible. Dad also would tell me to take an interest in his things and take care of my sisters.

The genocide

The thing that hurts me most is the way my parents were killed. I was told that when the attackers came to get them, my mother had been sick with malaria. She didn't have any medication and she had been shivering and vomiting all night. When they came that morning, my older brother was mopping the floor and listening to the radio, even though they were hiding. What hurts the most is that they shot five bullets at my father and he lay there in agony for two days with no medication. Two days later, when he was starting to feel better, they came back and finished him off. That hurts me and I always feel that it would have been better if he'd died right away without suffering so much pain.

I had gone to my grandmother's place before the genocide started. They said there was no security here in Kigali, so the best thing was to split into two groups. Perhaps then some of us would survive. So I was in Gitarama at my grandmother's.

I heard that the attackers killed the people in a terrible way, including my parents. They made them walk for maybe five kilometres, about 100 people, and they were shouting at them and beating them up. The way they were killed hurts me a lot. Even on the day they killed them, they still ran after them, beat them up and insulted them first. They pleaded to be allowed to live but the killers refused. I think it would have been better for them to die straight away, on the first day.

My family was murdered by a soldier we didn't know. But I know that one of my Dad's very good friends betrayed them. Dad always went everywhere with him – to family functions like weddings or traditional engagement ceremonies. They would have a drink together every evening. He was head of the *Interahamwe* [Hutu militia] in Kicukiro. He didn't help my Dad at all; he betrayed him. We even used to hide in that man's house when it was getting less secure before the genocide. I remember a time when Dad asked his friend if there was anything he could do, if Dad could maybe pay some money so they wouldn't kill him. And another time, when he was wounded and sick after they shot him, Dad sent someone to ask his friend if he could do anything to help him. Still he did nothing. In fact he was the one who went ahead and told the other perpetrators that Dad was still alive. He told them to kill him, and his wife and his children, as he would certainly take revenge if he survived. So he sent the second group of attackers who killed Dad.

All I can say is that my Dad didn't have any enemies. He didn't even have any problems with the soldiers. People in this area liked him because he helped them out with their problems. He used to give them a lift in the days when he had a car; and when he didn't have one, they walked up to the taxi together. He would buy them a drink when he had money. Even the soldiers had no problems with him; in fact some of them were his friends. He was on good terms with everyone.

All my Dad's friends were people he met – some at work or in bars or on the streets. He worked very hard and was very intelligent; the people he worked with liked him. Even the man who betrayed him was his very good friend. Everyone liked him because he was always ready to help. Members of our family always came to our house to see him, to ask for help with money or simply seek his advice. There were always people here in our house.

People told me how my mother was killed. It was on the morning of 27 April, two weeks after the genocide started. She was ill and feeling weak. There were about 60 people together. She sat there for about two hours and some people were begging them not to kill them. They got her to lie face down the floor and shot her with a bullet in the head. That was how she was killed.

When I was in Gitarama, I saw many people being killed. I remember particularly a man found by the *Interahamwe* in his hiding place. Some of the attackers had clubs, others machetes. They ran after him for about five minutes before they caught him. Someone beat him on the head with a club while I watched. He just fell to the ground and died right away.

The other thing I saw was a girl who was also killed in a terrible way. They found her hiding place and also ran after her. She was left there in agony for about 30 minutes and I could see everything. I saw her dying but I didn't have the strength to approach her. They were still standing next to her – laughing and pleased to have found their prey. The attackers were very happy. My impression was that they were not at peace if they weren't busy killing. They had the power and were proud of it. Even after killing people, you could see them standing next to the dead bodies, like hunters who have just killed game. They were really happy.

I was still a child but I felt very sad inside. I was also scared – although it reached a point where all the fear disappeared. I reached a point where I felt as if I didn't know what was happening or where I was. Seeing a human being kill other human beings or run after them, seeing people dying or with machete wounds all over their bodies – those are things I wasn't capable of grasping or fully understanding.

I was so miserable. There was one day I kept feeling very sad without really knowing why. I felt very uncomfortable, very confused even though it had been a good day because no one was chasing after me. I had spent the whole day crying without really knowing why. It had been quite a peaceful day because no one had come to where we were hiding. But I wasn't at peace at all. I kept thinking about home, about my brother. I memorized the date when this happened, wrote it down and kept the piece of paper. Later on, I found out it was the time my family was murdered.

I didn't find out what had happened to my parents until after the genocide. I was so convinced they were still alive. I learnt about it later on in August. The people who knew what had happened didn't know how to tell us; they didn't know how we would handle it. One day in August when the genocide was over, my sister and I had a long conversation and she told me what had happened. We spent some months living on our own without any other members of the family.

After the genocide

I just can't get out of mind how my parents were killed, the ways in which people were killed. And yet they were innocent children, innocent women, innocent parents. And then surviving by jumping over dead bodies, not being able to sleep, and having to steal a jacket from the dead – all these are things I can never forget. I can't go to bed without thinking about them and remembering how my family and other people I knew were killed. It's not something I can ever forget.

Surviving has taught me the value of life. When you escape death, when someone was perhaps about to cut you down and didn't do it and you're still alive the next day, that's when you appreciate life. You realize that your life or other people's lives are of great value. You understand that everyone is affected by things just as you are. Now I think twice before I do anything that might hurt others. It has taught me respect for my own life and for other people's lives.

In Rwandan culture, when someone dies, people come and mourn with you. But they killed my family and threw them into some garbage. To me, they were not buried: that is actually one of the things that really hurts about the genocide. I wish we had at least buried them as a family. They were respectable and innocent people. Even my sister who was with them saw the way they were killed. Afterwards, some people showed me the place they were killed and we decided to exhume their bodies and bury them in a better way – no matter how hard that was. At least we buried them like everyone else is buried, in a way that honours them.

Can I forgive those who killed my parents and brother? That's very hard. I can't just say that I can forgive the person who took my parents away, the person who made me the way I am, who made me different from other children, who deprived me of my parents' affection and presence. Forgiveness isn't easy and it's not something I could do on my own. It's already hard enough to forgive those who killed other people. But forgiving my parents' murderer is a lot more difficult. It's something that would require a lot of thought – and for a long time.

To me, it's as if nothing has been done as far as justice is concerned. When you see someone who killed your family being condemned for something like five years, you know that sooner or later, the five years will be over and he will then be released. Yes, being imprisoned is a punishment, but personally justice hasn't come my way yet because I have never seen it. They have never tried the people who killed my family – I don't even know where they are.

I once saw someone who was present when they were murdered – even though he wasn't the one who killed them. I was so overwhelmed that I didn't know what to say. I felt that if I talked to him, I might say or do something wrong out of anger. So I chose to leave. He was going to be questioned in a *Gacaca* court. I didn't have the strength even to approach him and ask him anything. There was nothing to talk about. He knew who I was and I also knew him. Should I have greeted him? I didn't know what to do so I left it there.

Personally the genocide taught me the value of life; it taught me to appreciate having parents. Losing them is what makes you realize the importance of having them. The genocide taught me respect for other people's lives, as well as respect for my own life.

I don't think genocide is possible again here. From what I see, I don't believe it can ever happen again. When I look at the way today's young people really fight against it all – and really want to fight – and the way they remember it no matter how hard it is, I don't think it's possible. We need to do all we can to ensure it never happens again. I feel convinced that genocide will never happen again.

The future

As for my future, I believe it will be good. I want to be responsible for my life and able to help others the way we used to before. It will take a good education – this is a must. There are others who are poor, whose lives are worse than mine. I believe that soon I'll be able to help them out. I think the future will be better than the last ten years.

Rwanda is a small and beautiful country and I believe all Rwandans have to learn to love and help each other. They also need always to remember what happened – because when it all happened, people didn't love and respect each other. Nobody respected the lives of other people. It will take a lot to make this happen because every Rwandan has his or her own problems. But if people understood the challenges we are going through individually, we would be able to help each other more effectively.

The most difficult aspect of being a survivor is remembering what happened to you. Sometimes you remember so many bad things that it could destroy your life and stop you from doing anything. You could become a very wicked person because of the things you saw or went through. Being a survivor can make life very hard because of what you saw. It may change the way you look at people and can even stop you from loving anyone. You saw so much evil that you no longer fear anything. You may be woken by nightmares about people with machetes who want to kill. Or you may remember a child you saw being killed. Those are the challenges for survivors. It affects them for the rest of their lives.

My mother told me how I should behave in her absence. She told me, "You should love people and always think of living peacefully with people." I wondered why she said that to me, but later on, when she was no longer there, I thought about it again and realized how important it is. I always try my best to live on good terms with everybody. Even when somebody hurts me, I try not to focus on that. I try to love and understand people and the challenges they face in life. I really try to put it into practice.

Today I want to work hard and achieve something in life. I'm not a sad person; I'm not sorrowful. Even when something saddens me, I look for a reason to be happy. I want to work hard and get somewhere in life. I know no one will have pity on me just because I'm an orphan.

I've been working with Aegis Trust to establish the Kigali Memorial Centre because it's ours; we need to be the ones doing it. If I don't do it, who else will? Not everyone is capable of doing it. It's very sad spending all your time looking into the lives of people who were killed and looking at their pictures. But I do it – and I do it with all my strength because it needs to be done – so that even the people who want them to be forgotten will have failed. When the project is completed, I think it will have a lot of impact. It is very helpful even for us. When you want to remember your friends or family, you will be able to go there. That's why I give myself fully to that project because it will be a great help. It will even show the international community that the genocide actually happened.

After ten years, life is still very difficult. Some people think the genocide is over and there's absolutely no problem. In fact, now after ten years, some people are starting to realise the consequences of the genocide. They are beginning to understand what genocide is. People are still hurting. When someone tells you that they have been unhappy for ten years, they mean it. Ten years later, life is tough and it is still too soon. We still have a long way to go although we are trying to move forward and I believe God will help us to do so, and to help one another. Survivors are not living in good conditions; the orphans have a difficult life and need other survivors to share their challenges and victories. We survivors need each other. Very few people who aren't survivors can actually help a survivor. A survivor is better able to encourage another survivor because he or she can relate to what they are going through, and can show them that it is actually possible to overcome the problems. Sometimes hearing about the challenges faced by other people makes you feel that your own are less important. It instils some strength in you. At least, that's my opinion!

Yves in Kigali, 2004 © Aegis Trust

Pierre, 2006 © Aegis Trust

PIERRE KAVUBI

My heart still bears a lot of pain

Before the genocide

My name is Pierre and I was born in 1960 during the days of King Kigeri. My father was a member of the UNAR party [*Union Nationale Rwandaise*, a political party for the King]. That's why Dad called me Mugabowakigeri. We fled to Uganda, then I came back to Rwanda in 1965 with Mum and my brother. Dad stayed in Uganda because he was scared to return. He tried to find a way to come back later, but was caught at the border. He was arrested among those they called *Inyenzi* ['cockroaches', derogatory term for the Tutsis] and imprisoned in Ruhegeri. When they released him later, he'd been tortured a lot and he died of his injuries in 1974.

I started school in 1966. The teacher who registered me when I started in Primary One refused to write the name Mugabowakigeri, so he called me Kavubi instead. By 1973, when I was in Primary Six, that's when they started torturing Tutsis. We weren't rich, but they came and burnt our house and destroyed the few things we had. It was at night and my parents went to hide in Kamonyi parish. I was lost on the way so I hid in a nearby bush. In the morning, the attackers were looking for us and they got me. One was holding a machete and hacked my arm. They took me to the local leader, a member of the MDR [*Mouvement Démocratique Républicain*] Parmehutu party, but he said I was very young and they should leave me alone. I lived in his home for about a month, separated from my parents.

After some time the situation calmed down and we were able to go home. Our house had been demolished, but Dad sold his cow and rebuilt it with grass roofing. I was in Primary Six by then and the leaving exams were in May. I wasn't able to do them because we were in refuge, so I had to leave school. I started a normal peasant's life.

Time went by and we were still persecuted; we wouldn't go to collect water because kids would stone us and say, "You're from UNAR." We weren't considered like others. We didn't have proper rights as Rwandans. We were like cursed people. They called us children of *Inyenzi*.

When I was 19, I left the village to come and live in Kigali. I did some technical courses and got a job later. I worked until October 1990 when the *Inkotanyi* [RPF] war started. Things didn't go well in Gikondo where I was living. I was renting Buhake's house and he told me to get out of his house. So I took my wife and three kids. We had nowhere to go, but our Catholic neighbour got us a house in a banana plantation. We were attacked three times while we lived there and I was arrested once. I spent about 15 days at the stadium before I was released.

In 1992 several political parties were formed, including the PL [*Parti Libéral*], which we joined. We thought it was going to change some things about the Government and help people get rights in the country as citizens. But if you were in the PL, you were considered a Tutsi.

The terrible things happened at the beginning of 1994 when a party called CDR [*Coalition pour la Défense de la République*] was formed. That's when all the parties joined together and started fighting against the enemy – the Tutsis.

The genocide

Then the crisis happened in 1994. It was night and we heard shootings all over the city. In the morning, Andrew, my neighbour, came and told me that President Habyarimana was dead. When the shootings stopped, I went outside to see what was happening. I saw another neighbour, an MDR party member, but when I greeted him, he didn't reply. Then I knew things had got worse.

Around nine o'clock that morning, a group of people ran past my home. They attacked my neighbour, Haridi, and started destroying his fencing. Haridi ran away and they burnt his whole house. Then they headed for my house. I hid behind the house and heard them asking my wife where I was. She told them I had run away. "We'll find him when we come back," they said.

The attackers left and started killing other people. At first, I hid in the home of a Hutu, but he told me to find a way to escape and join the people from my church. So I went to the house of a Congolese man called Musiwa; we were the same religion. I spent a night there, but in the morning I heard people banging on his neighbour's doors. Then they killed the man and his wife.

I realised they might find me in Musiwa's house – and kill him and his children as well. So I decided to go back home. When my wife saw me, she burst into tears and said they were hunting me. Suddenly, a group of attackers appeared and found me there. One of the *Interahamwe* [Hutu militia] was going to kill me, then he said, "If I save you from dying, will you buy me a beer?" So I agreed and we went to get one, but all the bars were closed. That was 8 April 1994.

On the way we met a policeman smeared with blood who was holding a gun. "Stop!" he said. "I was told this place is full of *Inyenzi* – in that house over there." So the *Interahamwe* and policeman went to see if there were any *Inyenzi* there and I immediately ran away.

I went to a Congolese family, but they were too scared to hide me. So I ran towards a church and a man was guarding the building. I asked him to tell my wife that I'd passed by there and was going to Masino's where I worked. I wanted her to know I'd be safe there.

I carried on till I reached a place where we fetched water – and I found some people there sharpening their machetes. They stopped me and asked, "Where are you going?" I told them I'd come for some water. They asked for my ID card and one of them realised that it said Tutsi on it. They asked me where I came from and where I was going. "I'm not an *Inyenzi*," I said. But the man with my ID card told them it said Tutsi. They tied me up and started beating me. "Even if you're going to kill me, first ask people if I'm an *Inyenzi*," I said. They took me with them and we met an old man. He said he knew me and because of the way he spoke to them, they stopped beating me.

We carried on and got to SGM [in Gikondo] where I saw a lot of corpses. But just as they were going to hack me, some policemen came and ordered them to stop. "Where does that man come from?" they asked. The policemen asked me for my ID papers and I gave them some documents I had – the attackers still had my ID card. When they checked the papers, they found out I was a Tutsi. But there were several other papers – my work permit, tax card and others. Then the policeman said, "Look, this man you want to kill because he's an *Inyenzi* – he pays tax and I bet none of you do that." Then he turned to me and said, "They won't kill you."

The killers left me alone although they were still nearby. I moved on, but when I reached the *Ecole Zaïroise*, they blew whistles to alert others. So I ran fast past the school. Then I met some people that I knew, Mutatwa and Kandida. I went and hid under the bed in Mutatwa's house.

He told me to keep quiet and so I stayed there. Five days later, Mutatwa left; he was Congolese and I never saw him again.

I stayed in the house alone. On the fourth day, I heard a knock at the door. I was dying of fear. But when I looked around the curtain, I saw it was my wife. Then we cried together as she told me how all our neighbours had been killed. She said they would have killed her as well, but they were still waiting for me. Then my wife and children joined me there. It would be better than dying alone.

People from my church found out we were there and brought us tea and food at night. Other people who lived around there knew as well. There was a man called Sylvère, the CDR area head. He knocked one day and said, "We know you're living there. Just give us some torch batteries so we can keep watch for any *Inkotanyi* who might attack." I told him I couldn't find any batteries because it wasn't my home. Then Sylvère told the *Interahamwe* that he had a 'cockroach' hiding in his area.

The attackers came early next morning. They broke the windows with their guns and shot into the house. The kids were crying and screaming. The killers came inside and tied me up. They took my wife and pushed her to the floor. They took all my family – my kids, my wife and her sister who lived with us. First they took us to a man called Tharcisse Rubwirizi, a journalist for Radio Rwanda who lived in Gikondo. Then they took me to Kongole, the new burgomaster, but he told them to take me away.

That's when they raised their machetes and started hacking me. Someone hacked my fingers. Then they took us inside Rubwirizi's gate. It looked like a butcher's there because there was so much blood. They untied me and started hacking again. They took my children first, starting with Saremu, my third-born. They hacked him and dumped him in a pit. Then they hacked the second one, a girl, and dumped her as well. Then they got the third one, a boy. They hacked him and he collapsed, so they moved on to my wife. She was silent as they hacked her. Then it was her sister's turn.

Finally they came to me and said, "We wanted to hurt you by killing your family first." Then they started hacking me – I have 14 machete scars on my body. I fell down on my stomach and they carried on hacking my back. Blood was flowing from the back of the neck and they didn't know they hadn't finished me off. That's the good fortune that kept me alive.

They pushed me into the pit, where I found my kids crying and other people dying. When I realised I'd been dumped in a latrine, I saw some light in front of me, coming through a small hole. I was very hot and badly injured, but I tried to climb up. I managed to get out.

When I got to the top of the pit, there were no *Interahamwe* there. I pulled myself up and went into the annexe building near the pit. Then I slept very deeply and woke up again around seven in the evening. I couldn't work out what had happened because they'd smashed my head. After about an hour, I came back to my senses and remembered it all. Then I tried to move my head a bit, but it wouldn't move. I tried to feel it with my hands, but my arm wouldn't move because my bones were broken. Then I realised I couldn't move my head because it was stuck to the floor with blood.

Eventually I managed to move my head. I thought the *Interahamwe* might come back again and tried to move. I leaned on the wall and pulled myself up. The lower part of my body was fine, but my head was smashed up and I had bled a lot. I fell down and hit my head again. I was unconscious again for a while.

I lay in a small water ditch and it was raining. I was thirsty. The water was flowing over me and I sucked some into my mouth. I felt dead. Around three o'clock in the morning, I regained consciousness and found I was wet all over. I struggled away from there and moved bent double. I could hear people snoring – I think some *Interahamwe* were sleeping outside.

I went back to where they had hacked me and looked for some clothes to put on, but everything had been looted. Then I moved slowly, aiming to get back to Masino's. I spent the whole night walking. I doubted whether I'd be able to get in there. Then I remembered a place where a tree had fallen on Masino's fence. I thought the white guy was still there and maybe they would shelter me. I climbed on the fallen tree, rolled and fell into Masino's compound.

The people inside were scared when they saw me, but they knew me... I was head of their workshop. They told me that things were tough and the white man had left. The perpetrators had already been to search for people there – they would still find me. I asked them just to hide me in the cellar. I would probably die there but it was better than dying in the street. So they hid me there and I covered myself with some sacks. Then I slept.

In the morning, a watchman called Bosco – also a Tutsi – came and I asked him to help me clean my wounds. They were full of mud and dirt from the latrine. But while he was doing that, we heard someone knock at the door. He opened it, thinking it was one of the white men, but it was a black guy wearing a CDR cap. "Didn't we say you were hiding *Inyenzi* here? Now I've caught you red-handed? Wait there!" Then he left. "Now I'll be killed as well," Bosco said. "They've been wanting to kill me and they've got a reason." So I said I would go and hide in the bush. "If they come looking for me, you can say I escaped or tell them I wasn't even there. That guy never saw me."

They put a ladder up to help me escape, but I had a broken hipbone. I couldn't climb it, so I told them just to leave me there. I went beside the swimming pool. There were cypress trees around it and I hid under a tree and covered myself with leaves. I thought I would probably die there. I could hear a group of *Interahamwe* coming. They shouted, "Hands up all of you! Bring out the *Inyenzi*." The watchmen said there were no *Inyenzi* there. The *Interahamwe* searched everywhere, but couldn't find me.

They carried on searching that night – in the grass and in the house. Then they left and told the watchmen to carry on searching because they would come back next day. Around two o'clock, the watchmen found me. Then I said, "Listen, you all know me. You know I'm being hunted because I'm a Tutsi. But I never hurt any of you. So please don't tie me up, just let me sit between you and you can watch me till morning." So that's what they did.

In the morning, the *Interahamwe* came. Samuel, head of the group, took my hand and said, "Now I'm going to kill you and nothing will happen to me. Because killing you is like killing a cockroach – it's not like killing a person." He looked at my fingers hanging loose, almost cut off. Then the watchmen wanted to please him so they took off the old blanket and showed him the cuts on my back and head. He was shocked. "This guy's already dead. I won't dirty myself killing him. Go and dump him in the waste in 'Camp Zaire'." So the watchmen carried me on sticks like stretchers and dumped me there.

I just slept. Then about one in the morning, there was firing and shooting in Camp Zaire from a mounted gun. The person operating it saw me, but they just went on bombing the area. I had to leave because I thought they might kill me. I knew there was a roadblock near Rwandamotors where they were killing people. So I thought, "I'll go there. Maybe they'll kill me, but it's better than dying here."

I went onto the main road. I wouldn't call it walking because I was pulling myself along. When I got near the roadblock, my heart advised me, "Don't take yourself to the killers, wait for them to get you. Don't go there." So I took the short cut and went via Bayirashi's. He was a Tutsi but his brother had become an *Interahamwe* as a way of saving his life. He told me, "Find a way out of here because they'll come soon. If they find you here, they'll kill me as well."

When I got to Inyange, there was a gang of people sitting there. They were taking a rest from killing people. They stopped me and asked for my ID. They asked me what had happened to me and I said I'd been hit by a grenade and was going to hospital. But they could see I'd been hacked by machetes. They took me back to the roadblock, but I was fortunate because the Tutsi who had become a perpetrator was in charge. If he could tell you were a Tutsi, he'd pretend to look at your ID, then tell the *Interahamwe* to tie you up. Later he would let you go. He was shocked when he saw me.

He ordered a passing car to stop and take me to the Red Cross. The journey was very dangerous and we had all kinds of problems, but eventually got there. Then getting inside was difficult. I had to get past two Habyarimana soldiers who were on guard and another person on the door who didn't like Tutsis... He refused to open the door for me and I pleaded... Suddenly a white guy appeared and ordered him to open up very quickly. That's how I got to the Red Cross. The white guy asked me what had happened and I told them the truth.

They operated on all my injuries and dressed the wounds regularly. I was hacked all over my body. I heard the patient beside me say, "That guy's going to die, why do you want to put him by my side?" At first they fed me on drips, then later they brought me tea.

After about 15 days, that place was bombed – and a miracle happened. The bomb fell near the injured children and among the kids there I saw my son. He recognised me and ran to hug me. As I recovered, I went to check on him and he improved slowly. Then we were moved to another room – but we had problems there because the *Interahamwe* had authority to enter. They would come and take people. Luckily, I'd helped an *Interahamwe* in the hospital and whenever they came to take people, he said I wasn't a Tutsi. So they left me; that's how I survived there with my son.

From there, they took us to a camp called CARE and the Red Cross hid those with machete cuts in a cellar. There were less than 50 of us and some died from their wounds. When the whole city of Mburabuturo seemed to be captured by the RPF *Inkotanyi*, the Red Cross had no way to fetch water, food or firewood. We were asked to write down which side we wanted to go to – Habyarimana's or the RPF. We chose the RPF – by then it was about 20 June.

They brought a vehicle and first took those going to Habyarimana's side. Then they came back and took us to the RPF. But as we got in the lorry, the *Interahamwe* were just behind us in a car, watching ... We set off. On the way, the car behind overtook us and stopped on the bridge in Kanogo. They told the people there to stop the Red Cross lorry because there were *Inyenzi* inside. They'd heaped soil on the road to stop us. They asked the driver, "Who's in here?" and he replied, "Patients I'm taking to the Red Cross at King Fayçal Hospital." Then they climbed into the lorry and said, "They're not patients. They're *Inyenzi* from Rebero." They started to hit us and were planning to kill us. But suddenly we heard someone say, "Stop that! Get out of the lorry. These people belong to the Red Cross. Let them go."

They finally let us go after that white man intervened. We didn't know where we were going. We just knew we were going to find the *Inkotanyi*. It was very dangerous. Suddenly the lorry stopped and everybody was thinking, "This is the end." But then we heard another vehicle and someone laughing and speaking English. We were confused. Then a soldier climbed into the lorry and greeted us. We finally realised we had reached the *Inkotanyi*.

After that, we were taken to King Fayçal hospital and registered for treatment. But we told the *Inkotanyi* that we wanted to be taken far from there. "What we've left behind us is horrible, you've really helped us." Next morning they took us to Gishushu and after about six days, soldiers came in and said, "Shout for victory! Kigali is captured." We were so happy. Two days later, they told us we could go home because the war was over.

After the genocide

I went to see where we used to live, but the house had been demolished. Then I rented a house in Gikondo and started living there, but after a while I realised Gikondo was bad for me because I used to get traumatised. I met people I'd seen on the roadblocks or others who belonged to parties that encouraged the *Interahamwe*. So I moved to Kimironko.

After the war ended, those who saw people kill or hurt their families were asked to report them to the authorities, so they could be arrested. But after some time, those arrested were out of jail. Later, we knew that the perpetrators used the trick of changing their names. After being released, they would go and live in a different area, but you would still meet them in the city.

When they were released, they never came to us and said they were sorry for what they did. Instead they said, "We hope you realise that all you did was a waste of time. We've come to live with you and we'll live in peace." So they came to live alongside us, but up to now, we have never had peace. Because when they left prison, they never asked the victims for forgiveness.

Unity and reconciliation? Reconciliation is a very clear process. Generally, someone has to admit that he or she betrayed his fellow man and ask for forgiveness... He should say, "I'm really sorry for what I did to you and now I wish to be forgiven." There's no way that unity and reconciliation will come out politics. It's not enough for perpetrators to negotiate with the Government. That's not reconciliation at all.

Up to now some survivors still say, "I wish I had died," because those who did wrong are better off than those they hurt. Sometimes they ask us to convict them in *Gacaca* courts [traditional Rwandan local courts], but when you go there and point out someone who attacked you with a machete, they say you are a liar... And on your way back home, you might be ambushed and beaten. For survivors, the genocide still seems to go on – in our hurt and injuries.

Today

After the war, I started working as a mason again. But I'm handicapped by my injuries. My backbone was damaged and I can't use my hands because of my injuries. I was hacked in my joints, on the shoulders, elbows and ribs. I can't do any job that needs physical energy. So I had to learn to interpret house plans and now I get part-time jobs building houses. My life goes on...

My surviving son is traumatised, but fortunately performs well at school. He never wants to cut his hair because the scars on his head make him feel inferior. His left arm is paralysed and he's not able to do a lot of things. He doesn't like talking about the catastrophic things that happened to him. He's so sad and lives with a lot of sorrow. To me the genocide never ended because my heart still bears a lot of pain.

After the genocide, I used to think I would leave Rwanda because all my relatives and friends had been killed. I was the only one left. But later I realised that as time goes by, things will change. Then later, I found two young survivors from my family who had joined the army. They helped me gather up some things – I was able to get a mattress where I could sleep.

Up to now, survivors still have a miserable life style. They are sick from their injuries and the children need help to go to school. They have lived through a catastrophe. Their loved ones were killed; some women were infected with the HIV/AIDS virus; others lost their husbands at an early age. Children became orphans. I imagine they wonder in their hearts, "Where will it end?" But I would advise them to be strong and patient.

In Kinyarwandan there's a very meaningful word, *sakidi* (destiny). God is aware of those who did those deeds. No one but God should take decisions over anyone's life. So let's wait for destiny. Someone may boast that he was released from jail and is now back home, dancing with joy. But he should know that there will be a Judgement Day. And it is written in the scriptures, "Before you reconcile with God, first reconcile with your neighbour."

Today I'm 44 years old. Since the day I was born, I've seen lots of things, especially issues based on ethnic groups. Those things hurt me so much. I think we should all ask ourselves these questions: When I was born, did I choose to be in this ethnic group? As I grew up, did anyone of a different ethnic group help me? That might help people understand that no ethnic group is above another, that no group should be hated. If people were free of this ignorance, nobody could convince them to kill someone just because he's short or tall! Or hurt a kid just because he was born in that family. Instead, people should focus on the future and help one another to build a united country.

Pierre, 2006 © Aegis Trust

Ernestine, 2006 © Aegis Trust

Ernestine Mudahogora

Surviving in Ntarama

Before the genocide

My name is Ernestine and I was born in Bugesera, in Ntarama district. My father's name was Peter Karinamaryo and my mother's Veronica Mukagasisi. There were seven of us in my family but I am the only one who survived. I was 18 at the time of the genocide.

My family was originally from Ruhengeri, but we moved to Bugesera in 1959 to escape the Hutu persecutions. When we were young, our father used to tell us about the very big forest where they lived and how it wasn't easy to flee from there.

People used to tell us about those days, but for us children it was just history. We never thought that something like the genocide would happen. Similarly, our children will probably see the 1994 genocide as just history.

We grew up normally until the 1990s, and then in 1992 the atmosphere in Bugesera became negative; the Hutus were burning Tutsi properties. By then we lived in Ntarama district, which was out of town. Our area was a kind of camp or agglomeration, a place where they put all the Tutsis who had migrated there. People used to build their houses close to each other.

In 1992, the killings hadn't started in our neighbourhood yet – they started in the areas of Mayange and Musenyi where Hutus and Tutsi Abamere [a Tutsi clan from Bugesera] lived. Some of the Hutus were locals and some from outside. We were lucky because they stopped in Nyamata and didn't reach our village. But we were well informed about what was happening and the people in the areas they attacked fled from their homes to our village. Life went on although it was very tough. There were always rumours about Hutus burning Tutsi properties.

So we grew up knowing that the Hutus had no sympathy for us. We didn't have any hope of living with them as a community. But we didn't believe it would end in the way it did.

The genocide

We were at home on 7 April 1994. That night we heard that the President's plane had crashed. My brother came in screaming, "We're all dead. I heard that Habyarimana is dead." I was still very young; I wasn't mature enough to understand current issues. I replied carelessly, "Oh, if he's dead then we're finally going to get some peace." My brother replied, "That's what you hope. All I can assure you is that we're going to die." We kind of joked about it.

The following day came, but we had no problems until night fell. The next day we started hearing terrible rumours about houses being burnt here and there. Things continued and to us it seemed as if the genocide had started. But in reality it had only started in Nyamata, Kayumba and towards Maranyundo. My home village, Ntarama, was only attacked later on.

People were confused and started moving about. They would accuse each other of being cowards. Some went to Nyamata while others came to Ntarama. It continued like that for a while.

In Nyamata, things were getting worse as the days went by. There were horrible shootings and killings in the church. The survivors fled back to where they had come from. All the Tutsis in Nyamata and other areas had been killed. That was when they started attacking the remaining areas.

My uncles and aunts were living across the valley, so they came and lived in the neighbouring houses. Sometimes it was OK for one or two days, then things got bad again. One day, after about two weeks, the *Interahamwe* [Hutu militia] had killed all the people in Nyamata – all those in Kayumba forest and everyone in the church. They had killed everywhere else and the next place was my home village. I remember some people saying, "The attackers have come through the coffee plantation." That was just below our home and I wondered what was going to happen. I couldn't imagine what killings were like. I thought they were impossible. People were screaming, "They've come." And then they fled through the forest to Ntarama church. Those who could still defend themselves with bows and spears fought off the attackers, but they started to lose courage when they saw about ten or twenty of their number being killed. They started to scatter. The strong fighters fled towards Gitarama and Kabwayi; a few helpless people were left behind.

My brother was among those who managed to flee. He came home and told us, "We can't defend ourselves; they've killed most of us. They've killed the strongest men we had. We should all find our own way now." "Where are you going?" I asked him. He told me, "We're going to look for a safer place to take refuge." "Won't you be killed there?" I asked. "I don't know," he replied. "But goodbye for now. If I survive we shall meet again." Those were the last words we heard from him as he walked away and left us.

Things had started getting worse. We used to feel comforted by the fact that the strongest men would fight back, but now they had left us. Then, one day, we were all carrying on life as usual. My family was out of the house and I was the only one left at home with my mother. A group of attackers came from the coffee plantation in the valley below our home. At first I decided to stay at home, but then my Mum called me. She said we weren't going to die there alone; we would leave. But some elderly men and women who couldn't flee decided to stay and die there.

We ran away and reached a small forest just below our home. We heard the perpetrators amongst the cattle we had left behind. They hacked the cattle and then killed the elderly people who had stayed in their homes. We hid in a bush near our house because the attackers were coming close.

Then we ran to the sector offices at Ntarama church. Even as we were running, we could hear some *Interahamwe* behind us saying, "They went through here. There they are." Others came into the bushes searching for us, but luckily they found property – suitcases, bags and so on – that people had hidden there. We heard them saying, "Hey! I've found some treasures here." So while they concentrated on what they had found, we fled. That's how we managed to survive that day. We ran to Ntarama church.

It had rained heavily. It was about four o'clock in the afternoon and getting dark. People were coming and going. Some said they were going to Kigali; others went to Ntarama church because some people had been able to survive there for a few days. It was so scary.

I had run away with my older sister. I told her, "Let's not spend the night here; it doesn't look safe. How can we sleep here?" Then some policemen came and called to everyone, "What's all the noise about? Why are you running away?" And the people replied, "We're running away from the Hutus. They want to kill us." So the policemen said, "Calm down, it's over now. Gather together in one place, there in the church, so we ensure your safety."

Again I told my sister, "I hope you heard what the policemen said. You can guess what will happen next. You'll see whether those who spend the night here survive till tomorrow. Let's go to the schools." We left immediately and ran to the schools.

Just after we left, they threw grenades at Ntarama church. They killed almost everybody – there are just a few handicapped survivors. Anyway, we continued and went to the school. It was the only safe hiding place then for those who had managed to survive Nyamata or the other massacres throughout Bugesera. We spent the nights in the school and during the day we would loiter in the swamps. We never slept in the swamps because the *Interahamwe* went home around four o'clock. Then we could go back to the school.

After we'd been three days at the school, a certain group of attackers called *Simusiga* came [the name means literally 'I cannot leave the Tutsis behind']. It was 15 April 1994. They came in many buses. They had come to kill us. The buses came straight to the school building where we were hiding. The attackers killed many people and only a few were left. We were near the swamp at the time and that's where they found us. Some old people committed suicide. They said they had survived the machetes of 1959 and the machetes of 1994 would not kill them. They dived into the water and were carried away.

I ran away and hid in the bush near the swamp. The *Interahamwe* immediately ran after me. It hadn't rained that day. It was around midday and the sun was shining brightly. That's when the *Interahamwe* came and killed many people – including my cousin who was slightly older than me. Later I discovered that they had hacked me. I didn't know when it happened, but I guess it was around midday. I touched myself and saw blood. I wondered if it was possible that they had cut me and I was still alive. I always used to imagine how one day they would bring a machete and hack me. I didn't know how I would react. I wasn't sure then whether I should hide in a sorghum plantation, but I just kept on running.

At some point, I penetrated another area of bush where the perpetrators found me and started hacking me again. I collapsed. I finally managed to leave that place around six o'clock in the evening when the killers left to go home. Perhaps it was the wind that brought me back to consciousness. I heard people moving around and started calling. But maybe those people thought I was with the perpetrators. Instead of coming close to see, they ran away. And then someone came and said, "Oh no, Mudahogora has been hacked. Look how badly she's hurt!"

You can imagine what I looked like, considering the scars I have now. I looked like a dead body with blood all over my face. I heard someone say, "She's taking her last breath; there's no life in her." I was with my sister's three-year-old boy; we had hidden together in the bush. When I opened my eyes, I saw him seated beside me; he wasn't hurt at all then. He died later. I was the only one left with him, but I couldn't help him get food and later he developed anaemia and died. He was sitting there with his eyes wide open just beside me. I watched him for a while, wondering what would happen to him. By chance, a kind woman who lived nearby came and carried him away on her back.

I was left alone there; everyone had gone. No one bothered to carry me away from there. I tried both my legs and found I had a little strength left in them even though I was injured. I knew that when the wounds are still fresh, it's still possible to move around. The risk was that I might suddenly fall over because of losing too much blood. So I tried walking and I managed it. The pain hadn't started by then so I started running after the people. I didn't want to be left in the bush alone.

Everybody was running and I was left behind. I remembered that when the *Interahamwe* came back and found you still alive, they had to finish you off. I survived that day. I pulled myself up to the school buildings, but by then all my brothers had fled to Gitarama. I was left with my sister, the second eldest in our family; the rest had been killed, including my third brother. There were still some survivors at the school. They had seen that the killing had become very intense and said we should start sleeping in the swamp. Otherwise, the *Interahamwe* would find us and kill us at the school.

When we got there, one of my uncles saw me and said, "Look how badly injured she is. We can't leave her alone here because once they find her, they'll simply finish her off with torture. So let's take her." We used to have some Hutu neighbours who lived in the centre of Bisigara. When the war got tough, they went to help their fellow Hutus and left banana leaves on the doors of their house. It was a special sign; when the perpetrators came, they didn't destroy those houses. So my uncle said they should carry me to one of those houses with a banana leaf on the door. No one would go in there. "God will take care of the rest," he said. So they took me there to hide.

There were other Tutsis who came to hide in that house. They would spend the whole day in the swamp and the night in those houses. I was lucky to have other people with me, but I spent the daytime alone in the house. One day, they went to the swamp and came back in the evening with my brother. After that, he used to bring me some sweet potatoes in a small bucket, but he never stayed to sleep in the house. After a few days, he left and never came back.

One day a certain *Interahamwe* came who used to work part-time as a gardener at home. I don't know why he came; perhaps he had come to loot because he knew that house. He came with some other people and I heard them bang on the door. My heart was beating very fast from panic. My wounds had started festering and there was pus all over. I was in so much pain; it was almost beyond death. I was feeling stiff. I just thought he was going to hack me again on those wounds. He pushed the door open and then said, "Oh my! Is that what you look like now?"

I don't know what kind of God had worked wonders on him, but he never hurt me. Instead he brought me some juice. I couldn't hold anything, so he held it for me and I took big sips. I'd spent weeks without eating anything. Later he told me he was going to get me some medication for me. Three days after he left, the RPF troops [Tutsi-led Rwandan Patriotic Front] came. And I thought, "All the people have been killed. I'm the only one left."

The next morning, the gardener's wife came to me and said, "Do you know what's happened? All the *Interahamwe* are gone and the *Inkotanyi* [RPF soldiers] have come." She asked me if I wanted to be carried to the roadside because there were other injured people there – some with worse injuries than me. She said, "You should join the others and not remain behind alone." I agreed and she walked me to the road.

I was feeling desperate because my arms had started rotting. They were so weak and I couldn't lift my arm at all. It took us about four hours to get to the house there. Then we heard people walking around, asking if there could be anybody inside the house. They pushed the door open and came in. I was the first person they saw. I was in a better condition than the others because my legs hadn't been hacked. Some of the others were horribly injured – hacked around the neck, on the legs, on the head and arms as well. Two of them were dying after weeks of hunger and thirst.

After the genocide

I was eventually taken to hospital where I received treatment. I was in a lot of pain because one bone was badly broken and my wounds were rotten – they were about a month old. They had to clean them, give me medicine and dress the wounds. After about two months, I got well again and continued to live in Nyamata. So many people passed by but I couldn't find any of my relatives. All my aunts who were there had been killed. I started thinking about what to do and where to go.

I finally decided to come to Kigali to see if I could find any survivors. A man who had come from Bugesera gave me a lift, and that's how I came here. When we got to Rwampara, I found that one of my aunts was still there. That gave me some hope since at least I had someone to stay with.

I stayed with my aunt until she died in 2000. I lived there with a few of my cousins who had also survived. When I found my aunt, she thought no one had survived. She was surprised to see me and although she saw how much I had changed, she was happy that I was at least still alive.

Tharcisse, 2003 © Karen Kessi-Williams

Tharcisse Mukama

How death became a way of life

Before the genocide

My name is Tharcisse and I was born in Ruhengeri. I came as a refugee to Nyamata in 1959 with my two children, my wife, my mother and grandmother on my mother's side. Since then I've lived here in Bugesera, in the district of Nyamata. We've had several problems of wars in Rwanda that all took place while I was here in Nyamata. At the time of the genocide, I was 63 years old.

I was born in Ruhengeri and so were my father, his father and my great grandfather, so I was told. When I reached school age, I went to the church school in Janja and finished the 5th grade in 1942. I didn't go to high school. My father had died in 1940 and I was mostly raised by mother. At the time, my mother realised that I wasn't going to help her farm, so she took me to her friends who traded goats in Congo and she gave me some capital to start learning to trade. We would go and buy in the markets of Ruhengeri and Buganza and then sell in the markets of Gisenyi and Bizige. Whatever we had left over, we used to take to Congo to a tradesman called Fati. He lived in Junga and traded both in Congo and Rwanda.

Events of 1959

I worked like that and in 1950, I got some money together and got married. All the business I had done before was under my mother's name because I didn't have a wife and home. After I got married, I continued in that business, but working for my own home. Then came the events of 1959. No one was expecting something big that would stop people from moving around freely. That political war brought us here to Nyamata. There were four political parties: Linar, Parmehutu, Porsomo and Lader. Parmehutu considered itself to stand for Hutus, and so did Porsomo.

Lader did not segregate people. Linar wanted independence. Meetings were held, led by Parmehutu, and they would pass on the message of how they were going to chase the Tutsis away.

In 1959, King Rudahigwa died and Kigeri was put on the throne. Jérôme Bicamumpaka, (former Rwandan Minister of Foreign Affairs) opposed the new throne, but powerful Tutsis shut him up. Bicamumpaka then passed on the word to the people about how they should eradicate Tutsis.

The war then broke out in Ndizi, Gitarama. From our home, we could see clouds of smoke and couldn't understand what was going on. Some of the Hutus we were with knew what was happening, but the rest of us had no idea. The house-burning attacks came closer and closer to our area and the next thing we knew was that our houses were being set on fire by the Hutus amongst us. They were our friends and neighbours, but they had been taught the propaganda about Tutsis. Nevertheless, they didn't kill anybody then; it was just burning houses.

We scattered into the mountaintops, sat there and watched. They would loot and burn houses, but not kill. They would pass us by, but do nothing to us. In the morning they would use horns as sirens and then go to work. The only people who died here were Nkundiye from Kigarama and Munyarugarama from Bukonyi. They both died because they fought against those Hutus.

We all ran to the churches. The people who had gone to the provincial town were all packed in cars and sent off to Bugesera. We also got news that those who didn't own land should go to the provincial town, where they would be sent to Nyamata. I had my own land, so I went back to it. My neighbours saw me come back and helped me build a little house. Vitari Basekwa, the appointed leader of my hill, saw me and told me to go to Bugesera right away. I asked him to give me an extra day and told him I would be off first thing next morning. I didn't even sleep at my house that night. I took my family and we went to a Hutu friend's and slept there. Early next morning, they escorted me across the river, where I got a car and went to the town of Ruhengeri. When we got there, we found cars waiting to bring us to Nyamata. We got into them and left, and that's how I came here in December 1959.

They had sent us to this area because it was a bad place with forests, wild animals and the tsetse fly. When we came, there was nothing but a single road all the way from Nyabarongo River up to here. Branches hit us in the car as we travelled. When we arrived, they welcomed us, gave us milk for the children and some peanuts. We all lived in one big house with about 100 people, including children. They used to give us beans that didn't cook properly, so women and children started dying because of bad food. That was when my mother and grandmother died – in February 1960. We would go to the cemetery in the morning and leave about 8 p.m. They would bring one body after another to be buried – all because of bad food. We had two white men guarding us and they were the ones who gave us the beans that were impossible to cook.

In 1961, perhaps they were ashamed of our living conditions, and they decided to cut small roads perpendicular to the main road to Burundi. They gave us small houses, about the size of a table, 50 metres apart. That's when we went into the forest and started farming there. The land was fertile and we had good rain, so we had good harvests and settled there.

Events of 1963 and 1966

In 1963, those who had fled to Burundi in 1959-60 gathered together and attacked Rwanda from Kirundo. They were the people from Linar – Tutsis, but they also included Hutus, and the leader of the attack was called Kayitare. They took out the Gako military camp. They came here to Nyamata and people got excited, thinking that the King was right behind and they had won the battle. Then some cars came from Kigali. By that time the rebels (*Inyenzi*) had reached Nyabarongo; they fought there but ran out of ammunition. Then the rebels scattered, running in all directions and crossed back into Burundi. Then there were some killings of Tutsis – but that time they killed the rich Tutsis, certified teachers, and our chief whose name was Kamali. They took him there and shot him. But they only killed those who were educated and left the ordinary people. We stayed at home but other people ran to the church.

Later, they told people to return to their homes, and those who had stayed at home had the courage to go to the market. I had run away into Burundi for a week and reached a place called Murori. I came back at night to get my family, and people advised me to stay because no one knew that I had left. I decided to stay. Next morning I went to the market and people were shocked to see me, but I pretended to be surprised that they should think such a thing. It all calmed down, but people didn't understand what had happened – even though I and my family knew that I had escaped to Burundi.

In 1966, there was another attack in a place called Bweyeye, in Nshiri, Burare, just near Gikongoro. It reached us and there were killings again. That time, we ran to take refuge in the church. They killed selectively, picking out the people they called the rebels' accomplices. Soon it was all over and we went back to our homes. But every time we went back, we had to rebuild our homes. Every time they killed, they also looted and burned houses. If you had crops, you would come back to find empty fields. If you had a cow, it would have been eaten. If you had a goat, the same thing. You had to start all over again. That was the way of life for us Tutsis in Bugesera.

1973-1994

In 1973, Major-General Habyarimana removed President Kayibanda in an army coup. But it wasn't just a *coup d'état*. Whenever anything happened, the Tutsis in Bugesera would pay. So there were killings again, and we ran away to escape. The next thing we heard was that Habyarimana had become the President. He truly gave us peace and we settled. We forgot about everything and built strong homes. He gave us full peace and we thought of him as the true President.

In 1990 the Rwandan Patriotic Front [RPF] attacked from Uganda. We heard about it in our homes, and we also heard of young people sneaking off through Burundi and going to join the RPF. They started to search our homes, saying that we were accomplices. They would ask us where our sons were, and if you didn't know, that was it. You would be taken and killed. That's how it happened: we would hear of people being taken to be killed like that.

In 1992, the mayor of this district, whose name was Rwambuka, ordered the shooting of a businessman called Sebazungu who had a shop. They also went and shot a teacher called Aron who lived in Gatare. That was also the time they shot Antonia, the Italian lady who lived here. When people saw these two killings happening, before Antonia was shot, they ran to find refuge in the church. People lived there in the church and Antonia started sending reports abroad about what was happening. They suspected it was Antonia sending them, and that's when they killed her. Eventually, the news spread and the refugees at the church were released.

The genocide

Then in 1994 Habyarimana's plane was shot down. Then things got bad. People ran. They got here to Nyamata and were stuck because there were roadblocks so that no one could go back. The killings started on 11 April. They shot them, killed them with grenades and later went in with clubs and machetes to finish the job. That's how they killed them. There are a few people who managed to survive here – the militia thought they were dead – but most of them have lost a limb. When the RPF came, they set up a hospital and took care of them. The few who survived are the ones who tell us what happened. I ran away and survived in the valley where the grass is very tall. I didn't come here.

We heard about the plane crash from a neighbour. We were sitting outside somewhere and a neighbour came and told me that he had heard on the radio that people were told to stay in their homes. That was in the morning. We remained home all that day. On the first day after Habyarimana's death, nothing happened, but on the second day, the war broke out. At the time the soldiers weren't involved; it was the civilians who started burning houses. They mostly set fire to the grass-roofed kitchens because the main houses were normally roofed with metallic sheets. They started burning. We fought against them; we were fighting against Hutu civilians then. They ran off across the valley because they lost the fight. There were a few of us, so we grouped ourselves and worked together.

We fought for two days and on the third day around 11 a.m., the attackers went and sat down. We saw a car take off up the road. It had gone to the district office to fetch police with guns. Up to then, they had been fighting with bows and arrows, which we also had. The old men like me who had no strength would carry stones and pass them on to those who were able to throw them.

A policeman named Kabano came. They came down the hill and we did the same because we thought nothing of them. We got down to the valley, just near the grass. Our archers were in front. At that time we hadn't seen the policeman, Kabano. The next thing we saw was a man called Murekezi going up in the air, then we heard the gunfire and he fell to the ground. We saw him go up in the air and the bang came after. He was our best archer. Then they shot another man called Kazimbena.

When this happened, we immediately took off and ran. That was around 5 p.m. From where we lived in Nyiramatuntu, we went and got our families and crossed to Cyugara. They came and cut down the banana plantation. There were many people hiding in there and they were all killed. They burnt houses in Nyiramatuntu.

The next morning we saw fires everywhere and heard gunshots from all corners. Most of the people ran into the Ntarama church, but we ran into the tall grass in the valley and others ran to a place called Butera. Buses full of soldiers came, so other people told me. I went and hid among the grass. My wife was killed there; I don't even know when, but I heard she was killed there. She was with my children. People were being killed all the time. The only way we could tell people had died was when we regrouped in the evening after the militia had gone home. Then we could tell who wasn't there any more.

When the genocide began, I had eight children; seven with us and one son who was in jail in Kigali at the time. He survived and died later. He had become a soldier. Six of my children were killed in the genocide. The other one who survived, a daughter, lived in Gisenyi and after the genocide she came back. She had a Hutu partner and he had hidden her in his house. When they asked him where she was, he would say that she had left. Whenever they wanted to search his house, he would refuse. She told me that he dug a hole for her which he covered, and he would feed her in there. Afterwards, she refused to carry on living there and came back here.

Four of my children were killed in the grass. Two others were killed as well – one in a place called Karambi and the other here in Nyamata. The one who died in Karambi was hacked and she screamed out that she was Hutu. They left her where they had hacked her and then came back in the morning to carry her to hospital. When they got to the hospital in Mwogo, someone came out and said that she was a child of Mukama, a well-known Tutsi. That's when they killed her. After the genocide, they told me where her body was. I went to exhume it and buried her here.

I don't even know how my wife died. I don't know. The body of my son who lived in Nyamata was recently exhumed. The people came and told me that he was still whole. I felt sad and so I didn't even go to see him. I didn't have the heart to exhume corpses all the time. I heard that he was found hiding with some other people. They took him to the shop, asking him to repeat that he was an RPF supporter. They asked him for money because they knew he was a businessman. He reached in his pocket and gave them some. They immediately hit him on the head with a hoe. He was 19, born in 1975.

Before 1959, Hutus and Tutsis had got on well together. We inter-married, helped each other, and so on. There was no problem at all. Even after 1959, things got back to normal and there was no problem. The Hutus weren't mean; it was other people who taught them bad things. They taught them first to burn houses and then, thinking that was not enough, they taught them to kill.

Today and the future

In the future, I think things will get even better than they used to be, now that segregation no longer exists. In the past, we had our race written on our identity cards; first it said which clan a person belonged to, then later they changed it to the race. Today, it has been removed, and that's why I say that if things continue this way, they'll get better. We fight segregation today. People are one. Children are taught as one, taught the same things by the same teacher. So if people are united at such an early stage, they will not become separated again. Division is created by bad leadership. The Rwandan Government is fighting – and will continue fighting – against segregation. This gives me hope that we'll be as content as we were for a few short periods in the past, if not more so.

I do have hope in the future. The most important thing everyone asks for is peace – even if you have only a little to eat, to be able to eat it in peace. Even though I'm old, I ask for peace and I have it now. I am sad, but I have peace. I'm in a peaceful country.

I think *Gacaca* [trials in traditional local courts] is important and will unite people. It will cease the gossip and bring back peace among Rwandans because someone who wronged you can come up and make you understand that he has never hated you, nor wanted to wrong you, that it was all done because of bad governance. We can truly see that some people didn't like what they were doing. Some refused to go to the attack groups and were punished. Nevertheless, I think *Gacaca* will serve. It can't bring back what they took away, but if they come back and apologise and explain themselves, you might feel much better and probably forgive them. You might also feel that you can trust them never to do it again.

Nowadays I work at the memorial site in Nyamata. I started work here on 20 July 1997. Initially, I worked as a night guard and then in 2002 I started working on maintenance. I do maintenance and my partner gives tours to visitors, explaining what happened to us here and telling them the history of Rwanda. When he's not here, I give the tours. I don't do it because I like it, but I still need life. It's because I need the means to survive. Before the genocide, I had a shop and was a farmer. I had a bar and I farmed a big area of land. Sometimes I needed a car to transport my crops. But that's all in the past now.

I do feel sad working here, but I've got over the worst. Even if I was at home, I'd feel sad. It makes me sad but I have no other way. Sometimes I shake myself to get it out of my system. Even when I'm asleep, I sometimes think about it. My problems today are to do with my life and where I live. I'm renting a place now and I don't think I'll ever get myself out of the renting life. I can get by each day with my wages, but it's not enough to build a house. That's the only thing that concerns me these days.

The memorial site at Nyamata. 5,000 Tutsis were massacred in this church. © *Aegis Trust*

Spéciose, 2006 © Aegis Trust

We must keep remembering

Before the genocide

My name is Spéciose and I was born in 1954. I live in Kimironko now, but I used to live in Muhima. I was born in Ntongwe commune in Gitarama – that's where my parents used to live and where they were killed during the genocide. I got married in 1974. At the time of the genocide, I was 40 years old.

In 1959 I was only about four years old when my family moved and I can only remember a few things. There were political parties like UNAR [*Union Nationale Rwandaise*], Parmehutu [*Parti du mouvement de l'émancipation des Bahutu*], MDR-Parmehutu [*Mouvement Démocratique Républicain*], RADER [*Rassemblement Démocratique Rwandais*] and APROSOMA [*Association pour la Promotion Sociale des Masses*]. MDR-Parmehutu was a Hutu party and UNAR was for Tutsis. Members of the UNAR party were on the King's side, and so the Hutus were against UNAR.

Then later the Hutus became more powerful than the Tutsis because they got support from the Belgians. They abused the Tutsis and destroyed their houses. On Tutsis' gates there would be a white cloth and on Hutus' a red one. The colours were to help distinguish between a Hutu home and a Tutsi home. Even Hutus from other areas would know which were Tutsis' homes and burn them. They would eat the cattle and even kill the Tutsis. That's why some people fled in 1959 and the situation continued like that till the 1960s...

My family fled in 1963 after our home was attacked and burnt. We fled to a bushy hill called Ikibanda. We had a lot of cattle and so we migrated with them. Even when we migrated, our cattle were being seized and eaten, our houses burnt and demolished and Hutus were killing Tutsis.

After some time, we left Ikibanda and went beyond Kinazi to a forest called Nyabusunzu. Many Tutsis gathered there with their cattle and children because most of their houses had been burnt at the same time. Some Tutsis went to Bugesera and others to Sainte Famille church. In the past, people had fled to the church on several occasions. They were fleeing from the Hutus. It was always the Hutus killing the Tutsis.

I also remember events in 1973 because I was a young woman then. Kayibanda was still in power and Habyarimana was chief commander. I remember they attacked our home village on 28 February 1973. They burnt and killed so many people then. I had a brother-in-law whose shop was destroyed, but he managed to escape.

That time we fled and came to Biryogo in Kigali, but we spent less than a month there. Then they made a patrol to capture all the Tutsis and take them to Bugesera in Maranyundo. I was among the people in Maranyundo. They transported us to the bush there in trucks and minibuses and gathered us in Muhima prison – it was a police station then.

I remember that was the time when Habyarimana wanted to overthrow Kayibanda. He sent cars to the forest and came in a helicopter himself. Then he ordered the police that no women should sleep in the forest. The men were left there and the women went back to town. But they would come and take away the men and boys left behind, one by one. They had a list of the people and would come and ask for someone. At first the Tutsis thought the Hutus were saving them from that bush – until they realised what was happening. Generally, very few people survived from there.

Some Tutsis fled then and we went to Kamonyi church in Gitarama, but then the war ended. They said – as they always did – that there was some stability again and we should go back home. We went back home and reconstructed our houses, but others carried on and went into exile. My brother was among those who didn't come back home.

But the situation didn't really improve. The Hutus continued to mistreat the Tutsis. We were oppressed and tortured a lot. Then in 1990, when the *Inkotanyi* [RPF army] invaded the country, the Tutsis were subjected to serious torture. They were imprisoned, accused of being traitors and some were killed. Houses were burnt. After Bucyana's death [President of the CDR party of extremist Hutus and *Interahamwe*], we were attacked and robbed, and my husband was beaten. We were thrown out of our house. That was the beginning of those tortures.

This continued right up to 1994 when Habyarimana's plane crashed on its way from Tanzania. Then they said that Tutsis were responsible for

Habyarimana's death. "So they must pay for it," people said. Then Tutsis were killed. When it came to 1994, it was a catastrophe. Unimaginable... It was one clan trained to kill another. And Tutsis were killed so painfully with so much torture. Some were drowned in rivers and lakes; others were thrown into latrines or pits.

The genocide

Habyarimana died in a plane crash on 6 April 1994. I think it was announced on Radio Rwanda on a Wednesday around nine in the morning. Then they started killing Tutsis who lived around Kanombe – areas like Kabeza, Kicukiro. Soldiers took over those areas and killed all the Tutsis. Suddenly the killings spread everywhere in the city. It was just through God's grace if you found a hiding place.

They came to my home on the day after Habyarimana's death, 7 April. My husband had money, so he gave them some and they went away. The following day, they came back again – on 8 April. Again he gave them some money and they went away. On 9 April, they came again and he gave them more... And again on 10 April, he gave them money.

When they received that money on 10 April, they held a meeting – they were always having meetings. And in the meeting they said, "Although that Tutsi gives us money, even if he gives us a million, we'll still kill him, with his wife and those children of his." Our neighbour was in the meeting and afterwards he came and told my husband, "Listen Michael, you're my friend and we have no grudges between us. Let me find you a way to escape because they just said that they're coming back right now." So he helped my husband escape. Then he came back to me and said, "Listen, I don't want to see your dead bodies here. So you must leave this place in about ten minutes because they're on their way back here." "Where can I go?" I asked him. And he replied, "I just beg you to leave this place because I don't want to see your dead bodies."

So I set off along the Gakingiro road with my children. I carried on and went via the police station because at Manumental there was a horrible roadblock that nobody could escape. So I said to myself, "I'd rather pass via the police; I'd rather be shot than hacked." When the policemen saw the kids, they asked, "You kids, where are you going?" I was carrying another baby on my back. And they asked again, "Are you an *Inyenzi* [cockroach]?" But the children said they weren't.

Then they asked again, "Is that your mother?" and I said, "Yes, I'm their mother." The policemen laughed mockingly and said, "Go and die at other people's hands." So we carried on towards the market. There we met young *Interahamwe* [Hutu] militia who were carrying knives – the oldest was about 14. "Who are you?" they asked, and I replied, "I'm a human being." One of them retorted, "Listen to that Tutsi arrogance! Do you think we can't see you're a human being? We're asking if you're a Tutsi or a Hutu?"

"I don't know. Call me whatever you want."

One of the young militia showed me his knife stained with blood.

"Do you see this? What is it?"

"It's a knife."

"Don't you see the blood stains on it?"

"Yes."

"Do you see that crossroads?"

"Yes."

"Do you see other people lying there?"

"Yes."

"I'm taking you there right now."

"Do as you wish."

When you were in the hands of people like that, there was nothing much you could do. You just became desperate and your fear disappeared. Even those who were killed, died strong and without fear. You were sure you were in the hands of hell. No one would come to your rescue. You would just say a simple prayer, "God, take my life as you wish."

Suddenly a policeman who used to come to our home appeared. I begged him, "Nkyesha! They're going to kill me and the children..." "Who?" he asked. And as he asked the question, the first boy disappeared and another one followed. In no time, just the two of us were left there. It was that policeman who took me to Nyarugege commune.

When we got there, we found that soldiers [a presidential guard unit] had seized the gate to the commune. They had retreated to Nyarugenge after being defeated by the *Inkotanyi* in Kimihurura. The house was full of their wives and children. I remember there were many people who were seeking refuge there – about 180 people. But they refused to let us in. They said we should go and join the *Inyenzi*.

We spent three days outside the district office. In those days the militia and ex-Government soldiers used to come and slaughter people.

Others were kidnapped and taken to undisclosed destinations. At that time, there was a seminar being conducted at Kabusunzu that brought together people from all provinces and ethnic groups. Those who had identity cards showing that they were Hutus were given transportation and other necessary facilities. Those identified as Tutsis were put in buses and taken to the place to be killed.

A group of *Interahamwe* came to kill us, including a taxi driver called Kadahwema, a notorious killer from Gisenyi. He wore a military uniform and was armed with a gun. They killed a lot of people, mostly men, and the rest of us were taken to Gakinjiro. There, we were put in a line and they started killing the men. Then our turn came. But before they killed any of the women, one of the *Interahamwe* said, "We'll finish them all off later. We must first escort Habyarimana on the day of his burial. I order you now, don't kill those women. Take them back." That was how we and several other people escaped from that pit.

We carried on awaiting our fate. We would think each day was our last. We thought that if you survived the night, you would die at noon. We lived in this state until the RPF [Rwandan Patriotic Front] soldiers invaded and liberated us. They took us to St. André secondary school and that was the end of war.

After the genocide

I found out afterwards what had happened to my husband. Michael was an accountant in a Kigali hardware store and knew a lot of businessmen. So he sought refuge, but later a soldier called Rurangiza from the presidential guard unit captured him. He asked him what he was and when Michael said he was a Tutsi, the soldier mocked him and said, "I've killed so many Tutsis. You're going to be my last victim." He fired his gun at my husband's head and my husband collapsed. He was later taken to hospital with some other wounded.

Survivors from Kigali hospital told me this story. There were several people in the hospital injured like him. They just used to cover them up without giving them any medicine. Later, another notorious killer called Kamashini came and took them away. He was the one responsible for all the killings at Kigali hospital. He took them to Kigali military camp where they were hacked to death with bayonets. After the war, Michael was exhumed and reburied in Rebero.

I also lost my baby who died and was buried in Gakingiro. The baby was still young and feeding on breast milk; he died of hunger. And I lost my niece, her husband and two children who lived in Cyahafi. They were hacked and their bodies dumped in a latrine. They were exhumed by Ibuka [Rwandan survivors' association] and taken to Gisozi memorial site for reburial.

My sister who lived in Gitarama was also killed. Her husband organised her reburial ceremony. Other family members were killed in Butare, but they haven't been exhumed because no one knows exactly where they were dumped after being killed in Nyamure. A lot of people were killed there. I realised that when I attended a burial ceremony. But I can't tell if my people's remains were among those we buried that day. I don't know.

After the war, we left St. André and went back to Muhima, to an abandoned house. We lived there till the day AVEGA [Association of Genocide Widows in Rwanda] came and found some American benefactors who built the first-phase houses for us. The second phase was built by FARG [*Fonds d'Assistance aux Rescapés du Génocide*].

Life continued and the children started going to school because FARG was giving out scholarships. Though we're still poor, I thank them because our children are studying well. Generally, our problem is poverty, like elsewhere.

Unity and reconciliation are not easy to achieve. Reconciling with someone who killed your people is next to impossible. I can't even imagine the beginning of an act of reconciliation. I can't imagine someone who killed more than 20 of your family members standing before you and asking you for reconciliation. How possible would that be?

Maybe the Commission of Unity and Reconciliation will succeed, who knows? Though it will require a lot of time. It seems impossible to achieve their goals in a short time because the perpetrators still have strong hatred. Whenever they see you, they try and show they still hate you. So how can reconciliation take place?

What do I think of the *Gacaca* trials? Past experience of *Gacaca* is different from today. It used to take place when someone grazed his cattle on another man's crops or if two people had fought. Then they would both go the *Gacaca* courts and later be reconciled. But I had never heard of *Gacaca* to try killers... I don't even have words to say what I think. That so-called *Gacaca* came into existence to set the perpetrators free. Those who would admit they had killed 100 people would be set free. I hear that in *Gacaca* the perpetrators ask for forgiveness. What about those who have already been released? Did they ask for forgiveness? If so, whom did they ask? Was it the Government or the people whose loved ones they killed? That's the question. *Gacaca* for killers! It's unbelievable!

Today and the future

As for the future of Rwanda, all Rwandans should come together to try and build our nation. But this will only be achieved if they try and eliminate the habit of not punishing the guilty. The most important thing is to set up a culture of punishing those who harassed and killed others. They should be punished accordingly and in public, for others to see and learn a lesson. If we stop that habit of not punishing, then we can build our country. People have to learn to live peacefully with others, without killing.

My advice to young Rwandans is that first of all they should learn how to love. Secondly, they should put a lot of effort into education because there will be no bright future for them if they don't go to school. They should avoid hatred amongst themselves in their lifetime. Children should experience love and be taught about love rather than hate. They should avoid saying things like, "Look at that Tutsi," as they used to before. Hatred must be uprooted and people must only think of themselves as Rwandans. Every human being has a right to live. No one should be killed. That's the most important thing for young people to learn.

The children who lived through the genocide were left in misery, homeless and without parents. They must be strong and patient, and take care of their education. Life may seem meaningless to them, but they have to be strong because there's no alternative. They should make friends with other survivors and talk about their problems. When you meet people who have experienced the same problems, you feel relieved because you can talk about your difficulties to someone who understands them. It helps children to know there are other people who faced the same problems.

The perpetrators? I wonder what I would say to them?... I couldn't say, "Never do it again," because if they had a chance, they would repeat it today. Most of them don't even admit they participated in the genocide. They deny it, yet we witnessed them doing those deeds. What kind of advice can one give such people? They should repent for their sins and feel it deep inside their hearts. They should tell the truth and ask for forgiveness. They should repent before God because those they killed were God's creatures.

The hardest thing that everybody faces is having lost their loved ones and learning to live without their family. It's hard to carry on with your life, especially on special days. For example, some children grow up and reach the time for marriage. Then they say, "I wish at least I had an aunt or one of my parents." Everything reminds us of those terrible days of genocide.

Personally, when I have a lot of problems – let's say the children need books or pens, or some money for school – that's when I remember and life seems hard. Sometimes I get worried, "What will they eat tomorrow? Or for dinner?" Then I think that if they had a father, I wouldn't be this worried. Well, I'm not alone in this; it's the same for every parent who faced that genocide.

When I feel like that, I think about the orphans around me. Over there in that house, there are four or five orphans living together. The oldest has to act as parent to the rest, to be in charge of the whole home. Then I think about their example and that of my fellow survivors. Considering other people's lives helps. We live in a residence for survivors. It's useful because we are neighbours and we all have the same problems. You see other people being strong and say to yourself, "I must try and be strong as well." All those who faced the genocide have to be strong because as the years go by and our children grow and go to school, our problems will go on reducing.

I met some Jewish survivors of the Holocaust. One of them said, "My grandparents were victims of the Holocaust. From what we saw and heard about the genocide, we thought we would find that people had gone crazy here. We thought it would be very hard to get close to you. But you look surprisingly good! You're still smiling!" But someone else came and told us he didn't agree that what happened here was genocide. That denial hurt us terribly because we couldn't imagine why people would deny it.

One of the things that keep me strong is commemorating the genocide. That's why the history of these killings should never be forgotten. Not only my testimony, but everyone's. The events must be written down in books so our grandchildren will be able to read about it and know what happened. All future generations should learn that there was genocide here. We must keep remembering our loved ones who were killed – and what happened to them.

Spéciose, 2006 © *Aegis Trust*

Odette, 2005 © Aegis Trust

Odette Mupenzi

It's hard to keep hoping

Before the genocide

My name is Odette and I was born in 1975. We lived in Nyamirambo, a suburb of Kigali. My father was a businessman and my mother stayed at home to look after the family. I had four sisters, Chantal, Marie-Cécile, Marthe and Safira, and two brothers, Félicien and Cassien. Before the genocide, I was 19 and a student. I was really fine.

Before 1990, life was good. We lived alongside the Hutus with no real problem, although we all knew that no Tutsi child could be admitted to a public school. My older sister was very smart and passed the Primary Leaving Exams, but the school administration gave her place to a Hutu child. And Tutsis were not allowed to do some kinds of work – there was nothing we could do about it. Despite this, there was no other major trouble.

Then in 1990, there was a rumour that the *Inkotanyi* [RPF soldiers] had attacked and it was obvious that the neighbours' attitude changed. There were divisions based on ethnic groups. And when war broke out in October, people started being arrested on the streets and abducted from their homes. One day, my Dad was taken to the regional stadium in Nyamirambo, but he managed to escape and come back home when the militia were out looking for more 'traitors' (*ibyitso*). Anyone who was a Tutsi was in danger, but the soldiers concentrated mostly on men. My Dad and brothers hid most of the time and the rest of us had no problem. Because we lived near the stadium, we could hear people in agony, crying for help. 1990 was the beginning of systematic torture and oppression.

The genocide

I was at home when the genocide started. When President Habyarimana's plane crashed on 6 April 1994, an announcement was broadcast the following morning forbidding anyone to go out. So we stayed at home. A few hours later, we started hearing cries from our neighbours' house – it was as if they were being beaten.

Our house was close to the Josephite seminary school, so we used a ladder to climb into the school compound. The brothers welcomed us and we stayed there one night. The following morning, we heard gunshots outside, then a few hours later, the school was attacked. The killers knocked at the gate, but the brothers refused to open it. Then the attackers jumped the fence and came in screaming, "We know there are *Inyenzi* ('cockroaches', meaning Tutsis) here." We were hiding in one of the classrooms, except for my brothers who were on guard outside. My Dad was with us in the classroom.

The killers kept banging on the classroom door, but no one would open it. Eventually, they said, "If you don't open this door, we'll destroy it." When my Dad heard this, he told us to hide under mattresses because people thought that a bullet couldn't hurt you after going through a mattress. From my hiding place, I could see two soldiers and some of our neighbours who had become *Interahamwe* [Hutu militia]. They were the ones who ordered my father to open the door.

The killers grabbed Dad as soon as he opened the door and started hacking him with machetes. When my Mum saw this happening, she acted with great courage. She rushed to take hold of the soldier's gun, but he pushed her away. Then the *Interahamwe* hacked her with their machetes till she lay unconscious.

I was hiding under a mattress just below the window. Suddenly I heard the glass smash. I was in such a panic that I hadn't heard the gunshots outside. As I raised my head to see what was happening, a soldier outside saw me and showered me with bullets. He hit me on my jaws, on my arms and chest. My injuries were terrible. I felt so weak that I lay down. I could hear other people near me praying, then suddenly it all went quiet. The other people were dead.

Finally, the *Interahamwe* came into the classroom to check if there were any survivors. I was breathing heavily, but trying hard not to make a noise. They still saw me. They hacked me with their machetes – I still have the scars on my head. I must have fallen unconscious then because I can't remember what happened next. When I woke up, I found myself lying amongst dead bodies.

The following morning, one of the religious brothers came. He looked at me in the light of his torch, lifted me back on the mattress, then left. He came back later with people to give us medicine and we spent the whole night and following day there. The *Interahamwe* didn't come back because they thought we were all dead. Those who could still walk left the school and went to hide somewhere else. I couldn't do that – I couldn't move at all.

Three days later, the Red Cross came and took us by car to Kigali hospital (*Centre Hospitalier de Kigali*). On the way there, we were stopped at a roadblock in Gitega. They were looking for Tutsis, but I looked like a corpse and the other wounded were in a very bad state. The *Interahamwe* got angry with the Red Cross staff and shouted at them, "We're killing *Inyenzis* and you dare to take them to hospital?" But after a short argument, they let us go on to the hospital.

When we arrived there, the doctors couldn't do much to help me because of my terrible injuries. They called for a specialist surgeon, but he didn't come that night. In the meantime, my wounds had started to go bad. I could see maggots moving in the wounds on my chest and armpit. Thank God, they weren't in my mouth – the acid in saliva stops that happening. The next day, they took me to the operating room, washed and treated my wounds, then covered them.

We felt safer in the hospital, but the following day, the soldiers came back. "Why are you healing 'cockroaches' when we're destroying them?" they asked. They ordered us to leave immediately and the doctors said there was nothing they could do. They put us outside in a tent.

Luckily for me, one of the nurses working there was Jeanne, my uncle's wife. She came and looked after my wounds outside – until someone reported her for helping an *Inyenzi* and she had to stop. It was the rainy season and water ran through our tent. Our wounds really began to stink, but the doctors had been warned not to look after those 'cockroaches'.

Some soldiers from Kanombe had taken refuge in the hospital, so the *Interahamwe* and *Inkotanyi* [RPF soldiers] were both firing towards us. The soldiers started blaming us, saying the 'cockroaches' had probably revealed where they were. Every night the killers abducted people from our group, but they left me alone because I looked almost dead and my face was really swollen. My younger sister was taken, but she was saved by a soldier who knew her. He just told the others to let her go. Some of the doctors even handed patients over to the killers.

As the war came closer to the hospital, people had to be evacuated. The doctors went first, and then cars came for those who were seriously ill.

I was so sick that a Hutu doctor took pity on me and put me in a car with other patients. We drove towards Gitarama, but on the way the car was stopped by *Interahamwe*. They were looking for Tutsis, but with my swollen face, they didn't waste time on me.

We were taken to Kabgayi hospital where they laid us down outside on the balcony. There was no one to look after us there, but I started thinking about my older sister, Safira. I hadn't heard from her since the war began, but she had been studying to be a nurse in Kabgayi. Perhaps she might still be there? That thought gave me hope and a bit of life.

The next morning, some people came and removed our covers. "She's dead," they said when they saw me. In fact I was starving because I couldn't eat anything. But I could still see with one eye and when I heard some student nurses coming, I forced myself to look for Safira. I couldn't believe it – there she was! She passed by me but I couldn't speak. I just pulled on her uniform. She looked at me, but didn't recognize me at first. When she realised who it was, she ran away and locked herself in a room, sobbing.

The doctor and other nurses were shocked to see my sister run away in tears. I could hardly speak, but I somehow managed to tell them she was my older sister. Then they took me inside the building and tried to put me on a drip, but they couldn't manage it – my veins had sunk too deep. The only way was to feed me with a syringe. Even this was difficult: I could just swallow a little, then the rest would pour out of my mouth. The doctor said I was totally dehydrated – that was why they couldn't find a vein. He asked the nurses to carry on feeding me with the syringe.

A little while later, Safira came and washed me. The dressings on my wounds were green with infection and my sister was scared I might get tetanus. I spent that whole day drinking water through the syringe and the next day, my veins started to show. Then, after a lot of trying, they found a vein in my leg and put me on a drip with antibiotics and medication. Safira took great care of me and had me moved to another ward. Two days later, the *Interahamwe* invaded.

Kabgayi hospital was near the Red Cross, so Safira and her friends carried me on a stretcher. We went through shooting, but reached the Red Cross safely and found lots of other patients there. Safira stayed to work for the Red Cross and really took care of me. The nurses used to feed me on milk mixed with biscuits, passing the mixture through a syringe into my mouth. There was no other way I could eat. It was too painful even to wake up! Safira was always there for me and fed me like this until I could sit up.

Then the Red Cross had to leave because the fighting was coming closer. They organized a convoy and we moved to Nyanza prison where there was space. My sister was still with me and the Red Cross treated us well. If it hadn't been for Safira, I would have died in Kabgayi with the others. I was still in dreadful pain: my jawbones were smashed to pieces, but there were no specialist doctors to help me. My sister used to dress my wounds every morning and evening. That was all we could do. There was no radio, nothing! All I could do was sleep.

I stayed with the Red Cross for the rest of the war and was safe there. There were even *Interahamwe* casualties at the Red Cross hospital, but they were in such a bad physical state that they weren't dangerous.

After the genocide

When Nyanza came under RPF [Rwandan Patriotic Front] control, we had to move because the place was mined. The Red Cross moved us to an orphanage in Rilima and we stayed there for the whole of June. A month later, the war was over. Then the Red Cross took the most seriously injured patients, including me, to King Fayçal hospital in Kigali. Safira was still with me, but we had had no news of the rest of our family since I had left my Mum and young sister at Kigali Hospital and the others at the seminary school.

My sister started work in King Fayçal hospital and was able to continue taking care of me. A Belgian doctor operated on me to remove all the fragments of bone and dirt deep in my wounds. That was why my wounds hadn't been healing.

Safira had a friend at the hospital who was being helped and supported by some people in Switzerland. They wrote to say they were coming to visit Rwanda because they wanted to understand what had been happening in our country. Safira's friend asked if I would like them to visit me as well. Perhaps they might be able to help me?

That was how I came to be visited by a man and woman from the Swiss charity organisation called *Sentinelles*. They came to Rwanda in August and visited me in hospital. My sister took the dressings off my wounds, which had still not healed after all those months. They told me, "We can operate on injuries like yours in Switzerland. It's just a matter of surgery." They took photos and all my medical details back to Switzerland with them.

Switzerland

In November, *Sentinelles* sent a representative to Rwanda, looking for me. He talked to my sister because I couldn't speak very well at the time. He told her to make sure I got my passport and visa as soon as possible. The group in Geneva was going to arrange for my operation.

I left for Switzerland on 30 November 1994, escorted from Kanombe national airport by a *Sentinelles* staff member. I couldn't travel on my own. The escort fed me water all the way on the journey with a syringe.

When I arrived in the Swiss hospital and the doctors saw me, they said my injuries were extremely serious and I might not survive. I had also been shot in the nose and the wound was badly infected – with the result that I had water in my ears and forehead. They were amazed that I was still alive and promised to do what they could.

The next day, the doctors operated to remove the liquid from my head. I didn't feel any pain during the operation but the following day, it was terrible and I was in agony. They had to convince me that the doctors knew what they were doing! This went on for three days until I began to get used to the pain. I couldn't feel anything any more; my whole body was numb; it felt dead. I spent all my time just lying there. All I could do was sleep.

I began to feel better afterwards, but of course I still had the terrible wounds on my jaw. I stayed in the hospital recovering and people from *Sentinelles* came to visit and support me with everything I needed. A few days before Christmas, they decided to discharge me so I could spend the holidays out of hospital. But when they removed the dressing from my wound, I started feeling dreadful pain in the bones again. So the doctors arranged for me to go and stay with a Rwandan lady in France. She would give me my medication for the pain.

That was how I went to France in December. Soon after I arrived, I started to be very ill and needed the painkillers. The more pain I felt, the more I asked for the tablets – and the more the lady gave me. I finally overdosed. My heart almost stopped beating and I was unconscious. The lady immediately called the hospital in Geneva and I was taken back there. From then on, I stayed there in the hospital.

After some time, the doctors operated again and removed other bone fragments from my jaw. Then they rebuilt my jawbone using another piece of bone, securing it with a piece of metal. Later they took flesh from my thigh to fill the cavity of the wound. They tried putting nails in my mouth to make the bones go back to their normal position. It was all extremely painful – almost unbearable – but it did gradually start to get better. The people were very kind to me. They gave me soft food through a syringe because I couldn't chew. They took good care of me and *Sentinelles* also carried on visiting me.

After my fourth operation, I spent another six months in hospital. Then the people from *Sentinelles* came and said, "You've had quite a few operations now. The doctors think they've given you enough anaesthetic for the moment. They want you to go back home to Rwanda and visit your Mum, but come back in six months." They said they would do three more operations to sort out my remaining injuries. I hesitated because I knew how hard it would be to go back to Geneva after being in Rwanda. But *Sentinelles* reassured me and told me not to worry about money issues.

Back in Rwanda

I came back home to Rwanda and to my remaining family – there was only my Mum, my older sister, Safira, and my younger sister left. All the others had been killed. I was supposed to return to Geneva six months later, but after three months at home, I became very ill with boils on my neck.

One of my uncles was a doctor and he helped me go to hospital with this complaint. After six months, when I should have gone back to Geneva, my uncle wrote to *Sentinelles* for me, explaining the situation. They replied that the difficult operations had already been done in Switzerland and the rest could now be done elsewhere. *Sentinelles* had done so much for me, but now it was up to my own country.

My uncle continued to treat my painful boils. They eventually healed, but then I became seriously ill again. The flesh the doctors had implanted on my mouth started to swell up.

I went to seek help from an association called "Kanyarwanda" and that was where I met Sister Cécile. Moved by my situation, Sister Cécile took me to hospital. She bought disinfectant to clean my infected mouth and did her best to find a way to send me abroad for treatment. Then, after some time, Kanyarwanda offered to pay my medical bills abroad. Sister Cécile sent details of my case to a hospital in South Africa and they agreed to do three operations for an estimated cost of $6,000.

South Africa

I travelled to South Africa and the hospital asked me to deposit the operation fees at reception. They said that if the treatment cost less than the deposit, they would refund the money. So my first operation was carried out and I went to recuperate at the home of someone Kanyarwanda found for me. When I went back for a consultation, the doctor told me to go home to Rwanda because the doctors needed to wait three months before they could do the second operation.

That was fine, but when I asked for the receipt and remaining refund, they told me to come back next day. When I did that, they said there was no balance – the money paid was the equivalent of my treatment. That day I had gone to the hospital with a doctor friend. He just could not understand how my surgery could have cost that amount of money and asked them to explain. I think the doctors felt ashamed because they asked us to go back again next day. That time, they gave us a refund of $2,000, along with a sealed letter for Kanyarwanda. They said the receipt was in the letter. We were late and in a hurry because we were returning to Rwanda that same day, so we didn't open the letter.

Back in Rwanda

When we arrived in Rwanda, I gave the letter to the association, but unfortunately there was no receipt inside. Instead, the letter thanked them for sending a patient and said they were happy to give me further treatment. But Kanyarwanda was angry at the loss of so much money and even wanted to call the hospital and challenge them. But someone told them it wasn't the first time this kind of thing had happened, that the hospital wasn't reliable...

Soon the hospital in South Africa sent another letter, saying they needed $15,000 for my next operation. The association was shocked by this demand. Its members became discouraged and I never went back to South Africa.

Back at home in Rwanda, Sister Cécile kept on trying to help me. She called a German friend of hers who was a nun and we went to see her. Cécile told her all about my case and the German nun thought there was a way out – she thought I could be treated in Germany.

Sister Cécile then went to the Survivors' Fund, FARG (*Fonds d'Assistance aux Rescapés du Génocide*), and told them my story. FARG agreed to pay my travel to Germany and Sister Cécile assured them that the rest would be fine.

Germany

That was how I found myself travelling to Germany, escorted by a German nurse who was going home on holiday. But there was a problem: the nun hadn't told her German colleagues I was coming, so when I arrived at the convent, they could hardly believe what was happening! I knew they were angry even though I couldn't understand what they were saying in German. I wasn't welcome; there was something wrong.

Another Rwandan lady, also there for medical services, explained that they were arguing about me. They didn't want me to stay there. I had to phone Rwanda to try and sort the problem out. It was all very difficult, but eventually the German Sisters agreed to look after me.

They took me to hospital and the doctor there told me, "There's no problem. I'll operate on you and afterwards, you'll be able to throw away that scarf round your mouth." He said it would need three operations.

I went in for the first operation and afterwards, the Sisters told me I could go back home to Rwanda: there was nothing more to be done, enough was enough. But then I sank into a coma and the Sisters took me to another hospital. When they saw how ill I was, they phoned Sister Cécile and told her to come quickly. By the time she arrived, I was conscious again. Although I was still very ill, the Sisters told Cécile that she had to take me back to Rwanda; she couldn't leave me there any longer.

Pain at home in Rwanda

That's how I came back to Rwanda with Sister Cécile. I went straight away to tell the FARG representatives what had happened. They said they would talk to the German doctors and send them money for the remaining operations. They asked me to go to the Medical Commission to get the authorization. One of the Medical Commission doctors told me, "There's a group of specialists coming to Rwanda in July. You should wait till they come. They'll probably take the metal out your jaw, then we can see what to do next."

All this time I was in terrible pain. It was so painful that I couldn't sleep. I lay all night long looking at the ceiling or wandering around the house. I was in agony but the plan to go back abroad for treatment had failed. The Medical Commission refused to stamp my authorization.

In desperation I finally went to see a doctor at King Fayçal hospital. He told me that my jaw was infected and the best way to cure it was to remove that piece of metal. I had no choice. I even accepted that I might die.

Afterwards, the doctor told me that if he hadn't removed it, I would have developed cancer. That piece of metal was originally supposed to be in my mouth for six months. It had been there for five years.

I waited for those other doctors who were supposed to come in July. They never came. But at least the pain was reduced.

Today

These days I've begun to suffer pain again and I don't have a doctor in Rwanda following my case. They all tell me to wait, that specialists are coming. My whole life revolves around my illness. I have headaches and fevers, but all I can do is sit at home.

Since this happened to me, my whole life has changed. Before the genocide, I had big ambitions. I always wanted to have a good job and be independent. I like studying and dreamt of being a nurse.

But today my life is full of pain – too much pain, psychological and physical. I'm not supposed to move a lot or do anything requiring energy. I have to rest all the time and just sit around. I'm handicapped for life. Safira has three children now, but she's so disturbed by the trauma that she can't settle anywhere. It's hard to keep up your hopes after a disaster like this. I just try to rejoice in the morning sunrise, that's all!

I'm supposed to wear a piece of cloth around my mouth. I just move it aside occasionally when someone asks me to show my face – but it has to be someone I know very well. I certainly don't want the perpetrators to gloat over my disfigured face. All I can do now is trust in God. Perhaps one day I might not need that cloth any more...

Amazing news

Towards the end of December 2005, an Aegis staff member came to visit me in the evening and told me something I've been dreaming of for years. Softly, she told me that Aegis Trust and some other people in the UK have managed to gather together the money for me to have another operation – and a new face... I stared at her. It was as if I was dreaming! I went to bed and the following day when I woke up, I couldn't help wondering if I had dreamt it all... I sat down and remembered everything that had happened, everything that had been said the previous evening. Then I realised that I wasn't dreaming at all.

I would like to thank all the people who have contributed towards raising the money for further surgery. I am so happy to know that some people think and care about me. And I am very excited at the thought of getting back the face I lost.

There are not enough words to show my gratitude, but may God bless all the benefactors who cared about me.

Thank you.

Freddy, 2005 © Aegis Trust

I want to see us build our nation

Before the genocide

My name is Freddy and I was 18 years old at the time of the genocide. I lived with my parents and four sisters in Kibuye. We were all very happy together.

My Mum was the person I loved most in the whole world. I still remember everything she used to do – perhaps because I was by her side all the time. She was a very kind and generous parent, very sociable, with lots of friends. She used to tell me, "Life is about making friends and learning to live with people. When you know how to live with people, you'll never fail to do anything." And she would say, "It's not good to be selfish, you should always share with others." She didn't have a lot, but she gave a lot to those she lived with. And now I can see the fruits of her actions. All the people helping me now do it in my Mum's name. They tell me, "You'll never lack anything as long as we're here."

My father was a very quiet man; he wasn't very talkative. From what other people have told me about his childhood and education in the seminary school, he showed tolerance with all types of problems. He used to console others by assuring them that, "The first thing is to have faith." He was reserved and patient. He was never discouraged when he faced difficulties. Those are the things I remember about him.

I had four sisters who were all killed during the genocide – killed in a terrible way, some of them dumped alive in the latrine. Of all my sisters, I remember Angélique best. Sometimes there's a special bond between two siblings. I was much older than Angélique but we really loved each other. In fact, she would have missed school if I hadn't taken her myself. I used to run along, carrying her in my arms and she'd tell me she was having lots of fun. I finished primary school when she was just starting. She used to tell me that when other kids at school wanted to fight with her, she felt very safe just knowing I was around. I was everything to her. She trusted me completely and at home she used to tell me all her little secrets.

I remember that I was very boisterous as a child. My Mum would tell other parents that her son was so lively that he was always breaking things in the house! Nothing made me happier than playing football. I joined a senior team when I was still in primary school. Playing football is one of my best memories.

I have other special memories of the times when my parents got paid. My Mum was a primary school teacher. Whenever she got her pay, she used to ask me to meet her in a place called Rubengera at around 1 p.m. Then she used to buy me milk and cake – I was still a child at the time. When I was at secondary school, she once bought me a bottle of beer, but she didn't let me finish it. She wanted me to know that there are many stages in life, that I had moved to a time when she no longer considered me a child. She could confide in me. She told me lots of things that day.

She talked about the treatment of Tutsis in Rwanda. She told me how she had passed her Ordinary Level Examinations at school, but no Tutsi ever passed those exams again until six years later when she was a teacher at the same school. She said, "I'm the only one who is educated in my whole family. My brothers are intelligent, but their fate is to become cultivators. Hutu children got into schools, but they were no cleverer than my brothers. But Freddy, you'll complete your studies, I can assure you of that. And I'm asking you to take care of your family just as I'm doing." She was supporting her brother Edward at secondary school in Zaire at the time. It was very hard for her to look after our family and his schooling, but she was doing it. She wanted me to know all this, to learn how to behave in such situations.

She went on to say, "I want you to behave like your father. He's one of the people I most appreciate for their patience. I sometimes give him a hard time and I always realise it when it's too late, but he always responds perfectly to the situation. I know you like football," she continued, "but don't let it stop you doing school work." I hadn't done very well in class that year; I'd got 65% whereas normally I got a distinction, 75-85%. She thought it was because of football. "Please, I beg you, nothing must take your attention away from school. You have to complete your studies so you can make something of yourself in the future."

The genocide

My strongest memory of the genocide, the one that hurts me most, is the night of 13 April 1994. That was the day they came to kill my family. I was away from the house, in hiding, but Mum came to find me. She knew I was very hungry because by then nobody could cook any food. There was practically nothing left in the house. By then people had been bribing the hungry *Interahamwe* [Hutu militia] with food – to let them live a few days longer. At home the only thing we had left was beans. Mum knew I didn't like beans and so she brought me some vegetables and passion fruit. She told me, "I couldn't find anything for you to eat... The people I told you about – the ones who don't like us – took everything away from me. I don't even have anything to give my child." Then she added, "Try and eat this, it will be OK. Be strong." Today, passion fruit still reminds me of that last meal my Mum gave me.

I also remember that before she was killed, Mum told me I had to be strong. She said that if my sister and I survived, I had to be a man. Those are the two things still on my heart to this day.

I was there when the perpetrators came to kill my family. They came saying, "We're tired, we'll take these two fat kids [Freddy and his sister] later." So they took the younger ones; my sister Rosette and I were left behind. We saw them being taken with our own eyes and they were killed not far away. We couldn't see it happening, but we could hear them screaming... They took Mum far away to kill her. Later at night, I went with another boy to find her body. We rushed there and buried her. We simply covered her with soil. So I saw my Mum's body, but not the rest of the family. I just heard my sisters being killed. I didn't see my father killed – people told me about it later.

I know some of the killers very well. One of them wanted to rape my sister, but he didn't succeed. I know the people who took them away. They were our neighbours, among them a man called Benoit who had been our neighbour for years and owned a shop nearby. He was Mum's friend and he even used to lend her money for me to go to school. They got on very well. He was one of the leaders of the group that took them. And there was another young man called Kanani – Mum had been his teacher in primary school. Some people inside the compound tried to fight off the killers, but it was Kanani who held on to Mum when they took her out of the house. Later, he let go of Mum's hand and she ran away. But they found her again and she was beaten to death with clubs.

Those memories usually come back to me in April. That's when I have nightmares and I see people killing other people... I see *Interahamwe* killing people. But otherwise I'm lucky, I rarely have nightmares. Another thing I keep remembering is how they used to chase people from their hiding places in the bushes and run after them with dogs. Once they caught them, you could hear the screams that meant they had been killed. The killers ran after people as if they were animals. Tutsis were no longer considered human beings then. The killers were like animals as well. They acted as if they were killing something else, not human beings.

It's hard to describe how I felt during the genocide. I was so afraid. I used to imagine a machete cutting my neck all the time – or my neck on the ground. All the time I was hiding in the roof of someone's house, my heart was full of fear. They sometimes used to let me sit near the fire because I was freezing in the cold. I used to hide behind a big sieve (used for sorghum) so that whoever was making the fire couldn't see me. I was so afraid and lost all hope of survival. But then I reached a point where I wasn't scared any more. I was no longer afraid of death. Death or life, it meant nothing any more.

Sometimes my sister and I would walk along the road. We walked a lot but we weren't afraid of passing the roadblocks. There was only once we were frightened. That was in a place called Mwendo in Kibuye. They took us up to the roadblock and asked us if we were Tutsis. We told them we weren't, but they looked at us and said we must be Tutsis because of our soft hair. They told us to stop lying to them. They asked me to dig my own grave and I refused. They said the burgomaster would judge our case and took us to the commune. We ended up spending a night in a cell because the burgomaster was drunk. But I wasn't afraid. I had lost my fear after my parents were murdered and after all the terrible things I had experienced. Only my sister Rosette and I survived.

After the genocide

I personally believe that surviving was partly a matter of luck – but it's also a great responsibility because many survivors are very poor and don't even have life's basic necessities. That's why those who have something to share need to feel responsible for those who have nothing. I also think surviving is a privilege because when I consider what happened in Rwanda, all the determination of the killers and their accomplices, it's a miracle that some people managed to survive.

It's hard for other people to understand our experiences. Obviously not everyone can understand what I went through. Some people didn't even want me to live – they still don't want me to be alive today – and they're not happy to see me prosper. Those who went through similar things do understand, especially those who share our lives daily.

In the future, I want to carry on working to help survivors. I'll need to invest a lot more effort into it because I know survivors have many problems. So I'm ready to work for them my whole life. I was lucky; I'm not handicapped, so I want to make use of my luck to help others.

It's difficult to forgive and I don't even know where to start. Who should I forgive anyway? The former Government? Individuals? I look around and I don't even know where to start because so many people were involved in the genocide. Personally, I'm not ready to begin that journey of forgiveness.

Forgiving is difficult, but it's not impossible because the few genocide survivors can't develop Rwanda by themselves. We all need to combine our energy to develop the country. But I think it's better for those who committed the crimes to start asking for forgiveness. They should come to us to talk about it. Let's say if it's a Hutu who killed, he should come and say, "I killed people and I am really sorry." They should show us that they are truly sorry. Then things could proceed.

And the countries involved should also use their power to help survivors in need. I'm not among them because I'm not handicapped; I'm able to work for myself. But what about the orphans, the kids who look after themselves and have other responsibilities as well, how do they survive? The countries involved should do something to show they care about them.

I personally would like to thank those who founded AERG, the Association of Student Survivors of the Genocide [*Association des Etudiants et Elèves Rescapés du Génocide*]. I think it's a very worthwhile association and has achieved a lot. It helps people believe that although they have lost their parents, friends and fellow students are there to help. As long as that association operates, I hope that orphans will stop considering themselves as orphans, that they'll find that AERG is there for them – and that they'll find peace. I know this from experience; I lived there for a long time and found peace.

What can we learn from the genocide?

I think we can learn from the genocide. A lot of people had to grow up very quickly. They had to take on responsibilities while they were still young. Their experiences made them forget they were still young. It wasn't a good experience but it taught us important lessons – about knowing who you are, how to behave and consider others.

There are also lessons for the international community – that it's very important to keep one's word, that they did very little to save people who were dying in our country. They also need to know about the survivors, that they need to live a good life. The international community needs to know that the genocide actually happened. It should show respect to the victims and acknowledge that those victims were innocent people.

The future

I dream of having a family one day and I'm sure I'll achieve it. I'll teach my family the morals my parents taught me when I was young. The first thing they need to know is that a parent's word is of great value. They need to keep that in their hearts.

I want to help other survivors as we join together to fight against the consequences of the genocide. I dream of a developed Rwanda and I'm determined to fight all genocidal ideologies. I want to see us build our nation. We can only do that if we consider the younger generations and work to remove all bad ideologies from their minds.

I WANT TO SEE US BUILD OUR NATION

Freddy, 2004 © Aegis Trust

Henriette, 2006 © Aegis Trust

Exile in Burundi

Before the genocide

My name is Henriette and I was born in 1972 in Butare province. My father's name was Antoine Rutayisire and my mother's Thérésie Mugorewishyaka. I was the firstborn of the family and I had two brothers and three sisters. I was 24 at the time of the genocide.

My parents were farmers; we had cows and land. Life was not too bad... it was interesting and happy for us because both my family and extended family lived in the same neighbourhood. We children were allowed to spend the night in another family member's home. We had so much freedom and that was really good!

The whole family would gather at Christmas and other feast days to share and socialize. That was really fun! The kids from our extended family never wanted to leave our house because Mum took such good care of them and gave them all they needed. Mum never worried about anything in life; for her everything was simple and straightforward.

I knew about my ethnic group when I reached Primary Four at school. The teacher told pupils of one ethnic group to stand up, and so I stood up without having a clue what it was all about. When I got home, I asked my parents about my ethnic group and they told me I was a Tutsi. But that wasn't enough for me. I was so curious about it that whenever I went to stay at Grandma's, I used to ask her about it.

Grandma's house was a shack then, but she told me that they had been rich before 1959. They used to have a house built of bricks, but people had destroyed it and almost beaten my grandfather to death. He didn't die immediately, but the pain was so intense that by the time he was taken to the hospital, it was too late.

In 1990, I was studying in a boarding school called Remera Rukoma in Gitarama. That year, the RPF [Rwandan Patriotic Front] troops had invaded the country and, as a result, Tutsi students were threatened, beaten and sometimes killed by their fellow students... I remember that at mealtimes there were 15 of us around the table and we used to have fun passing meat from one person to the next. But in 1990, things fell apart. No one wanted to share with me any more. Whenever I passed by, people would call me a 'snake'. They even spread a rumour at school that I had some poison and was plotting with a group of other Tutsi students to kill all our Hutu colleagues.

The rumour was so intense that the headmaster organized a meeting and asked students to write down the names of all the suspects. My name was listed at the top as the Number One Suspect, probably because I was very tall and looked more Tutsi than the others. They hated me!

The following day, a delegation came from the Ministry of Education, along with armed soldiers and many other important people. They called me into the headmaster's office for questioning. I was so scared. They asked me questions like, "Tell us about the *Inkotanyi* [RPF soldiers], what mission did they assign to you?" But at the time I didn't know anything about them. Whatever I told them, they said I was lying! I cried... they wouldn't believe me.

After questioning me, they sent me back to class. When I went into the classroom, the teacher, who was Congolese, gave me a terrible look and said, "You witch! No witch of a student will ever succeed in my classes." From then onwards, all the teachers started to hate me. I remember there was one teacher who liked me before because I was smart in lessons. He called me over one day and said, "Henriette, why did you get involved in all this?"

Because I was at school, there was no way that I could let my parents know what was happening. At the same time, people had started to threaten our family; soldiers would go to our home and search for guns, and some people from my extended family were arrested as presumed 'traitors'.

On my way home at the end of the first term, I went to see my Aunt Marie Rose, who lived in Nyamirambo, Kigali. I told her what was happening. When her husband came home, she told him the story and he replied, "Things are going to get worse. It would be better if Henriette could study near here, where you could keep an eye on her." Marie Rose's husband was aware of what was going on; he was a Hutu from Gisenyi and influential in the MDR [*Mouvement Démocratique Républicain*].

When I got home, I told my Mum, "I'm not going back to that school," but she insisted. "Look, my dear, you can't stay at home and we don't have the money to send you to a private school. Be strong, my daughter, and go back to school." I finally agreed, but just before I left to go back, Mum told me, "If things get worse, write to me. But don't say you're being threatened, because if someone intercepts the letter, we'll all be in trouble. Just say 'the kid is still sick.' I'll understand that and then I'll ask Marie Rose to go and pick you up." Things at school got worse and worse, but I never told my parents. I didn't want to upset them.

The following year, I moved to a school close to Marie Rose's house. It wasn't a boarding school, so I was living at my aunt's. There were plenty of roadblocks on my way to school and I was stopped every day. I was always late at school because of that. Then Kigali started to be affected by the chaos: people were being murdered, buses were exploding here and there...

I went home during this period and Mum told me, "We're trying to arrange for you to go to Burundi. We're doing this because young girls and women are the most targeted group in this war and we don't want you to get hurt." But going to Burundi was very dangerous and a lot of people were killed trying to get there. It was really hard to find someone to help who wouldn't betray you.

Fortunately, a Burundian Hutu businessman agreed to help two of my cousins and me – all girls. It was very complicated because we needed people who lived near the border to accommodate us for few days before we crossed over into Burundi. The problems came when people noticed us. I don't know how they did, but they always knew we were there and so we would have to move back for a couple of days. Then we would try again, staying in a different house near the border. Altogether we slept in five different houses over about two weeks as we tried to find a way of getting into Burundi without being noticed.

We finally found a way in December 1993, but we had to cross the river Akanyaru, on the border between Rwanda and Burundi. There was no boat, so we paid two men to carry us across the river on their shoulders.

Exile

There were already some Tutsi refugees in Burundi. They helped us until I met an old man who had been adopted by my grandparents. My face looked familiar to him; he stared at me and asked, "Who are your parents?"

When I told him, he said some members of my family were living in Burundi. He offered to get in touch with them so they could shelter us. The old man went to Bujumbura and told the family members that we were on our own in Ngozi. A few days later, we went to Bujumbura and lived with them.

About four months later, some people who had fled from Rwanda told us that all my family had been killed in the genocide. That message hurt me so deeply. I had never felt so much bitterness in my life... I decided never to go back to Rwanda. There was no point in returning because no one had survived.

But three months after the genocide, I received a letter from my younger sister, Chantal. I don't know how she managed to trace me, but I got the letter. She told me, "All our family has been killed... Aunt Marie Rose and I are the only ones who survived. Why don't you come back? I need you, please come back." I was so happy to know that at least someone from my family was still alive. I decided to come back to Rwanda.

Return from exile

Back in Rwanda, I went to where we used to live. The whole place was a ruin; you couldn't even tell there was once a house there. Chantal told me she had seen some of our family's bodies. She told me whenever she heard how other children in the family had been killed. I never believed it. I was still hoping to see them some day.

I remember that the UNHCR [the UN Refugee Agency] used to display pictures of orphan children coming back from Congo... I always went to see those photos, hoping to find the faces of my younger sister and brothers. But soon people told me how they had been killed. After that, I lost all hope. Then we arranged a funeral to bury our parents and relatives. We exhumed their corpses from different places and put them together in one place – at a cousin's place.

After the genocide, life was so hard! There was trauma, pain, hunger and sorrow each and every minute of every day... I just didn't know how to help my remaining family without a job. So I started looking for a job and fortunately got one. The salary was very insignificant, but it helped us to carry on somehow.

Today

Today I work as a guide at the Kigali Memorial Centre, where I meet many different people, especially survivors. My work has helped me a lot to understand the pain of genocide survivors. I never used to like interfering in people's personal affairs before, but today I feel it's my responsibility to hear people out and help them as much as I can.

There are thousands and thousands of people struggling to live today because of what they went through during the genocide. I believe that everyone in the world has a role to play in helping them. Help is not always financial. Even listening to them is helpful. Survivors have no one to look after them and moral support is always much appreciated.

Henriette, 2006 © Aegis Trust

Jeanette, 2006 © Aegis Trust

JEANETTE NIBAGWIRE

I'll never teach my child to hate

Before the genocide

My name is Jeanette and I was born in 1983. I was 11 years old at the time of the genocide. My home village is in Bicombi commune, in the rural province of Kigali.

Before the genocide, we were six children at home with our Mum and Dad. We lived in peace with our neighbours. There wasn't any problem between us. We used to share everything. If my parents made the local beer at home, all the neighbours would spend the night dancing at home with my father. No one could tell that one day the same people would turn their backs on us and kill us in such a painful way.

Before the genocide, I remember people saying, "I'm in such and such a party," but I never heard of anyone being killed because he belonged to a certain party.

The genocide

Everything bad started with the death of President Habyarimana on 6 April 1994. When he died in the plane crash, people started saying, "Since he's dead, other Tutsis must die." They said they must hunt all the Tutsis wherever they were. But I was very young; I was only 11 years old then. All of us in the family tried to ask Dad why they were going to kill all the Tutsis. But he couldn't find an answer to that question, so he said, "It's true, that's the way things are... If you happen to die, may God receive your souls in heaven. There's nothing else I could wish for you."

We spent the night of 7 April at home because things hadn't got worse then. The following day, we were separated from Dad and went to hide with Mum. The men would stay behind to fight. That's how people lost sight of family members. I never saw or heard about my father again.

All six children in our family hid here in the swamp for about a week with our mother. The *Interahamwe* [Hutu militia] came looking for people hiding in the swamp. When they found us, we were taken to the road. They asked us, "Where are you from?" We told them the truth.

Among them, there was a man who used to be one of my father's friends. He interceded for us, "Please leave these children and their mother. Their father has been a very good friend to me. Let others kill them instead of us." So they left us alone.

Then another man among them said, "I'll take the girl to my home because they never kill girls in my home village. Don't worry, she'll be okay. If you survive the war, you'll be able to see her again." That's how I went and lived with him. My Mum took the rest of the kids.

But later, when the *Inkotanyi* [RPF soldiers] came, that man changed. He told me, "Your people have come now, so there's no need for you to flee with us. Go and join your mother." "But I don't know where she is. I don't even know if she's still alive. How can I join her?" I asked.

The man was constantly telling me to get out his sight and when I realized how much he was insisting, I decided to leave. I thought that maybe he would react and kill me himself. The *Inkotanyi* had come, but I couldn't tell who they were. I didn't know them. So I continued fleeing with other people who lived in that area. We walked all the way from Rwamagana to Karembo.

We reached Karembo at around six o'clock in the evening and spent one week there before the *Inkotanyi* arrived. I was with a group of people but I didn't know anyone. I couldn't find anyone to ask for something to eat. I used to go to a place where they peeled cassava and I ate the peelings. Or sometimes I would uproot sweet potato stems and eat them. The closer the *Inkotanyi* came to us, the further we would flee. I was with Hutu people who were scared of the *Inkotanyi*.

On the second part of our journey, we walked up to a place called Sake where there was a roadblock. It was a tough roadblock: children with no families and anyone with no identity card would be killed. There was no excuse, no discussion. So when I reached that roadblock, I was wondering what to do. Fortunately, it had been raining previously and I had helped a lady to carry her wet clothes. I went next to her and said, "I'm alone and I don't know where my family is. If they let you pass through the roadblock, please don't leave me behind." She agreed.

When the *Interahamwe* told people to go through the roadblock, she presented her identity card and they let us pass. It was around 6:30 p.m. A lot of people were killed at that place – and their corpses thrown into the river Kanyaru [at the Rwanda-Burundi border]. We camped around there for about week.

I was starving to death. One lady said to me, "Little girl, I always see you alone. Don't you have people who came with you?" I told her, "I'm not with my family. We all fled, but we suddenly lost each other." And then she said, "Come with me; we'll go and beg some food." We went and asked some other people for food, then we went back and the lady prepared it. After eating herself, she refused to give me part of the remains. She said she wasn't going to sweat for me. "Stay there. I don't care if you starve to death or not."

I was starving so I decided to go back to the people who had given us food. I told them that the lady had refused to give me my share. They were hurt; they were very good people. They sent me to another lady who was their neighbour and I stayed with her then.

When the *Inkotanyi* arrived at that village, they said that the people living there should join others in the camp, so then we set off. There was another roadblock that was also very difficult to pass through. Those who didn't have identity cards marked Hutu, or those who weren't old enough to have one, were killed without any discussion. If you didn't have a family or a father to declare you on his identity card, you were killed.

I decided to go back to the lady I had begged food with... because her identity card said she had three kids, yet she was only carrying one baby. I said to her, "You see, I'm not old enough to get an identity card and things are really bad down there. Please let's go through together." She agreed again.

I helped her with her paper bag of clothes and we crossed together. The other lady I lived with in the village continued her journey to her home village of Gikongoro. But the lady who helped me pass the roadblock often used to fall ill, so she couldn't walk fast. I hurried up and left her behind. I realized that if I walked at her pace, all the other people would leave us behind. We would be on the road alone and the *Interahamwe* would come and kill us. I caught up with the lady I'd lived with in the village and she said, "Now you can come with me."

We went together to Gikongoro where she was born, although she had got married in Bugesera. When we reached her father's place, he wasn't happy to have me there. Every morning he would wake up and stare at me. Every day he would ask his daughter, "Where did you get that kid from?" And she would say, "I've adopted her." Her father would complain, "I don't like the idea of living with someone I know nothing about." "Are you crazy?" he would ask her. The lady kept quiet and tried to divert his arguments.

But the old man wasn't at ease. About a week later, he woke up very early one morning and went to his sons who were taking part in the killings. He went and told them, "Come and kill this kid because I don't know who she is." He incited them and left them sharpening their machetes. He immediately came and told his daughter that he had left them sharpening their machetes to kill me. She was terribly hurt and advised me to leave before they came and killed me there in her presence. "It would hurt me terribly to see you being hacked," she told me sadly.

I left immediately. I don't know what happened after I left there. Maybe they came and couldn't find me there, who knows? When I reached the road, I didn't feel like carrying on towards Congo, so instead I went back the way we came. I had a feeling that I should go back towards home – so that if I was killed, I would at least die on my way home, rather than walking away from home. I was very tired.

When I reached the road, I met the *Interahamwe*. They were asking the people who were fleeing to present their identity cards. When I saw them, I got so scared and stood still in one position. They asked me, "Why did you stop?" "I feel very tired; besides I'm waiting for someone," I replied. Then they asked me where I was coming from and where I was going. There was a centre that we had passed through on our way there and I had memorized its name. So I said that was where I was going. Then they asked me about my home and my father's name and I replied. But they didn't trust me. They ordered me to sit to one side and wait. They said they would come back to my case later.

They went on asking people for identity cards. I imagined sitting there waiting to die and I decided immediately to leave. I stood up and walked away. I waited to see if anyone would follow me but no one did. No one told me to stop or say where I was going. I simply walked away and passed the *Interahamwe*.

Just ahead I met a man who had a machete. He asked me, "Little girl, where are you coming from?" I told him what I had told the previous group. He kept on asking me a lot of questions, and then I asked him why he was asking me all those questions. "If you want to kill me, go ahead because I've already died of pain and struggle." Then he said, "I'm not intending to kill you but just tell me where you're from." I told him that my home was in Kigali-Ngali. I even told him all about how I had fled. But I never told him where I had come from just then. I just said that I had lost sight of my family when we fled: that was why I was going back. He asked me where I was going and said that if I met other people on the way, they would kill me. I replied that if they killed me, I would just call it my last day!

We carried on walking together. Slightly ahead, we met another man and the first one said, "This kid lost her family when they fled and because of that, she refused to carry on fleeing with the other refugees. Why don't you take her to your house?" I decided to stay with that man. I thought that if he killed me, I would be lucky because he would be disturbed by the smell of a corpse and would have to bury me. That's how I came to live with him.

At one point he stopped giving me food. Another time we went to dig in a valley where he had an Irish potato garden. We had gone to harvest there, but when I dug into the soil, the hoe broke. "What's wrong with you?" he asked me aggressively. "Do you think I'll carry on joking with you?" And he lifted me up and threw me in the river Rukarara. He said, "I could hit you with this hoe blade, then throw you in here, and no one would ever accuse me of killing you. Did you know that?" I did my best to dig but I couldn't manage it – and I was beaten every day.

Another time while I was still living with him, I went to a sorghum garden to look for sorghum stems. He caught me eating them and said, "This time I'll kill you." He locked me in the house and went out to sharpen the knife. He came in saying, "I'm going to kill you, that's it." Then his wife came in and said, "You don't know that girl very well and now you want to kill her. Why do you want to shed her blood? You've tortured her enough, why don't you leave her to die another death?"

He immediately slapped his wife and she ran away. I asked him to forgive me that day and kill me the next. He was very annoyed, so he went and cut a big branch of a tree and whipped me. He whipped me almost to the point of killing me. Then I was left there suffering from the beatings. I knew I had nowhere to go. I kept wondering what to do.

I went to the man's neighbours and asked them to take me in. They told me not to mess with that man. They said they could take me in, but if he ever saw me, he would kill me. But there was a woman who lived some miles away who had heard about me and the way I was being treated. She came one morning and found me alone at home. She asked, "Where's your home, little girl?" I told her that my home wasn't there; it was in Kigali-Ngali. "How did you get here?" she asked me. "I fled here." I replied. "And what's it like for you here?" she asked. I replied rudely, "I know they sent you here to spy on me and see if I go around telling everybody how I'm living in this house. Do you want to help them kill me?" She told me to calm down and tell her exactly where my home was, then she would take me there. I asked her to stop lying. "Where would you take me? I'm almost dying. Can you find a place to take me?" I asked her.

She was very hurt, but told me a time to go to her home. There was a place where I used to milk a cow to feed the man's baby and so she told me that I should go there. Then someone would take me to her place. On that day, very early in the morning, I woke up at 4.00 a.m. as usual. I went and knocked on the door where I was directed, and a girl took me to the woman's home.

When that woman saw me, she was very sad because I looked like a street kid. My hair was long and messy; my clothes were very dirty because no one used to wash them for me – even street kids looked better than I did. She trimmed my hair and washed me. My clothes had lice in them but she boiled them in water. She went to look for flour to make me some porridge because I looked dehydrated because of the way I was living. She dressed my injuries and took care of me.

I spent a night there and in the morning, one of her neighbours came to the house. "I heard there's a kid here," he said. "No one knows where she's from, so I've come to kill her." The woman pleaded with him, then went to the local leader. She explained the situation and the leader called for a meeting. I was present and the woman as well.

That woman didn't have any children at home; she had one boy who didn't live with her. The leader said, "This woman has no children and now they even want to kill the girl she's adopted. But if anyone touches or kills her, they will be killed as well." So then I was free to live and I stayed there until 1995. Later in August, some of the woman's lady relatives came to visit and found me there. They asked her, "Where did you get the child from?" and she told them she had adopted me. Then they asked me, "Where's your home?" I told them, and they said the place sounded familiar to them. They said that when they came next time, they would let me know if my family had survived or not.

Reunited

In November 1995, they came back with my mother.

When my Mum saw me, she burst into tears. The first thing I asked was, "Did any of the others at home survive?" She told me that all those I knew at home – Dad, my brothers and sisters, my relatives – had all been killed. "Only you and this baby I'm carrying in my womb survived. I was pregnant during the war." She told me that one cousin had survived as well – we were the only ones in the whole family. I was so upset and I cried as well.

After that I went back home with my mother and life continued. Mum told me how the others were killed. My Mum wasn't a Tutsi; she was born in a Hutu family. After we were separated, they went and hid in the bush, but after spending many days there, the kids were starving. Mum decided to go to her uncle's – he lived nearby. She thought, "Because he's my uncle, nothing will happen. I'll go and ask them for food for my children."

When she got there, her uncle chased her away. "Shame on you," he yelled at her. He asked her where the kids were hiding and lied that he would bring them food. My Mum told him where they were hiding, thinking that they would really take food for her children. Instead, he went and called a group of *Interahamwe*. They found the children in the bush and killed them all. They were going to kill my Mum because she was pregnant with a Tutsi baby, but they forgave her and let her go.

We don't even know where Dad was killed. We don't even know what happened. All we know is that he was killed. I used to ask Mum, "Where did Dad die?" And she would tell me some place called Nzige. During the period of collecting people's bones, we went to find the man who had killed him, but he was already in prison. When we tried asking people who lived around there, they said they didn't know where our father's remains were.

Today and the future

When I got back home with Mum, I went back to school. Before the genocide, I was in Primary Four, and when I started school again, I went to Primary Three. I carried on studying and completed primary school successfully. Then I went on to secondary school and eventually did my secondary-school exams.

The future? Only God knows that. I can't plan anything because I don't know what tomorrow will be like. I was hoping to save money so I could go and thank the lady who got me out of the man's house. But a few days ago, I was told that she had died. That's all I had planned so far. If I can find her children, I will thank them instead for the great thing their Mum did for me.

Reconciliation? Take the example of my Mum's uncle who killed his own nieces and nephews because they had a Tutsi father; they killed their own blood. To tell the truth, I can never reconcile with them. Whenever we meet, I always turn away. I avoid looking at them and they are always afraid. We go to the same church but I cannot reconcile with them. Maybe I could be reconciled with those who never hurt me directly...

Although people talk about reconciliation, to me it seems very far off. I know in the churches they teach about reconciliation among the Rwandans. But for me... well, we can meet on the road and talk, but I can never feel at home with those people like it used to be before the genocide.

As for the future, although our children will have to hear about it, we should avoid them growing up in the same chaotic environment. I guess that would be better for the future. As a parent, I will try and tell my child what happened, although I'll never teach my child to hate those that I hate – because even God doesn't allow that.

Nowadays things in Rwanda aren't the way they were in 1994. Instead people are trying slowly to become reconciled. That's all I can hope for the future – for people to unite and be reconciled so they can live in peace.

Jeanette, 2006 © Aegis Trust

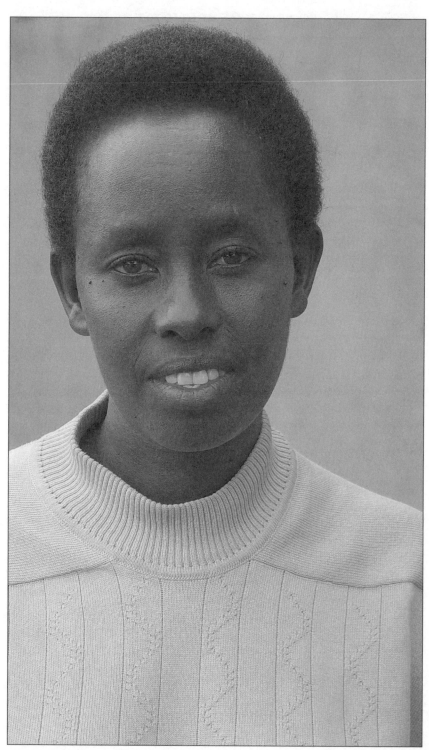

Béatrice, 2006 © Aegis Trust

BEATRICE NIKUZE

Look to the future

Before the genocide

My name is Béatrice and I was born in 1967. I got married in 1987. We had no children until 1990 when I gave birth to my firstborn son. He was our only child. At the time of the genocide, I was 27 years old.

As a child, I remember hearing about previous tensions when we lost some family members in the 1970s. I remember my uncle was taken to Nyamata. We went there to see him and found him with a group of other Tutsis who had been captured. They were put in a very small building with no opening. They were of mixed ages – women, children, boys and men. They suffocated to death. They sprayed them with an insecticide called DDT and my uncle was beaten to death.

We stayed in Nyamata for a month, then went back home to Kanazi. My father fled to Burundi for a long time, but came back when I was six years old when the situation had improved. It was peaceful again then, but the men and strong boys used to patrol at night. That's all I can recall. My father died before the genocide began.

Then people started having meetings, but peasants like us didn't know that they were dangerous. We never thought anything bad would come out of the Hutus or the Tutsis. Although I'd seen some of the Hutus' deeds in the 1970s, by then I'd forgotten everything. I couldn't differentiate between the Hutus and the Tutsis because they used to be very sociable and intermarry. Later on, I knew about all the political parties, and some parties joined together and started fighting against others. It was all very confusing, especially for the peasants. During that time of multiple parties, whenever the MRND [*Mouvement Révolutionnaire National pour le Développement*] and MDR [*Mouvement Démocratique Républicain*] held meetings, many people would die. Strong boys would be taken and you waited in vain to see them come back. They would kill young men and their bodies were discovered later. There was a lot of chaos; it was a dangerous period.

By 1990, my husband worked at Rwandex [a coffee factory], but in 1992-1993, at the time of multiple political parties and when ethnic tension intensified, he lost his job just because he was a Tutsi. Even after he was expelled from work, some people carried on harassing him. I remember one day when he was coming from his temporary job, a gang of people arrested and threatened him. They didn't do him any harm except that one tried to beat him up. From that time, we carried on suffering discrimination. Criminal elements would regularly attack our home and threaten us. As the terror grew, we decided to move from Kicukiro to Remera, where we thought it would be a bit safer.

Around 1993 or 1994, we went back to live in Kicukiro. But ethnic tension resumed when Bucyana [President of the CDR party of extremist Hutus and *Interahamwe*] and Katumba [an important CDR member] were assassinated. Every time something awful happened in the country, the Tutsis were always the scapegoats and were mercilessly killed. So we sought refuge in the parish of Kicukiro where many families from Nyakabanda and Kicukiro had gathered. I went with my mother and brothers. At first my husband went to a different place, but after a few days he joined us at Kicukiro.

The genocide

We'd been there for two months when President Habyarimana died in the plane crash. After his death, a priest called Patrice told us to go to ETO school [*Ecole Technique Officielle*]. When we got there, a group of people – including Mr John from Nyakabanda – came and took my husband, seemingly to collect some property he had left at home. Nevertheless, I knew they were going to kill him because these were the people who had hunted him in the past. Later, a lady called Bibi came crying to me and said, "Your husband Masabo was murdered along with a boy called Ndohera. John killed them."

We remained at ETO under the protection of United Nations forces, but after a short time the police came and told the UN soldiers there was no need for them to continue guarding us. The police said they would ensure our safety themselves. The UN forces packed up and left us at the mercy of the mob.

As soon as they left, the policemen took us to Sonatubes [*Société Nationale des Tubes*, a factory and the surrounding area] where we stayed a short time. A man called Rusatira came and said, "Take the garbage to Nyanza" [where there was a waste tip on the outskirts of Kigali]. By 'garbage', he meant us. Many people started showing their identity cards claiming that they were Hutus, and the police started sorting out the Hutus and letting them go. The rest of us were taken to Nyanza.

When we were taken to Sonatubes, my brothers and some other boys had been kept behind at the parish. Whilst we were in the factory, my older brother came running and told me that the rest of them had all been killed. They had hacked him as well, but he was still able to run away although he was bleeding. The others had been thrown into a pit.

So we were taken to Nyanza. I was still with my Mum then, but my husband had already been taken. There were so many people going to Nyanza. On the way there, we were stopped at Kicukiro centre because there was a traffic jam. In front, there were military tanks surrounded by *Interahamwe* [Hutu militia] with machetes and clubs. Some of them suggested we should be killed there at the centre, but it was later agreed that we would be taken to Nyanza for execution. In fact many people were killed on the way; others were kidnapped and taken to an unknown destination.

When we reached Nyanza, they gathered us in one place and started throwing grenades at us. After many people had been killed and others injured, their leader said there was no need to waste their ammunition. He said machetes and clubs would easily execute us because we were wounded and very weak.

But before killing us, they first sorted out the young, energetic boys and men and killed them right away. Then, instead of killing us in small groups, they finally decided to do it all at once. They started hacking us. But around 2.30 in the afternoon, they got tired. They had taken us there at around eight or nine in the morning. That was when I managed to crawl towards a nearby bush with my child. My mother hadn't been injured, but she had passed out when Nyiramutangwa was killed on top of her.

I crawled slowly and finally reached the bush, although I had already been hacked on the head and back. But after the *Interahamwe* had killed all people on the field, they surrounded the bush, looking for those who were in hiding. They shouted, "Come out and join the others." Then we were put on the field with the corpses and they started killing. People were screaming in agony; babies being hacked to death; young women being raped and murdered... I remember Oliva who was murdered so maliciously. She was raped first, then tortured to death. It was a horrible scene. And Cécile, who was accused of going to visit the RPF [Rwandan Patriotic Front]. A soldier called John told Cécile, "I'll kill you myself." And he did horrible things to her. I could hear her crying for help from where I was.

I don't remember the dates well, but I remember entire nights went by as we lay there with the corpses. I was with the nephew of Burakali, who survived and is now married. He had a serious neck injury but we crawled together towards a nearby orchard. My mother was still alive but she had been lying among the corpses for all those days. The militia came and stepped on me. One soldier called Matayo [Matthew] saw me and said, "How come Masabo's arrogant wife is still alive?" "Take her and kill her with the others."

All the militia were searching for people who had hidden among the bushes. So they took me with my baby on my back. My clothes were all stained with blood. They took us to a certain place and kept us there, to be killed later. The militia took the corpses and used them to block the road from Kigali to Bugesera. They arranged the bodies in stacks to sort out those who might still be alive.

Just then, while we were still piled up the dead bodies, gunshots were heard from Rebero hill. The militia said, "*The Inyenzi* ['cockroaches', Tutsis] are coming before we've finished our job." Then they started firing bullets and killed a lot of people. One of Bazatoha's daughters called to the killers, "We're still alive, come and finish us off." They killed them using screwdrivers as I watched in horror.

Later on, I was able to stand up. My mother was still alive and she spoke insultingly to the killers. She was with an old man called Apollinaire Ntasingira who had become desperately bold and started abusing the killers. He said, "You dogs will die. You can't kill me. You've been dogs ever since you started." The killers got angry and shot him dead right away – and my mother as well. I begged them to kill me but they refused. John and Mathew said they would kill me themselves.

At around five in the morning, RPF soldiers attacked and the killers ran away. But as they retreated, they took some women with them. I don't know what their fate was. Many people, especially the young boys, had been killed the night before. The killers had worked hard that night to make sure of killing us all before the RPF army took over.

When the *Inkotanyi* [RPF soldiers] reached us, they said, "Whoever still has any strength left, should come with us." I tried walking but couldn't stand up. I'd been shot in the leg although I hadn't felt it till then. I only knew I had injuries on my back and head. So the *Inkotanyi* took us to Rebero, where they washed and shaved many of us.

We then left Rebero for CND [*Conseil National de Développement* where about 600 RPF soldiers stayed to ensure RPF officers during the Arusha peace process] and later headed for Kabuye. On the way, the *Inkotanyi* did a lot for us. Some people were pushed in wheelbarrows. Others walked until we reached a place where they put us into cars to take us to Kabuye. By the time we reached Kibari in Byumba, we started to hope that we would survive. People were no longer being killed. We were no longer in the hands of killers and rapists.

After the genocide

We had a good life when we reached Kibari. We were with the *Inkotanyi* and they fed us and dressed the wounds of those who were injured. Later on, we were taken for treatment at King Fayçal hospital. I was a patient there for a year and a half. They operated on my back and head because I still had some injuries.

Later on, they got someone to nurse me because after the operation, my leg was raised up and I couldn't move. But that nurse didn't give me the necessary care. She treated me so badly – she used to hurt my leg on purpose. When she was mopping the floor, she used to shake the other side of the bed so I would feel a lot of pain. She kept on doing those things and calling me a Tutsi. She was a Hutu and wasn't happy looking after a Tutsi patient. She still had the Hutu ideologies and couldn't avoid telling me what she thought. She just hated me because of my origins and tribe. Eventually, I talked to the people in charge of the hospital and she was fired. After that, better nurses were recruited.

I stayed there until the time in 1995 when people who had places to go to were asked to leave. I started thinking about where to go and couldn't think of anywhere. I was using crutches and still had my child with me. But I knew a priest called Diyo who lived in Kicukiro. He had seen me at the hospital and he said, "Béatrice, come with me. I'll take you to my chapel, you can live there."

So I agreed and went to live with him at the chapel. I spent seven months there and he took good care of me. But then he told me that he was leaving for Europe. After that, I found some of my family members who had survived – some cousins living in Kibagabaga. They came to look for me when they heard where I was living. They asked me to live with them and I joined them in Nyakabanda.

The time came when they too had to leave for Europe. They left me in their house, but came back later and sold it. So then I rented a place because my injuries still hadn't healed completely and I still had to go to King Fayçal hospital. I was a patient there for a year and a half. They operated on my back and head. My leg still had bullets and fragments in it. I had another operation and once again my child was with me. That's the kind of situation I lived in. Later on, once I started to get some energy, I looked for a house and started to rent.

Life has always been hard for me – before and after the genocide. Afterwards, I often wondered how I was going to survive with my child, but there was no one to help me. At that time, I hadn't yet been to the associations to know what was happening. All I knew was that they were giving out food like yellow maize flour and cooking oil. We used to go to Kicukiro to get it. But because I was weak, it was sometimes impossible for me and I just couldn't go to get my share. Life was a struggle for everyone then.

At last I began to regain some strength because my head and back were better. I still had a problem with my leg but I used to go and get the wound dressed. I had crutches and could walk with them. Once I crossed the swamp and came across a field with beans and other crops.

I decided to look for a part-time job and found one as a gardener. I was in a very bad condition and used to go to work on crutches because I needed to earn the money for rent. I worked in various different gardens – some belonging to those who had killed our people. One man said to me, "I never thought that one day someone like you would work for us, considering what happened in the past." Taking a job with a Hutu farmer was brave; it was a risk, but I was desperate. But even though I worked for them, they never paid me. Besides five kilos of beans they once gave me, they never gave me any money. I worked for almost a month for them.

I still didn't have the money I needed for the rent. The landlord told me, "It seems you're not going to get me my money." I had paid him two months and asked him to be patient with me. This difficult life carried on.

I stopped working in gardens and in November 1995 met a soldier who asked me, "How do you survive?" I told him everything. And then he told me where to find a job in Kanombe. I got the job and worked there, even though I was still limping. Then I told the soldier that I had another problem – accommodation. I had left the house I was living in. He found me a place in Kanombe military camp, so I could work and live in the camp. That was when my life – and my child's – improved. I think that job as a nurse in Kanombe came to an end in 1997. So I started looking for another means of surviving.

By then, my injuries had healed completely and I was fine. In the same year I heard about an organization called Avega [Association of Genocide Widows]. A lady called Astérie found where I had moved to and came to ask about my situation. When she asked me about my life, I just looked at her. I acted very hostile and said, "What do you want to know? Do you want to bring back my life?" She kept quiet but came to visit me about three times. She was hoping to get me to talk and later on, I did. She told me that she was a genocide widow as well. We chatted and she told me about her experiences during the war. Her story was just like mine. She was a widow and had lost seven children in the genocide. She had survived because some white people had hidden her, then later taken her to Italy.

Astérie took me to Avega where they asked me details about my life. I told them everything and they said they could get me a house in Kimironko. I started living there in 1997; I was the second person to get a house there. Avega then continued to help me; widows would visit me regularly and they would talk about different aspects of the genocide, including the trauma.

After the genocide, I was able to exhume some of my family members and rebury them – except for my husband. I don't know where his body is. When Bibi came and told me he'd been killed, I couldn't go and see where they had dumped his body. So I don't know if he was eaten by dogs or taken in the cars they used for carrying corpses to lakes or rivers. The people I reburied were my in-laws.

Today

My child who survived with me is 14 years old now [2004]. She didn't study well and is still in primary school. She would have joined secondary school but because of the lack of school fees, she was left behind in school.

Sometimes I think how life would have been if I had family. If my family were still alive, there would be no problems. We would be helping one another. But we have to accept what happened and carry on living normally. Actually, my worries are reduced now because I have somewhere to live.

Can there be reconciliation? Frankly speaking, people reconcile after you have met and he or she asks for forgiveness. Personally, I would say that it was President Habyarimana's Government or regime that committed the atrocities. Personally, I don't believe I have any reason to communicate with the killers. None at all.

As for punishing the perpetrators, what can you punish them with? You can never change their ideology of genocide. I don't even think there is another way of teaching them not to kill. Because there are some who still kill out there; there are even some who encourage people to kill. So I can't imagine what can be done to teach them that killing is bad. I think the killers should wait for God's judgment. Even if you imprison them, it won't change anything. I still see people with the same ideologies. I don't know if there is any Commission that could teach and change them. I don't know.

The future of Rwanda? Considering life before the war and the way I see things nowadays, if people were honest, everything would be possible. If the people who still believe in killing changed, this country would become peaceful. There could be security and the orphans who are living in terrible situations would also be able to say, "There's peace now and we don't need to hide from people any more."

Today I would say to those orphans and to all young Rwandans, "Look after your siblings and be tolerant. What happened, happened, but instead of looking at the past, look ahead towards something that will be of use to you. Always aim at your own development so as to improve your standard of living."

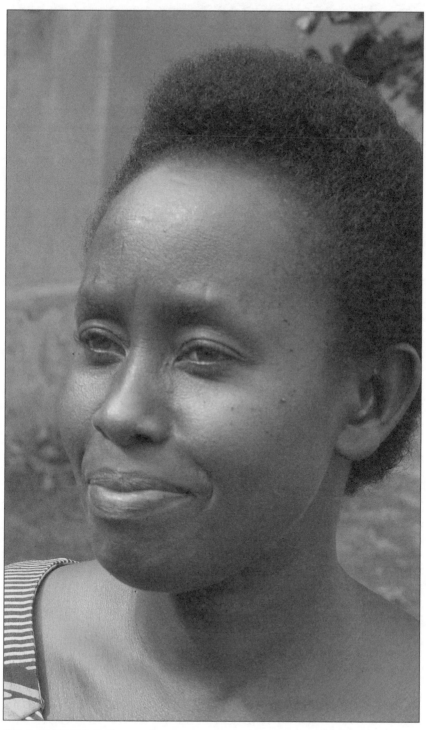

Béatrice, 2006 © Aegis Trust

Diane, 2006 © Aegis Trust

Diane Niyongira

Trying to be strong

Before the genocide

My name is Diane and I was nine years old at the time of the genocide. My father's name was Charles Butare and my mother's Agnes Mukamunana. We lived in Shyorongi in Kigali Ngali. My mother was a teacher and my father worked at the ministry in Kacyiru.

Life before 1994 was fine because I was with both my parents and my brothers and sisters. I had no problems. I used to hear about political parties and I saw people in secret meetings at home. The people would say that they couldn't sleep in their homes because they were afraid of being killed. I used to ask my Mum why, and she told me there was a group called Hutus who hunted a group called Tutsis. I wasn't worried about that because I was young. I knew that nobody could harm me when I was with my parents.

The genocide

Our father told us that President Habyarimana had died in a plane crash. But before that, there were several political organizations and whenever they held meetings, we would run away from our home because some people wanted to kill my father.

When the war began, the attackers immediately surrounded the place where we lived, Shyorongi, so that no one could run away. After a few days, we were told that the *Interahamwe* [Hutu militia] were coming so we should move from our houses and go to another sector for our safety. Of course that was a very easy way of gathering us together to kill us.

Many people went, but my father sensed the danger and said we wouldn't go and be killed in that sector. So we stayed at home during the day and at night we hid in the banana plantations. Those who went to the other sector were told to move on from there. They were taken to the bush, convinced that they would be safer there. But when they got there, some were shot and others were killed with grenades. Just a very few escaped, among them a child who was our neighbour. He came back and told us that they had killed his whole family. He then stayed with us.

The perpetrators sometimes came with soldiers to search for Rwandan Patriotic Front (RPF) army members who might be hiding in homes. They didn't find any the first time and so they came again a second time. They searched everywhere, even in the ceiling, but couldn't find them.

One night, they came to take my Mum and two sisters to kill them. As they were leaving, Mum asked them to give her a chance to say something. They thought she was going to say "Goodbye". But she asked them if she could carry her baby. And they replied, "If you have a baby, you can stay here. We'll just take the two girls."

So they took my sisters to the place where they intended to kill them, but when they got there, they told one of the *Interahamwe* to take one sister and kill her. That *Interahamwe* told my sister he wasn't going to kill her – she should go and die at other people's hands. So one sister came back home.

The other sister went with the perpetrators to find a boy they wanted to kill. When they reached that boy's home, they told my sister to go and knock on his door so they could kill them together. She went and knocked, but the boy refused to open the door. They told my sister to get out of the way so they could knock themselves. They wanted to break down the door. They knocked and then one *Interahamwe* who was standing behind asked my sister to go with him; he was going to save her life. She refused and said, "Don't take me to kill me where people won't be able to see. Just kill me here where they will see my body."

That man insisted that he wanted to hide her, not kill her, and she finally agreed to go with him. While the others were still struggling to get the boy to come out of the house, he took her to his home. After some days, when we thought she had been killed, that perpetrator came to our house and asked my father for money – then he could have his daughter back. My father asked, "Are you just making fun of me when I know very well you've killed my daughter?" The man replied, "I have your daughter and the only thing I need is money, then I'll give her back to you." Later my father gave him money and he brought my sister back the following day.

The days went by and the perpetrators came again. Other attackers and soldiers surrounded our place one morning at eleven o'clock. My father, mother, young brother and I went to hide behind the house and the other children went inside and locked themselves in. Then, when the attackers surrounded the whole place, they threw a grenade. My father had told us to lie down so it wouldn't kill us.

We were lying behind the house when they threw the grenade. It passed through the window and fell right in front of me. The explosion hit me on the head near my ear, and on my arm and leg. I was really badly injured. My mother lifted me up and took me to the side of the house. She asked me to be strong; she really thought I was going to die.

After the explosion, the attackers immediately went into the house. They got my brother and killed him. They also saw my mother holding me. They called to her. My mother had taught one of the attackers at school although he was grown up by then. She asked him, "Why do you want to kill me? Have I done anything wrong?" He just remained silent, then shot her. She fell down and died.

I sat there watching but I couldn't move. Then they saw my father as he went to hide my young brother in the kitchen. Father tried to jump over the fence, but they got him and beat him to death. When I saw that my father had jumped, I wanted to stand up and run as well because my wounds weren't so painful yet. I stood up, but the moment I tried to climb over, I fell down – fortunately behind the fence. Then I went into the gardens and hid in a sorghum plantation.

They got my younger brother as well and were going to kill him, but he escaped. They tried to shoot him but the bullets passed over his head. Then they got my older sister and killed her, and there were my two other sisters and little baby brother left. They shot the baby in the eye and left him crying. Then one of those men said he was going to take my oldest sister. He said he wouldn't kill her so he would get a wife for free.

The man took her and as they reached the road, they met other attackers. These men took my sister from him and killed her. So there was only one sister left – and the baby boy before he died. Then they told my sister to show them the *Inkotanyi* [RPF soldiers] in our house, but she said there weren't any soldiers there. They started hitting her with a gun to make her show them where the soldiers were hiding and she kept on saying she didn't know. They wanted to shoot her. She was so afraid that she grabbed the barrel of the gun. Then the attackers got annoyed and stabbed her in the head with a sword and she died. The baby was left crying until he took his last breath. I was still behind the fence although they thought they had killed everyone.

They looted, then destroyed the house. At around eleven o'clock, some children passed near the fence. I called to them because I was thirsty, asking them to get me some water to drink. They told me, "We're going to call the attackers and tell them you're still alive, tell them to come and kill you." I was frightened. I got up very quickly, but felt dizzy and fell down again. I couldn't walk. I crawled on my stomach to leave that place. I went to the roadside.

There was a long pit near my house. They took all those dead bodies and threw them into it. I stayed near the road. I fainted at some point, but I remember a passer-by took me to hospital. Mum's godson had been visiting us at home when the attack started. He was hiding behind the bookshelf. They threw a grenade and all the books caught fire as well as the clothes he was wearing. He was burnt down one side but didn't die. He was taken to the hospital in Shyorongi and so we were there together.

After three days, the war got worse and they said they were going to take all the patients to Gitarama. They brought a bus and took us all. When we reached a crossroads somewhere, people started shooting at the bus. With us, there were some perpetrators who'd been wounded in the fighting. A soldier was driving the bus. When we reached the corner, there was a car in the middle of the road blocking the way. We couldn't get past, so the perpetrators got off that bus, carried their people out and abandoned us in the bus while the firing was still going on. Later, they found they couldn't manage to carry their patients, so the soldiers came back, lifted that car blocking the way and threw it to the roadside. They came back to the bus and took us to Gitarama hospital. By the time we got there, I had passed out. The doctor was an *Interahamwe* and it was a military hospital.

They got us off the bus and took us into the hospital. They asked me what had happened to me and I told them that the perpetrators had hacked me. The doctors got annoyed and said they didn't want civilians there; they only treated soldiers. So they took us to Gitarama Kabgayi. We stayed there, but they didn't dress our wounds although our legs were badly injured. We were mostly pupils of primary school age. When they finally came to dress our wounds, maggots fell out of them. If they found it hard to treat you, they would throw you out of the hospital.

So we stayed in that hospital. The perpetrators would come at night and kill some patients. The soldiers wounded in battle kept on increasing in number so they removed us from the beds and put us on the floor so the soldiers had beds to sleep in. The perpetrators would come and tell us to get up and walk. If you couldn't walk, they would beat you and force you. One day a perpetrator came and took a girl who had previously been hacked and injured. He took her and killed her, then later came and ordered us to walk.

The following morning, the perpetrators heard that the RPF [Rwandan Patriotic Front] were coming to capture Gitarama and so they came and took all their soldiers out of the hospital. Only about five of us were left there. They refused to take us. They left us in the hospital and we heard the bombs passing over the building. To our surprise, that afternoon at around three o'clock, we saw the *Inkotanyi* [RPF soldiers] arrive. They asked us what had happened and we told them everything. Then they said they would take us to the Red Cross.

Our wounds had started rotting because they hadn't been dressed. In the evening, the RPF came back and looked for stretchers. They took us to the Red Cross in an area they had captured. The Red Cross started to take care of us. There were so many of us that they didn't have enough space for us all to sleep. We slept on stretchers.

Later on, the war got worse there, but luckily we were with the Red Cross and they took us to Butare. Doctors there suggested I should have an operation because my leg was rotten. They decided to cut it off because it had taken too long to heal. Another boy also went with me for an operation – his leg was cut off.

However, I was lucky – they operated on my leg and didn't amputate it. They decided to remove flesh from one side of my leg and add it to the deep cuts. Then I had another operation and they removed the shrapnel left in the wounds. They assured me that the rest of the shrapnel would come out without further surgery.

After some time, we were taken to Rilima because the Red Cross had moved there. They used to dress my wounds with a piece of cloth after applying some white powder to them because I didn't have enough flesh in the deep cuts on my leg. We stayed in that hospital and later they brought us crutches and taught us how to use them. We were told that when the war ended, we would be taken to our districts and then we would have to take care of ourselves.

After the genocide

When the war ended, I was still recovering from my injuries and they moved me to Kigali, with the boy whose leg was amputated. But when we reached Nyabugogo, he suggested we should go to his home in Gatsata because he knew that my parents hadn't survived. So we went together and found that his mother was still alive. I stayed there for a short time until my uncle in Remera learned that I was still alive.

My uncle came and took me to his place, and also took me regularly to hospital because my wounds hadn't healed completely. The doctors told me that the fragments of shrapnel are still in my leg, but I shouldn't worry because they will fall out by themselves. I stayed at my uncle's for some time. One night, robbers attacked us. My uncle was a businessman and robbers followed him as he bought some goods. They shot him dead. After his death, I carried on living with his wife but she later remarried. My cousin from Nyamata came for me and I'm now living with them.

I went back home once when we were exhuming my family's bodies and reburying them with respect. My uncle was still alive then. Now there are only ruins of my home. I don't like the place. When I go there, I feel very sad because of those ruined houses and graves. I can't live there now.

Before, I used to go and visit my younger brother, Emile Pierrot Mbarushimana, who also survived. After the war, some people fled with him and he only came back after my uncle died. It wasn't possible for him to come and stay where I was living. I could only go and visit him, but I hated that place. Later, they moved away and now I rarely go there – only about once a year. We still have a farm there that someone looks after for us. We'll keep it because that's where we reburied our people, so if we don't go there and tidy the graves, we'll forget them. We'll keep on going there, and when we grow up, we'll make the graves better if we have some money. They'll always remind us of our parents and family.

Today

I'm used to my life now, but I can't compare it with the life I had before the genocide. Then I had both my parents, but now I have none. When I think about my life, I remember myself before the genocide. I had no wounds and scars, but now my leg sometimes hurts and swells up because of the shrapnel fragments still inside. It also gives me a complex because when the boys at school see my leg, they ask me what happened. They ask me that question, even though it was their people who caused me that damage and so I feel offended. I just tell them I had a problem. If they insist, I walk away. Some girls get scared of my leg as well, especially when we're taking a shower. They ask what happened and I just tell them that something went wrong. You see! You can't compare the life I'm leading now with the one I had before the genocide.

I'm still studying now, but once I've completed my studies, I'd like to get a job and improve my life because it's been miserable since the genocide. I'd like to help those who helped me, not forgetting the orphans because I have experienced that life. Above all, I want to avoid being lonely, to be happy with other people because whatever happened has happened. I can't bring back those who perished. Instead I think about my future.

Of course I face problems every day. Sometimes my leg hurts and I get constant headaches. I can't read for long hours or memorize many things because I get these headaches. It reminds me how I was before and I feel bad.

Can I forgive the perpetrators? Since they intended the genocide to happen, I don't think I can forgive them. I feel as if I can't manage to live with them; it's beyond my imagination. You can't forgive someone who really tortured you, with all the after-effects it had on me. I might only have one leg now if the Red Cross hadn't helped me. When I remember all that, I feel it's almost impossible to forgive them.

But I think there has to be reconciliation because if it doesn't happen, the killers will murder more people. It can bring peace. It has to be. I believe there will be reconciliation and unity in the near future, and it will be peaceful.

If I had the power, I would help the people who went through those problems and were traumatized. I would console them and help them as much as I can. Maybe what happened to me will not happen to my own children – being victims of a genocide and leading a horrible life like mine. We have to find a solution so that it won't be repeated.

I'll never forget

I'll never forget it because if my children ask me what happened to my leg, I won't tell them that I was born like this! Or if they ask me about my parents, I'll have to tell them the truth – how Rwandan people were divided and it was decided there was a group of people who were to die and others who were to live. How they planned to wipe out one group, but fortunately didn't manage to do it. I'll tell them how the genocide originated, how our grandfathers told us the story of the 1959 war in Rwanda. At the time I wasn't interested in knowing. There were no photos or written history or testimonies that could show us exactly what happened.

I want people to see and remember all that happened, but most of all, they have to be reconciled with the people who wronged them. They have to love one another so that such a dreadful situation doesn't happen again. They should never forget an event like this. I'll never advise anyone to keep quiet and forget the genocide. Because it was planned. The Hutus wanted to kill and finish off the Tutsis. They planned it. It wasn't something that suddenly happened. There's no way someone can find himself suddenly holding a machete and hacking someone else! Even if he did, he couldn't have killed 100 people and still claim it was sudden.

But now I think the perpetrators have realized that one human being is like any other. They didn't have anything against each other to make them kill. They somehow failed to reach their goal. For example, the person who tortured me was aiming to kill me or make my life miserable, but maybe I am living a better life than he is now. So from that he may learn a lesson and repent.

In the past, the people of Rwanda were as one. They shared everything and had one language. Later on, division came among them due to bad leadership. People thought the Tutsis were not human beings, that perhaps they were like animals, so they decided to kill them using mostly machetes. Now there is peace again and people are beginning to live together in harmony. Those who were affected are trying to be strong and the perpetrators are trying to repent. People are trying to unite.

Diane, 2006 © Aegis Trust

Claver, 2006 © Aegis Trust

Claver Nkezabera

"Will I survive today?"

Before the genocide

My name is Claver and I was born in 1960. My Dad was called Murindabakenzi and my Mum Félicitée Mukarwemera. I live in Gasaka now, but I used to live in Sovu. I left there because of the war. I was 34 years old during the genocide.

I knew I was a Tutsi from the time I started to grow up. My Dad was a Hima [an ethnic group with similar characteristics to Tutsis, who live in Uganda]. He was called a Tutsi; they used to call him the 'Tutsi from Sovu'.

Before the genocide, there were times when we had problems, but at other times they would lessen. I was sometimes afraid during that period. The first signs I saw were people talking on RTLM radio [*Radio-Télévision Libre des Mille Collines*] and what I read in the newspapers. I heard about the radio announcements while I was working in Kitabi. I was going home by car with a man who told me what he had heard on the radio. He told me he'd like to kill such people [Tutsis] himself. He drove me from Kitabi up to Kigeme and all the way my heart almost stopped beating. If he'd known I was a Tutsi, he would have killed me.

I also noticed in the neighbourhood that people were no longer united. Those who used to work together could no longer work together. People changed. The Hutus would say, "Look, they're Tutsis, they're snakes."

The genocide

I remember that on the day President Habyarimana died in the plane crash, 6 April, they told us not to go out of our homes. I'd come from work in Kitabi and I spent a night at home. When they said nobody should leave their home, I never went back to Kitabi.

At home in Sovu, I saw people burning houses. They came in two cars, one carrying petrol. As they drove along, they poured petrol out, then others burned the houses. I realised things were getting complicated, so I left Sovu for Nzega. But when I got there, I found people were fleeing from there and so I went back to Sovu.

When I got home, I found they were burning my house. So I joined the people in my village to try and put the fire out. There were a lot of us and we really fought hard to extinguish it. It was getting dark and we kept watch. Then the people I was with said, "It seems we're fighting a stronger enemy." Then I went and woke up Mushana, a local councillor, and told him we'd been attacked by people from Bihanga.

Mushana was shocked and we rushed from Sovu to the commune. We told Semakwavu, the burgomaster, "Sovu is being attacked and they're planning to burn the whole area." He asked who the attackers were, and then Semakwavu left with us by car. When we got to Nzega, Semakwavu asked Mushana to join him in the front of the car and I was left in the back. They started chatting. We proceeded and then they stopped at a place called Kigema at Gasaka. They ordered me to get out of the car.

When I got out, there were people holding spears, clubs and swords standing there. I could hear shooting just in front. People gathered around and those who'd seen me get out of the car started asking, "Why did you leave the car?" I explained it was because I didn't have a gun, otherwise I would have continued with them. Even as I was explaining, I was very scared.

I ran away along the road leading to Gasaka. I ran and ran and ran. When I reached the settlements at Gasaka, I found Garusumiya and his group standing there, holding clubs. They asked me, "Why did you leave the car?" I said again that I'd got out because I had no gun and I'd decided to go through that way. Then I started to think that maybe Mushana had said something, or Semakwavu had asked him about me.

I carried on and made my way to Sovu. But when I got there, I found the attackers had already reached the town. We decided to try and protect our homes. But then a very big group of people invaded us... I stayed that night at Sovu, trying to bring all the cows together. I wanted to gather them and put them in one place. But I couldn't do it. Only two of us had stayed behind, but next morning we had to flee as well.

When we reached Nzega, we met Bihehe Gasana [Bihehe was a nickname. His real name was François Gasana and he was a local authority in Gikongoro]. He asked me, "How are things?" and I told him the situation was bad at home. He asked me again and I said, "They're burning our houses, they're chasing us... I don't know how things will end." Then Colonel Simba came and talked to Gasana. He was a colonel, a soldier, and later a Member of Parliament.

I saw the two of them talking and wondered, "What are these people talking about?" Then Gasana hit me lightly on the ankle with a stick. "Disappear from this place," he said, "because in a few minutes you may see bloodshed." I asked him what type of blood he was talking about and he replied, "You'll see a mixture of different blood." All the people had big sharpened sticks and there were so many of them gathered there.

I left immediately and he told me to go very quickly to Kirehe. I went and hid there in Boniface's house. But I didn't spend the night there because I decided to go back to Sovu. I found the town had been completely burnt – the whole area was burnt on 9 April. So then I stayed and hid in Kirehe. There were times when I hid outside, but sometimes I hid in a metal case. I hid there so long that today I've got a scar on my shoulder that looks like a scald.

After that, I left Kirehe and went back to Nzega. I never stayed in one place long. I kept on moving, searching for news of what was happening. But I never moved during the day, always at night. I found the whole area had been burnt – all of Gasaka and Gikongoro. I made a stop at Misago's place in Gikongoro because I was trying to go to Murambi.

In the past I used to bake bread for Gasana; he was a businessman. He warned me, "Don't go anywhere. If you go to Murambi, you'll die there." Then he took me back to Kirehe and I stayed there. But then the war started in that area as well. I spent three months there, but in those three months, I moved to so many places. I went to Kamegeri and other places. Sometimes I spent nights on the move, looking for new places, trying to hide myself so they would forget I existed. I was fleeing all the time with Boniface Nsengimana. He would say, "I'll go in front to let you know if there are attackers ahead. If so, we'll find another direction."

There was even a time when we went to Nzega together. I was going to hide at Athanase Ruzindana's but on the way, we came across a roadblock. That place looked very dangerous. I watched it from a certain distance, then dodged it. There was a fire at the roadblock and I can still remember the people making the fire. Boniface advised me that we'd better go back to Kirehe, so we did that.

I stayed there in Kirehe. I spent the first month hiding in the metal case, then later I hid in a ceiling and underground. I would hide everywhere. I even went into a bar where they sold local beer and spent four days there. During those four days, there was a snake that used to pass beside me, just on the pillow. I used to feel it every day about eleven o'clock and then again at three as it came back... Then I left that bar. They ran after me, but didn't catch me. They were shouting, "Catch him, catch him..."

I heard that people in Murambi had been killed. I don't remember the day, but someone told me that people had been killed there. Two men coming from Murambi passed by the gate and I overheard them saying, "Blood is flowing in Murambi." They even mentioned the names of some people killed... From Sovu, some people had gone to the Bishop's place in Gikongoro – Bishop Misago. But from there they were all taken to Murambi and killed. They had fled towards the authorities thinking they would help, but instead they were taken to Murambi to be killed.

The killings in Gikongoro got worse. Some powerful people were behind them. There were two Gasanas. One was Venuste Gasana and the other was François Gasana [Bihehe]. They would spend the whole day supervising the killings. They were the ones deciding which area to kill in. They would say, "We'll kill in this or that area, at this or that time, on this or that day." They were the two people who were so motivated to kill. They were both capable of shooting; they were very mean.

The Nzabamwita group of attackers had guns and I would hear them say it was Simba who distributed them. But I never saw him giving out guns. The Mudasomwa people were also very involved in attacks. As they came down the hill, they gathered up people and killed a lot. They killed everyone they met on the roads. Some of the Mudasomwa people were given cows as a reward for their serious killing. For having 'worked' hard.

I realized that the war was very dangerous in our area. Although some people survived, it was very bad. And the perpetrators were the authorities. We called for help several times but they refused to help. There was a policeman I met in Gatyazo; I didn't know his name. Semakwavu alerted him saying, "Sovu is under attack, what should we do?" The policeman replied, "Leave them, that's how it was planned."

The killings in Gikongoro were so horrible. It's terrible to hear people say they're still going on. I strongly believe that those killing today also played a role in the past. If they could kill then, why not now? We live in fear because of these killers in Gikongoro. Gikongoro was the only place where *Opération Turquoise* quickly intervened and rescued the killers. Even those arrested were allowed to flee. The French took them to Congo. I was here in Murambi when they took them.

After the genocide

I came to Murambi from Kirehe on 7 July 1994. We didn't spend many days here in Murambi. When I arrived, some French people came, but you would still see the *Interahamwe* [Hutu militia] boasting. Actually, it seemed as though they still wanted to carry on killing. The French would show us that they had arrested them, but they were only pretending. They would get them and take them away, but a few minutes later, we'd see the killers coming back. The following day, the French would say, "This time we're going to tie them up and dump them in Nyungwe forest." People thought it was true, but they just took them to their homes. That's something I observed myself.

Some cases against perpetrators weren't taken seriously and some of the accused were even released from prison. You'll find them in their homes. They were not brought to trial, nor did they confess. Instead we find ourselves living in fear of going to our home village because we might meet people like them. The killers are still out there, living freely. They should at least admit what they did and ask the people whose loved ones they killed for forgiveness.

I can't count how many people were killed in my family. There were very many because it was a big extended family – my mother's family, my father's, cousins, grandmothers. It was one big family on one hill. I am my Mum's only son, but my uncle had nine girls and one boy. We were not less than 60 people. Some of my cousins survived as well – about five of my uncle's children. They were hidden by a Hutu lady.

My whole family was killed here in Murambi, but I haven't identified their bodies. I don't think the bones should remain here. They should be buried – but in such a way that everybody is aware of it, and in the presence of the people who lost their loved ones here. There was a time when they buried some bones. That hurt the survivors so much because they had buried our people without informing us. They used prisoners or whoever to bury them. Life afterwards has been tough for survivors.

I was scared all the time during the genocide because I was hunted every day. They would never give up. I didn't even hope. I thought I would never live through it. I actually thought surviving was impossible. Every day I thought, "Will I survive today?" Every beginning of a new day, I wished it would rain because whenever it rained, I got some relief. Other times I wished it would stay dark because I always saw people being killed in the daytime. I used to think I would be the next one to die.

The worst things that happened to me? So many bad things happened. There was the poverty. My house was looted; I was constantly worried. I had a child who was living with her uncle and I kept giving some of my cattle as a bribe. Her uncle used to take the animals to the *Interahamwe* in exchange for her life. He and I used to discuss it. I would tell him to give them a certain cow today, another one the next day. We had to do everything to save the child. I always thought she wasn't going to survive. Those things used to worry me so much and kept my heart anxious.

The worst thing I witnessed was people being killed. I saw it with my own eyes. Another shocking thing was how they discovered me and ran after me. And hearing that all my relatives who came to Murambi were exterminated. Then there was the hardship of hiding in a place where I couldn't make the slightest move during the day. I could only move at night.

Justice and forgiveness

Justice? What I'd like to see is a way to unite and reconcile Rwandans. I hope one day to see the perpetrators accept what they did and be forgiven. All I want is to see those people being sensitised, so they stop their meanness, so they stop being bad and become normal... They have to be punished according to their crimes. Maybe that will transform them.

They shouldn't be released from jail. The ones who committed terrible crimes should be imprisoned for life, but those who assisted them should be imprisoned according to their actions. They shouldn't just release them as if they did nothing wrong. To me, reconciliation would be meaningless if they freed people who had never been pardoned or asked for forgiveness.

So far no one has asked me for forgiveness. But they know what they did was very bad and are ashamed of it. We can't be reconciled when they're like that. That's why they need to be punished and maybe learn from it. When I see people released, I just act normally because I'm powerless. There's nothing I can do. I'm left saying, "So be it, I'll continue to live with them and if they happen to say 'Good morning,' I'll reply." But when I see them living alongside us, I feel we're living together in hypocrisy. I think Rwanda today should head towards a justice that brings unity.

Claver, 2006 © Aegis Trust

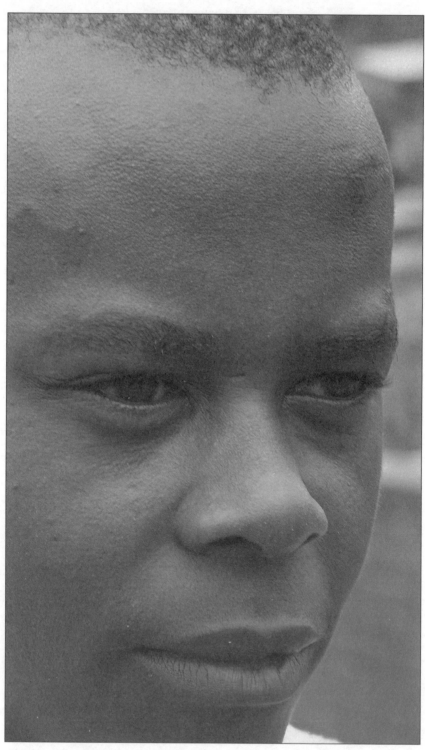

Claude, 2006 © Aegis Trust

CLAUDE NSHIMIYIMANA

Conflicts make us move backwards

Before the genocide

My name is Claude and I was 15 years old at the time of the genocide. My Dad was called François Macumi and my Mum Odetta Umulisa. We were three kids at home – all boys – and we lived in Kicukiro, in Ngoma district.

Before the genocide, I lived with my parents and younger brothers. I was in primary school. I had a good life with no concerns. We lived in peace as a family. But later on things changed. Bad times came from April 1994 – that's when we started suffering because of the genocide. People were hunted. I lost my family members. I had about 60 relatives but they were all killed. I'm the only survivor.

Even before the genocide, some families were victimized. Some families would have to move. They would be living on a certain hill, but then because people said they were *Inyenzi* ['cockroaches', meaning Tutsi] traitors, they would be forced to move.

My father used to work away from home. He used to go on long trips and sometimes the *Interahamwe* [Hutu militia] would attack us at night. They would bang on our door... but we had to be patient because the people we were supposed to report things to were exactly the ones who initiated everything. We had no way of defending ourselves apart from telling our neighbours. But the neighbours often had no means of helping you. We definitely used to get problems like that. In fact we were attacked three times at home before the genocide started – although they never harmed us.

They used to harass my father because he spoke his mind – and he had married an *Inyenzi*. He was someone who easily made friends, no matter what people's background was. There was no enmity between different tribes then; it was more between people from different regions and other things like that. First of all Dad was someone who didn't like the ideas of jealousy or ethnic or regional segregation. Secondly, he wasn't afraid of saying the truth; he didn't fear anyone and he would never support someone who was doing something wrong. So people thought he was against them. They would say, "Why doesn't he ever agree with our ideas?" He was victimized because other Hutus used to say, "He's our fellow Hutu but he doesn't behave the way we do." He would tell them, "That's not the way things should be."

During this period when people were suspected of being traitors, one of my relatives was beaten up to the point that he died after going crazy. His name was François and he was killed in the genocide in Gikondo. People used to be accused of being *Inyenzi* traitors or of having friends in exile – things like that.

The genocide

I remember that when we heard about Habyarimana's plane crash, I was revising my lessons and Mum was cleaning my little brother up in the sitting room. My Dad owned a small bar where he was having a drink with some other people. When we heard that Habyarimana was dead, I could tell there was a change on my parents' faces. Although we were young and they didn't tell us exactly what was going on, I could feel the tension in my parents and in everyone who was at home.

They said, "Let's wait and see if we reach the morning peacefully." All we could do was flee. I remember my Dad saying, "It's over now." They were saying we should flee to the ETO school [*Ecole Technique Officielle*] in Kicukiro because it was the only place people could hide [because the UN was there]. A neighbour couldn't hide you because you knew that some of them could actually be the ones to kill you. People would kill in their own neighbourhoods.

We decided to flee in the morning, but some people were killed that particular night. We heard gunshots the whole night and some of our neighbours had already put roadblocks on the streets near our home. That's how they started killing people.

The morning after Habyarimana's plane crashed, I remember Dad tuned into Radio Muhabura to listen to the news around five in the morning. Then Evode called – he was my brother's godfather. As they talked, he told my father how things were, and he said we had no way of escaping. There was no way we could walk up to the CND [*Conseil National de*

Développement, the building where about 600 RPF soldiers were staying during the Arusha peace process in 1994]. It was impossible.

Dad tried making phone calls and people outside the country would also call him, asking about the situation in Kigali. They would say, "We've heard that Habyarimana's plane crashed, how are things over there?" We were waiting to see what would happen because people had been forbidden to leave their homes. Nobody was allowed to go out, although those who were wise had already sensed what was going to happen.

Dad received several phone calls from inside and outside the country and he told people, "I'm at home with my family but we don't have a way out. People are being killed in front of my house. Things are horrible here."

One of our neighbours was married to Mum's sister, who was pregnant and carrying twins. That neighbour had several other brothers and they were all together in the same house. Dad told him, "There's no way you'll manage to hide your wife. You'd better bring her to our house and leave her here. The rest of you should find your own way. Whoever survives will tell the story." That's what happened. They brought his pregnant wife to our house and the others started fleeing in different directions. Some other people decided to join us at home saying that if we were meant to die, we would die together. Or if we were meant to survive, we would also survive together. But as people kept on coming to hide with us at home, the *Interahamwe* were also planning how to attack us.

They were afraid my Dad would fight. And when they came to attack our home, he did try to fight – but there were too many of them, about 200 people. Some soldiers came first and then the *Interahamwe* followed. The *Interahamwe* were waiting to kill those who managed to escape from the soldiers. They used to call it 'finishing off'.

Some were armed; others were carrying clubs and many other weapons. They found us all at home. They first shot at our very big gate; they used so many bullets but it never gave way. For two days they fought to open the different gates around the fence. Then one evening they finally decided to climb over the fence and get inside the compound. It was a Friday around six o'clock. I don't remember the dates well, but I'm sure that two weeks had passed by then.

They entered our home by jumping over the gate, then shooting the front door open. We had locked ourselves inside the house. They ordered us to open the door, but my Dad said, "Whether I open it or not won't make any difference. They'll still shoot at the doors and open them by force." So he went outside and tried to fight the men in front of the house, but there were too many of them. He was shot and collapsed immediately.

Then the other militia came into the house and ordered everybody to leave. We went out – it was a very long line of people, those inside the house and the compound – all those who had sought refuge with us. Dad had felt sorry for people, especially the children and women who couldn't run. He had given them shelter. He'd never thought such a thing would happen.

As we went out, I heard people making a noise. After that I saw people holding clubs and smashing other people. Some were shooting and others would finish up using clubs and machetes... They got us out of the house. Then they shot every single person who came out – I was the fifth to be shot. They shot me as I was trying to escape. When I fell down, they maybe thought I was dead. They left me and shot those around me.

In the end one of them said, "This isn't enough, use a grenade." They threw one and I still have the scars from it; I have two fragments left in my arm. When they threw the grenade, I was hurt, but it just felt like an injection so I ignored it. I thought that if I breathed, they would hear me. So I remained in the floods of blood and kept quiet. My shirt was covered in blood and everyone lying on top of me had blood all over them. I just kept quiet. Then they threw another grenade and some of them walked over people's bodies, stabbing them with knives. I didn't notice one of them who came to stab me. Fortunately, he missed and hit the grass instead. I sensed that it was me he wanted to stab. He raised his knife again and stabbed me on the shoulder. When he saw me bleeding, he thought I was dead.

Then the attackers left. I watched them go. I lifted my head up a bit but everybody around was silent. They were all dead. I lay on the ground, then stood up to check if anyone else had survived. But there was no one – only floods of blood. I was numb. I couldn't think what to do, yet I needed to find my way out of that place. It wasn't easy to leave – it was difficult to find space to step on. I stood up... One thing I remember is that I went into the house and picked up a big blanket. It was raining. And I covered their bodies, and covered myself with a cloth that belonged to my Mum.

My Mum had been shot with three bullets and my brothers were next to each other – they'd been made to sit in a line. They had been smashed with clubs and shot in the head. There was a big stream of blood. My aunt, the one who was pregnant, was kiilled in the banana plantation. I couldn't do anything to help her.

I had lost my mind. I didn't know whether to go into the house and sleep. Sometimes people cry, but I didn't have any tears to cry, not even a drop. Instead I thought about what had happened to me and I suddenly felt so confused.

While I was still there, the attackers jumped back over the fence and got in. I'd left my shirt there on the ground... They fired a lot of bullets again. Several people watched over the bodies while others were looting our property. I watched them start looting. But I was hiding in a corner of the house. I had gone inside and got a cloth to tie round my wounds because I was bleeding terribly. Then I went out and stood there at the corner. There were some things they didn't manage to take that particular night. They came back the following morning, but I had left by then. I hid that night and was lucky to see a new day dawn.

That's when I got out of that place. By the time I left, no one was alive. I thought it was the end of everything. But then I realised I had to find a way of protecting myself, to see if I could survive. I'd left a green shirt on the ground where I'd been shot and the following morning, when some people came to loot again, they knew that someone had managed to escape. They tried to look for me but couldn't find me. The attackers even declared that anyone caught hiding me would also be killed.

But I didn't hide near there; I carried on fleeing. It was the rainy season and many people were fleeing. I carried on walking, but even as I went, there were some people behind me, trying to hunt me. We had houses in Gikondo and they even went to look for me there. They went to see if the caretakers were hiding me.

I looked for a way of going to ETO in Kicukiro, but it wasn't possible because I had no one to help me get there. I tried all possible ways but I failed. Then I started moving around. I thought there were relatives who had survived nearby, but they had all been killed.

I carried on moving around and the war went on. I would pass by dead bodies, people who were terribly hacked and couldn't do anything for themselves. I had also been shot on the back but I would try and walk.

I suffered... I went through so many problems – the roadblocks and things of that sort. Later, the *Inkotanyi* [RPF soldiers] saved me when we met at the place where they were fighting. I told them all I had been through and they helped me as much as they could.

After the genocide

That's how I survived and was taken to hospital. I was treated there for my injuries. But they only treated the wounds; they didn't remove the fragments inside. Then the war ended in July, but things like schools hadn't started operating. Then FARG [*Fonds d'Assistance aux Rescapés du Génocide*, funds for the assistance of the genocide survivors] encouraged us to go back to school. We started the registrations and the ministry split us up in different schools.

So I managed to study but because I had a problem with the wound on my shoulder, I wasn't very good mentally. Life went on like that. There were other children who survived. We used to meet and talk about what had happened to us and our people during the genocide. But those days were very bad. No one could imagine how someone could kill a person who wasn't fighting back. It's like killing a lamb. The killers were capable of torturing the victim as much as they wished.

When I went back home after the genocide, I found only corpses lying in the compound. I tried to get people to help me – some friends in the same sector who had also survived. They helped me cover the bodies with soil so I could think what to do next... By then, I couldn't identify my parents' bodies – except for pieces of clothing they had on. We didn't do anything special for their reburial ceremony. We just got some clothes, laid them inside the grave and covered them with soil. Then we sealed the grave with cement.

Today

Life is still very hard but there is peace in the country. People have problems like health problems but you keep trying to find a living. When I think about what happened during the genocide and how some people survived, I believe that God played his role. I can't say my current life is very good, but I can't say that it's too bad either. When there's peace in the country and one can sleep peacefully, then life goes on.

After the genocide, I went to Remera near IAMSA [*Institut Africain et Mauricien de Statistique Appliquée*, a kind of university], where the KIE [Kigali Institute of Education] is now. I met a man who had come from Uganda who knew my family. He took me to school in Uganda and I studied there for a while. Then I came back to Rwanda and started studying here. I started living a normal life again. One can never forget what happened but life has to go on. I didn't manage to finish school, but I reached a certain level where I'm able to look for a living. I would like to go back to school but I still have some problems. When I was in school, I used to have problems with headaches. I would be attentive in class, but all of a sudden I would get terrible headaches. And sometimes my arm would hurt so much.

The most challenging thing in my life after the genocide was living without anyone to help me in my plans, to help me work out how to get things I needed. That and all the terrible things I had experienced and seen. I saw so many people suffer. I saw the problems of orphans, including myself. But I've got used to a different lifestyle now.

The most painful thing is living without my relatives, with no family. Living with nobody to tell my problems to. And I'm hurt when I see the kind of life the orphans lead – when they weren't meant to live like that. Especially when there are three or four orphans who can't help each another. It's a pity.

What would my advice be after all these hardships? First of all, I would encourage people to keep up their morale. And I would tell them to use their time efficiently. If they have a chance to go to school, they should study. If they get a job, they should work. Anyone who has a chance should use it well. And I would advise survivors to try and get on with life. They should look for a living. But if they can never forget what happened, that's impossible.

As for the perpetrators, I think they should first admit their crimes, then the punishment could be reduced... They should admit that they murdered people and shed blood. After that, the rest would be easier. But they don't admit what they did, even when there are witnesses... Before I can forgive, the perpetrator needs to come and say to me, "Deep in my heart, I feel guilty. I did this or that to so and so, and my conscience is the best witness." If your conscience accuses you of what you did, then you must ask for forgiveness. Only those you offended can forgive you and it still doesn't clear away the crime you committed. But if you admit it, it brings about a change – it lightens the burden you were carrying.

I believe the reconciliation of all Rwandans would be a very big step forward. When you consider where we are now, there's no longer time for conflicts. It's time for all Rwandans to love their country. They should love each other as Rwandans. Rwandans should unite and come together in the development of their country. Conflicts and rivalry only make us move backwards.

CLAUDE NSHIMIYIMANA

Justice and reconciliation

In my opinion, reconciliation among Rwandans is possible. It will be a long process, but in the end it will happen. It's even taking place nowadays – people do interact although they belong to different ethnic groups. They talk with no problem. They visit each other. And when it's time to share, they share. Personally, I think that those who don't want to move forward and make that step are fools. Because there's no way you can live alone in this world; there's no way you can decide to live with only one ethnic group. In the past, some children weren't allowed to pass in school because of their ethnic group. To me, that's nonsense. It can't contribute to the development of the country. To me, saying that someone is from this or that ethnic group doesn't mean anything. Even the *genocidaires* killed some people who didn't belong to the Tutsi group. Some people were victimized because they had positive ideas.

I believe the *Gacaca* courts [traditional local courts] are a very good idea. I think it was important for the perpetrators to be judged by their local courts to which local people have access. It's better to keep people in prisons in their areas of origin. When they take the accused in their respective provinces, communes and cells, it helps the judges examining their cases. And it's easy for the witnesses to have access to the courts. To me, it's unbelievable that a neighbour could actually have the courage to kill his or her neighbour... That someone would come to your place and kill your whole family when in the past you went to school with their children, or when your families intermarried, or when they used to visit when you had a party at home.

In 1994 people were killed in an extremely horrible way. What happened will never be forgotten. Even my children will ask one day, "Dad, where is our grandfather or grandmother?" And I'll tell them that their grandparents were killed when conflicts arose in the country, when some people hated others based on their ethnic group or honesty about political opinions. I'll say that others were victimized because of their families... And it even went to the extent of families killing each other because of grudges that already existed between them. I'll explain how things were, how people hated each other in 1994. Then I'll advise my children never to follow such ideologies. I'll want to try and teach them the truth so they may never be affected in their lives as grown-ups. I'll tell them about it so they grow up knowing what happened. My point will be to avoid them wasting their own time doing the same things.

173

I'm thankful that the Rwandan Government of unity is trying to bring Rwandans back towards transparency. They're also trying to find a way of punishing the *Interahamwe* so that it all comes out into the open and in the future there'll be no more bad feeling among Rwandans. I believe the Government has played a great role and the country is now developing. New houses are being built; there is a change in the governance. Generally, things are changing for the better. And as years go by, the country will develop further.

Claude, 2006 © Aegis Trust

Marcel, 2006 © Aegis Trust

MARCEL RUHURAMBUGA

I thought my life was over

Before the genocide

My name is Marcel and I was born in 1977 in Mukingi commune, now known as Ntenyo district in Gitarama. My father's names were Hategekimana Gakuba and we were eight brothers and sisters in our family. I was the fifth born in the family. I was 16 years old during the genocide.

We lived in Rutagara sector in Bamagayo district. We were the only Tutsis living in that area. During the 1959 war, my Dad came home from school and found that all his brothers had fled. Grandpa was already dead and it was our Hutu neighbours who looked after Dad. They built him a house, gave him back the cows and when he reached the age to marry, they found him a wife. In other words, they were like his parents or his only relatives. They were the closest people he had. He always used to invite them on special occasions. That's how he ended up being the only Tutsi there.

Before the genocide, some things did happen, for example stealing or cutting people's banana plantations. There was scaring people, knocking on doors at night, but not serious torture like beating someone. And I remember in 1992, they came and searched our home. A cousin had come to visit us from Nyanza and they came claiming we were sheltering an *Inkotanyi* [RPF] soldier. But instead of searching, they looked for our local brew and started drinking. Then finally they left.

The genocide

I remember how President Habyarimana's plane crashed on the night of 6 April and we got the news next morning. The massive killings in our region started on 21 April, when many people were fleeing from Kibuye.

When the genocide started, things happened in the usual way. The neighbours took all our livestock. They gathered everything and said, "Don't worry, nothing will happen to you." They divided our livestock between them; some took two cows, others took three; some took goats, others hens. We saw them take everything with our own eyes. Then they moved us, saying they intended to hide us, but they weren't sincere. At first, we stayed in our neighbours' homes. Things continued like that till around the first days of May.

Dad was the first to be killed – at the beginning of May. First, they took all of us, saying they were taking us to the district offices at Mukingi commune – where they used to put people on buses and send them to Kabgayi. But then they took my Dad and Mum, my young brother, Serubibi Guido, and my sister, Marcelline Mukakimenyi. Somewhere on the way, they let Mum go; and one of the militia helped Serubibi Guido escape through the millet plantation because he knew what would happen to them. The other attackers looked for him, but they never found him. I found out later that they killed Marcelline at Karambo.

So they carried on with only my father. Then Dad was handed over to another gang of killers on Mwendo hill. When he saw the perpetrators with machetes and clubs, he decided to run away. The group that had taken him there acted as if they didn't want to kill him, but the other group ran after him and grabbed him. He couldn't run very fast – he was tired and a lot of people were chasing him. They led him towards Kiryango River and when they got there, they tied him up – his arms and legs were tied tightly. Then they threw him in the river and drowned him. It was raining heavily and the flowing water carried him along. His executioners threw stones at his head, saying, "He can swim. He might get out of the water." So they did that until he died.

About a week after my father's death, a soldier called Shyaka came. He asked, "How could you kill Nicolas and leave his children? Why didn't you eliminate them all?" Then the killers added, "Especially that son who goes to school. (I was in secondary school then.) He knows all the *Inkotanyis'* secrets. He's part of them so he must be killed!"

My older brother, Gabriel Burabyo, was hiding at Rusizana's house. One night Rusizana gave my brother some beer. Gabriel took it and got drunk. Then Rusizana made him talk loudly. The gang of perpetrators that worked with Shyaka climbed the fence and got inside. The last word I heard Gabriel say was, "Rusizana, why did you betray me? We fed on the same breast, how could you do this to me?" When they were babies, my mother had breastfed Rusizana and Gabriel at the same time like twins.

Gabriel was about 27. He fought the killers but they stabbed him. I heard him screaming. It was moonlight, so I followed them quietly to see how they would kill him. I didn't see clearly, but when we exhumed him and re-buried his remains, I realized they had stoned him to death.

The following day, around three o'clock in the afternoon, I was attacked in my hiding place at Munyawera's home. Then I hid in a shed, in a cow's manger and used manure to cover myself. Maybe someone saw me. I don't know what happened. I just saw people searching the house and they later came to find me.

There was Shyaka and his brother, a female *Interahamwe* [Hutu militia] and many others whose names I didn't know. They made me get out of the manger and took my clothes off – except for my trousers and shirt. They took me to a place called Kabuga, whipping my legs all the way, and I was subjected to the worst torture you can imagine. They beat me up, spat in my face and forced me to move on my knees and elbows. Shyaka asked me where my brother Gabriel was and I said, "Don't you know where you put him last night?" "Listen to that Tutsi arrogance!" he said. Then he kicked me in the chest. He laid me on the ground and hit me hard on my back. He grabbed me and hit me all over my body.

I sat there and after a short time, a boy called Joseph came. His father was hiding my cousin's wife. The perpetrators ordered Joseph to go and pick up the 'witch' hiding in their home and he brought her back with him. They made us sit there and they hit us. They tied our arms behind our backs. Then they took us to Mr Silas's ruined house and made us sit there near the septic tank. That's where they were throwing the people fleeing from Kibuye after they'd been killed.

I thought they were going to kill me. They made me sit at the top of the pit with my legs hanging over it. I was tied up. But none of those perpetrators wanted to kill me – I'd been at school with most of them. Whenever they told someone to kill me, I looked him straight in his eyes – and he backed off.

Then another group of *Interahamwe* came, Shyaka and Alex among them. Then Alex said, "Look at that cretin! I'll show you what I'll do with him." It was late in the evening and dark. Then he got a hammer and intended to hit me on the head, but somehow I moved a bit and he hit me on the neck. He hit me three times.

I don't know how I got into the pit. I don't know if someone pushed me or I went in myself. I only remember the moment I gained consciousness and found myself lying on my stomach among the excrement. The pit was a latrine that had already been used. Fortunately, the piece of cloth they used to tie me had come loose. I also noticed they'd had thrown bricks on top of me, but luckily, they fell to one side and didn't hit me. I don't know what they did to my cousin's wife. But I guess they raped her, then dumped her in the pit, still tied up. All her pelvic bones were smashed. She was in intense agony.

I tried to get out of the latrine by stepping on the bricks. I tried to get the lady out as well and untied her. I tried to make her stand, but she couldn't because her bones were smashed. She was screaming. Then I had to leave her because I could see she had no life in her.

I started fighting to get out of the pit. It was circular and about eight metres deep. When I almost reached the top, I slipped and fell back in. I tried again with some support from a stick. But then I fell back in again because all my clothes were wet. So I took everything off and was just in my underwear.

When I finally managed to get out, I was in dilemma wondering to go. I thought about going back to save the woman I'd left in the latrine. But I couldn't think of anyone to help me. Then I heard the same group of attackers coming back. They came up the hill and were all drunk. They were saying, "Those people we dumped in the latrine must have died." They came to the pit where the lady was still dying and said, "We should fill it up with about 20 more Tutsis."

The perpetrators approached the pit with torches and lamps. When I heard them, I hid in Silas's abandoned house. They held their torches over the pit and said, "They've surely died." Then they went back home. It must have been around two or three in the morning – the time when everything is asleep, when even frogs don't croak.

After the perpetrators left, I wondered where to go. "What kind of a life is this?" I thought. "Oh God, I wish I had died!" I was freezing and the injury caused by the hammer was swelling. My neck was swollen, almost to the size of my head.

So started walking. I wondered where to go and remembered a village called Buha where Karangwa and Rurangwa, some school friends of mine, lived. Those boys had become terrible *Interahamwe*, but I still decided to go there. I thought that even if they killed me, they wouldn't subject me to terrible torture first.

To get to their house, I had to cross the river Ruhondo. When I got there, I first rolled in the water to get rid of all the excrement and maggots.

Then I remembered that there was a camp of Habyarimana's soldiers nearby, in a place called Gafunzo. As I approached that area, I heard people shouting and smoking drugs. "They'll kill me," I thought, so I went back to our abandoned house. When our dogs saw me, they tried to follow me, but I chased them away. I passed though the bush nearby and made my way to Pascal's house – his wife was my godmother and my sister, Pélagie Mukaburabyo, had hidden there.

I decided to go there, but doubted whether they would take me in. My older and younger brothers used to eat there and then go back to their hideouts. They had a special way of knocking on the door. So when I got there, I knocked like that but no one responded. I knocked and knocked, but there was no reply. It was getting light; morning was coming.

Then my brother Michael saw me and came towards me. He said, "I thought they'd killed you. How did you escape?" I started telling him what had happened but he stopped me because it was a long story. He took me to a man called Nzaramba, whose wife was called Françoise. She worked at a hospital as an assistant nurse. I spent about three days there and she washed me and treated my injury.

Françoise took me to her father's place and I spent a few days there. Then I thought again of going to Mr Ndongozi's, those school friends of mine. By then my injury was getting better and the swelling reducing. So I crossed the river and went there. But instead of going to Mr Ndongozi's, I went to his younger brother's. He was called Aloys Ndanga and he was Dad's friend. He and Dad had given each other cows. [In Rwandan culture, giving someone a cow is a symbol of friendship and solidarity.] However, I doubted if they would agree to hide me. Fortunately, they welcomed me into their home and I stayed there until towards the end of May. I left when the whole family was preparing to flee after the *Inkotanyi* captured Kabgayi.

I told them it was okay; I would wait for darkness, then leave as well. The people who had sheltered me told me the *Inkotanyi* had captured Kabgayi and Ruhango and advised me to go towards those areas. They warned me of all the places where I might find the *Interahamwe*. In the evening, I left and went to Pascal's again. My sister was hiding there and I was sure that my brothers, Guido and Michael, were still alive.

I found my sister there and we spent the whole day together. Then, around midday, Habyarimana's soldiers came from Gafunzo and said to Pascal, "We've heard that you keep 'cockroaches' in your house." "How can

I keep 'cockroaches' when I've heard they slaughter people?" he replied. We were terrified.

This time I really thought my end had come! The old man was talking through the window and we were just behind the door. If they'd tried to open the door or break it, they would have seen us. "We'll come back and check," they said as they left.

So then we left the house and hid in a nearby plantation. In the evening we went back to Pascal's to get some food and then we started looking for my brother. But he was nowhere to be found. We asked the old man to help us, but we still couldn't find him. I told my sister, "You saw what happened during the day, we've got to leave now and take our little sister." She was about five years old and was also living in the same house. But the old man refused to let us take her. He said, "She's very young. I'll keep her and tell everyone she's my granddaughter."

So my sister and I left. I told her that if Michael was still alive, we would meet somehow. But when we got to Kigarama, my sister got very sick. I took her to a nearby house owned by a man called Ntakiyimana. My sister was shivering. I didn't know if it was malaria or something else.

We spent two nights there. He was a good man and even brought malaria tablets and painkillers for my sister. After that, he told us where to find the Rwandan Patriotic Front. We asked him if he knew where Michael could be hiding and he told us he had been killed. I tried to argue that he couldn't be dead because I'd seen him the previous day. But the man described him and insisted they'd killed him the day before and thrown in his body in the same latrine as me. We were very sad. After the genocide, when we exhumed his remains, I identified his bones from the trousers he was wearing. I think over 30 bodies were exhumed from that pit.

My sister and I met the *Inkotanyi* at Kazinganyoni, near Byimana. When we got to their roadblock, my sister was so scared because she thought it belonged to Habyarimana's soldiers. But I convinced her that according to the directions we'd been given, Habyarimana's soldiers weren't there. So we got to the roadblock. The soldiers suddenly appeared and surrounded us.

"Who are you and where are you going?" they asked. We introduced ourselves and they started talking to us. We told them all our experiences and they felt really sorry for us. After that, we lived with the RPF, then they took us to Byimana where we joined other people.

After the genocide

Frankly, I never expected to find any other family members alive apart from my sister who was with me. But after some time, our mother joined us at Byimana, although we found out that our other sisters had been killed. We don't know exactly how they perished, but we learnt later that the killers had taken all the children to Karambo to kill them, then thrown them in the river Kiryango – like my father.

My young brother, Serubibi Guido, is still alive as well. He'd been hiding at Mr Gwiza Dionizi's, where he met a lot of other Tutsi boys who were planning to join the RPF troops. He insisted on going with them, but he was too young to join the army. One day, when we were living in Byimana, those boys were walking around there and saw me by chance. They brought our brother to us and since then, we've been living together.

Later we heard that our married sister had also survived. We met her in Kinazi when we were going to Rwabusoro near Bugesera. That's how the five of us survived – Mum, my sister, my brother, our married sister and me.

In the end our neighbours had betrayed us. They had assured us they would hide us and look after our properties. Later they told us, "We must kill you!" But even before the genocide, you could tell from the looks on their faces that they were capable of killing us. They had had some skirmishes with my Dad in the past and it was clear they envied him for having a lot of land.

Our neighbours didn't kill us – because of the relationship between us. Even though we were the only Tutsi family in the area, they didn't take advantage of that. Fathers would warn their sons not to kill us because of the ritual pact of blood they had signed with our parents. But then some of their sons became *Interahamwe*. They even went for training and when they came back, they just wanted to finish us off.

The worst times for me? When they took me to that latrine hole, I thought my life was over. I'd just seen and heard what they did to my brother. All I could think of was what heaven looked like. I wondered why it took them so long to kill me. When the killer snatched a hammer, I thought he was going to smash my head and finish me off. Fortunately – I guess it was by God's will – he hit my neck instead of my head. That's how I survived.

When I pass by that pit now, I change a bit and behave differently. I feel strange. It's as though I lose my humanity. But I don't have a cruel heart, the heart to kill. I don't feel like talking to anyone. I just say a prayer, no matter how short, just a word of thanksgiving to the Lord. But if I see someone related to the militias at that time, I become aggressive. Sometimes I think of doing something horrible, but because it isn't in my nature, I just get over it.

Some people did help us during the genocide – yet we weren't friends. I can't tell why. Maybe it was by God's mercy. Pascal, for example, was my sister's godfather, but we weren't very close to his family. We never expected him to help us the way he did. Surprisingly, those who should have helped us – I mean our neighbours, those who were like relatives to us – they changed. The people we never expected to help were the ones who did.

Sometimes I try to understand those killers' minds, but I can't! I try to imagine how someone gets the courage to hold a machete or hammer and start hacking someone else. But it goes beyond my understanding. I can never understand the things I witnessed.

Today

Now, after the genocide, I'm the oldest son in the family and I've taken all the family responsibilities upon myself. I've had to grow up before time. Now I'm the 'old man' at home; I'm the one who makes the decisions in the family. So at my young age, I feel deprived of my freedom. I don't have time to enjoy life as I should at my age – playing around with fellow teenagers or doing other fun things. Instead I spend my entire time worrying about things that actually seem impossible to me, problems with no easy solutions.

Sometimes in class I'm absent-minded, busy thinking about my problems while others are concentrating. If my father or older brother had survived, it would be easier for me. I would be able to use my time in class effectively rather than thinking about family problems. Those are consequences of the genocide that affect me.

I do feel desperate sometimes when I think about my problems. But when I meet friends at school, I forget about it. Then the feeling comes back during the holidays when I'm at home seeing my family's situation. I get so desperate because I can see everything, but I can't improve it. When I think about my problems, I can't get to sleep until five o'clock in the morning.

Some things make me happy – like doing something to help a genocide survivor. It may be giving advice or helping with something. However simple it may be, I'm able to help. I think all genocide survivors, especially the young ones, should be given the advantage of a scholarship. Those who are still young should go to school and exchange ideas with different people. I think the Government should continue financing FARG [*Fonds d'Assistance aux Rescapés du Génocide*] so that the young survivors can continue their studies to higher levels.

We do find it difficult to adapt to this new life because we're responsible now for our young brothers and sisters. But we can come together as genocide survivors and help each other in associations like AERG [*Association des Etudiants et Elèves Rescapés du Génocide*]. We can get advice there which helps us fulfil our responsibilities for the family.

From what I see today, there's a change in Rwanda's leadership. During the former Government, there were several barriers. It was a problem to get a school if you were a Tutsi; it was hard to study. But today people have proper access to schools. There's also freedom of speech in our country and we can express our ideas without fear – which is a great change from the past. But some things haven't changed. We live together but we still don't trust each other.

Maybe reconciliation will be possible among our descendants if we tell them the truth and show them the right path. But it's impossible – or very difficult – amongst this generation.

Remembering the genocide

I know there are some people who deny that genocide took place. I would take them to memorial sites like Ntarama, Bisesero, Nyamata and other places like Gikongoro. And I would ask them a single question, "Why do you think those people died? Was it a thunder or floods? Did they commit suicide?" Then I would wait to hear their answer.

Memorial sites are important because they are the basis for our history. They will help us never to forget what happened in Rwanda. These sites will be there for years and years. Our children will see them; historians all over the world can come to research what happened. As part of the young generation, especially as a genocide survivor, the sites are there to remind us, so we never forget.

When I give my testimony, I feel as if I've given part of my burden to be carried by someone else. Instead of keeping everything to myself, I feel

I've shared it with someone. I feel it reducing in my heart and at such times, I even sleep peacefully.

I know it's very important to give my testimony so that the whole world, and especially foreigners, will see it. People have to know about the genocide in Rwanda and give it its significance. What I want to be remembered is the massive number of innocent people who were killed. Those people would have been helping the country to develop now. If you forget the genocide, it's as if you don't value human rights.

The message in my testimony for young people, especially survivors, is that they should never despair. We can't change the past. I'm not saying that we should forget and be reconciled. But we shouldn't be taken up too much by our past. It doesn't mean we should forget the genocide – we should always think about it because it makes us strong. Remembering gives us the power to fight against any future cause of genocide in Rwanda. We're the ones to give the genocide its importance. If we don't value it, no one else will. If we don't give out these testimonies, no one else will give them out. If we don't fight for the construction of memorial sites, no one else will. It's our task to stand up for our rights. We should have our freedom to live. To live again.

Marcel, 2006 © Aegis Trust

Olivier, 2006 © Aegis Trust

OLIVIER RUYENZI

There will be unity

Before the genocide

My name is Olivier and I am the son of Vénuste Karasira and Spéciose Mukakarangwa. I was born in 1984 and there were six children in our family. At the time of the genocide, I was ten years old.

Before the genocide, my mother was a teacher at Kicukiro and Dad was a businessman. Our neighbourhood was difficult because that's where some important leaders of the MRND [*Mouvement Révolutionnaire National pour le Développement*] lived. It was their headquarters. The flag used to go up every morning and everyone stood still till it got to the top, then went about their activities. It wasn't easy for Mum working in an atmosphere like that. They would raise the flag before she could get into the school courtyard. They even spat in her face and things like that...

There was one time they attacked us at home, saying they were searching for a gun. They said that we had one, but they couldn't find it. Dad's younger brother was suspected of being an *Inkotanyi* [RPF soldier] and they used to think we were in contact with him. They were very suspicious of us.

They would come and search our house – about twice a week. That's when we started to be afraid. They would make everyone sit down in the sitting room while they searched; then they went away having found nothing. They used to come in a group, saying that Tutsis weren't trustworthy. They suspected us of hiding people or maybe being in contact with soldiers.

The genocide

Two days after the death of President Habyarimana, we went to ETO school [*Ecole Technique Officielle*] where we found the UNAMIR soldiers [United Nations Assistance Mission for Rwanda]. We went there around one o'clock in the afternoon. When we got there, our houseboy went back home and found that our house had already been burnt. We carried on living at ETO along with many people from Kicukiro, the neighbourhood where we lived. People came to ETO hoping that they would survive. A few days later, on 11 April 1994, the UN announced that the UNAMIR soldiers were going to leave.

So the UN soldiers and white people left, along with the Catholic nuns who worked in a convent there. Some people tried to find ways of leaving with them, but it didn't work out. The *Interahamwe* [Hutu militia] were positioned at the fence of Don Bosco High School at ETO, surrounding the area. They came in as soon as the UNAMIR soldiers left and started killing straight away. We tried to escape with a group towards Amahoro Stadium, but some people were killed at ETO. As we headed towards the stadium, some were killed on the way, in Kicukiro neighbourhood. When we got to the Sonatubes factory [*Société Nationale des Tubes*], there were some Presidential Guards and a few *Interahamwe*. They gathered us all in one place and made us sit down.

We heard that the *Inkotanyi* [RPF soldiers] could see us there at Sonatubes, but they didn't have any means of getting to us. The *Interahamwe* couldn't figure out what to do with us and that's when they ordered us to continue walking towards Nyanza. We left for Nyanza, with some soldiers walking ahead of us and some behind. We walked straight towards Nyanza; those who were tired died on the way. At Nyanza, we found a roadblock with *Interahamwe*. They decided to leave us there – because it had been decided that Kigali city should be kept clean and they should stop killing people on the streets. It was dark and raining. They made us sit down and started throwing grenades at us. People were collapsing all around. A fragment hit my head and I felt very weak. When the killers were running short of grenades, they started shooting until they also finished all their bullets. Then they started looking among the bodies for people who were still breathing, and killed them.

By then, I was no longer with my father and brothers and sisters. But I was still with my mother, who was pregnant. Because Mum had been a teacher, when we were at Nyanza, some of her students who had machetes recognized her and protected her. They said, "This is our teacher." I was still very young and Mum kept urging me to remain silent. An *Interahamwe* came and realized that she was still breathing. He hit her on the back with a hammer. She was in a lot of pain but she didn't die right away. Another one came and hit me with the side of a machete, but it wasn't very painful compared with the pain from the grenade fragment. All this happened at night and I can't recall exactly what happened next, but I was told that Dad hadn't been injured. So Dad looked for us and took us to a place not far from Rebero where the *Inkotanyi* had a base. The *Inkotanyi* found us the next day.

They put us in a house nearby that belonged to some *Interahamwe*. The men and women who weren't injured took care of the casualties and cooked for them. One day, an *Interahamwe* came. He had followed the people who were cooking. He came in, saw a lot people there and quickly took the pin out of a grenade and threw it as people were screaming. It fell on a lady near me and she was killed straight away. The *Inkotanyi* came when they heard the grenade and the *Interahamwe* ran away. As he ran, he met some people who were cooking and shot a boy who was with my Dad. That boy died immediately.

As Dad defended himself, the *Interahamwe* also shot his right hand and it was almost blown off. Dad became very weak and fell to the ground, but he was still alive. When the *Inkotanyi* came, they followed that *Interahamwe* and killed him.

That same evening, they took us to Rebero where there was another group of non-injured people from our neighbourhood. Two days later, when the *Inkotanyi* saw that bombs were being thrown from the airport, they told us to go to Gishushu, to the offices of the *Conseil National de Développement* [CND, Parliament building]. We travelled in a Daihatsu. The *Interahamwe* were still throwing bombs there, but they didn't know that some *Inkotanyi* were scattered in the surrounding neighbourhood.

Some other people came and then we left for CND in a Daihatsu full of casualties. They kept on shooting at the vehicle because it was surrounded by *Inkotanyi*. When we got to CND, the casualties were taken inside and doctors took care of them. More people came to seek refuge there. A lot of bombs were being thrown.

Three days later, they decided to move us to Byumba. It was around three o'clock in the afternoon. The roads were safe; the non-injured went on foot and the casualties were driven there. By the time we were leaving, I didn't know where Dad was. As I said, he'd been shot in the hand and I was only with my mother. We didn't know what had happened to my younger brothers and sisters. But at Byumba hospital, we met up with Dad. He didn't know about my sisters either, but soon after we got there, we saw my two-year-old sister. She had been hit on the head with a club and was with some of our neighbours.

In Byumba it was like starting a new life – apart from the pain and seeing people crying and others dying from their wounds. It was a new life after the shootings, bombings, screaming... It was like going back to a normal life. There was a military camp nearby and the soldiers used to bring us food to the hospital. Mother was in very bad shape because she was pregnant and Dad's hand was almost cut off. There were some white doctors and Dad told them he didn't want his hand amputated. He could speak English because he had learned it at school.

The doctors told him there was nothing else they could do and they ended up amputating it. They were treating people very fast because there were so many casualties. When we found out that his right hand had been cut off and we didn't know where all my siblings were, we began to realise how hard life had become...

A few days later, some white people came to the camp. We were with other kids from our neighbourhood and they wanted to take us to Italy for treatment. The other kids had worse injuries than ours, so they took them first.

Later, when Dad was getting better, we thought of going to Uganda because giving birth in those conditions would be too hard for Mum. When we got to Uganda, some relatives of ours welcomed us and a baby boy was born a few days later.

After the genocide

By then the war had ended and Dad went back to Rwanda to check how things were. When he came back, he told us that our house had been destroyed. We had some neighbours at home with whom we shared everything. They had been killed but their house was still there. So Dad and I came back to Rwanda, but Mum, the newborn baby and my litle sister remained behind. They joined us later on. Then we returned to our normal life although there was still shooting here and there. After some time, we moved back to our own house.

We lived near the Kicukiro health centre and knew the nurses there. They introduced us to some Italian doctors who helped us get visas so that Dad and I could go to Italy for treatment. They operated on my head. I'd been treated in Byumba, but my injuries didn't heal right away because they were infected. The Italians took me to Italy twice. The first time, I had an operation and then when I went back, they did a check-up. A bone near my brain had been affected by a grenade fragment and they removed it. We agreed that I'll go back in five years' time if necessary so they can implant an artificial bone.

When Dad and I came back from Italy, we found that my younger sister, Diane, had returned after the genocide as well. She was fine and had only been injured on the head – she has a scar on her forehead. We kept asking people about my older sister, Florence, and found out that she had been killed. She had gone to visit my godmother during the holidays and all the family had been killed apart from the eldest child in my godmother's family. Florence was the only one killed of the six children of our family.

We also inquired about the rest of our relatives and discovered that only my Dad was still alive from his family – apart from his younger brother who lived in Uganda and his sister in Butare. The other two had been killed. In my mother's family, no one had survived except her. Mum herself had some grenade fragments in her leg, but she went to King Fayçal hospital for treatment and there was some improvement. She's getting better with time.

Today, my mother is a teacher at Saint Joseph's and father is a bank manager in Kicukiro. Dad can't do just any job because of losing his hand. We were lucky because he was very educated and that allowed him to adjust quickly to this new life.

I'm a student now. I'm studying computers and have just finished secondary school. I'm continuing with my studies. You have to look for a job – it doesn't just come to you. Then life will be good.

As a child, I remember I used to think that was just how things were in Rwanda, but as time went by, we saw things getting worse. You could pass by somewhere and witness someone being taken away to be killed in the open. It was beyond what anyone could handle. You reached a point during the genocide where you were insensitive to what was happening around you. It was as though you had stopped being human.

The perpetrators were people who lived in the same neighbourhood as us and so we knew each other. I can't recall their names but they looked familiar. We even used to play football together although they were older than us. It has, of course, affected us, but we need to endure life and accept reconciliation. Life goes on despite the scars that are obvious to everyone. I think unity will be difficult, but it will come with time. As people give their testimony or tell what happened to them in public, they will feel released. I believe one day we will reach unity.

But for reconciliation, the killer should be the one to make the first step. He will most probably be thinking that you're still holding grudges towards him, that you're still bitter towards him. He should come to you and tell you in detail about everything he did and how sorry he is about it all. It must come from the heart. Then you would feel that at least he's shown you that he's become human – as opposed to his inhumanity before. That could bring unity. But it won't come automatically. It will be built with time as people talk to each other and see each other.

The future

The future? I think the suspicion will disappear with time. But there are some things you simply can't erase from your heart. Some people don't believe we should live in unity. They can't erase what has happened, but I think it will come slowly.

Things have changed in the last ten years. In 1995, everything was still very fresh in people's minds. You would see someone and immediately suspect him or her of being something else... But as the years go by and things happen, as life changes, the way we think also changes as we learn new things. Perhaps at first I had a problem with going back to school. I kept remembering the events wherever I was – sleeping, walking or sitting on my own – and that was a big issue. But today, we talk about it. Survivors exchange ideas and share experiences; it removes a certain weight and one feels lighter. You start living with others in harmony.

Today Rwanda is very different from the way it used to be. Before, only one part of the Rwandan population could express itself freely, while the other couldn't. But today it seems more open to both sides. Before, there was so much division – people's ethnic groups were written on identity cards, for instance.

I believe in the future things can only get better. Our children will go through the country's archives and find out how things used to be. They will want to understand why things were that way. But development in the future goes hand in hand with unity or with understanding among the people. There needs to be tolerance among the people. Let's take the example of the *Gacaca* courts [traditional local courts]. Some people were killed and others were accused of murder. Maybe the ones accusing them are dying of AIDS. Maybe some people will be released because there won't be anyone to accuse them. But maybe somewhere in the village, there will be someone else on their deathbed, who was unable to go and accuse him. If the accused really has it at heart to be united with the people he wronged, then he can make a step towards that person and work it out himself. That way, I believe Rwanda will develop because there won't be any suspicion in people's hearts.

Young people should be encouraged to think through what happened – so it never happens again. They should keep it in their hearts so we never find ourselves in the same situation again. Genocide happened against the Tutsis in Rwanda just like there was genocide against the Jews in Europe. But now it is coming to an end because Rwandans are becoming reconciled.

The fact that we Rwandans are still alive and able to give this testimony and message shows there has been a change. That change needs to remain forever and even improve. The change is that people are free to express themselves today. I believe that's what development is all about and I believe there will be unity in Rwanda in this generation.

Rosette, 2006 © Aegis Trust

ROSETTE MUSABE SEBASONI

Innocent people shouldn't be killed

Before the genocide

My name is Rosette and I was 15 years old at the time of the genocide. Before the genocide I lived with my parents, my older brother and my four young sisters. At first we lived in Bujumbura, where we were born, but later we lived in Kigali. Then finally we moved to Kibuye. I lost my parents and four sisters in the genocide – in total, six people in my family.

My mother was a wonderful parent and I learnt a very good lesson from her. She was very good at looking after us. Her great example is still very vivid for me. She was very open with us; she used to tell us everything. We used to think it strange that she would tell us that she loved us. When we told people about it, they couldn't believe it because it's not something a parent easily expresses to his or her child [in our culture].

But she was a parent who knew how to look after her children. She was very sociable and people still say so today. People used to come home to seek her advice. She had many friends and there would always be visitors at home. We were used to people coming; some would come to live with us; others for help with school fees or some were domestic workers. If my Mum thought a worker was bright enough to go to school, she would take them to school. She took a lot of people to school; some went up to secondary even though they started as domestic workers at home. All I know is that Mum was a very wonderful parent. What I remember most is the advice she used to give all types of people – that was why most people liked her. She was humble and able to advise people.

My father was also a wonderful parent. After the genocide, people said a lot of good things about both of them. All I said about my Mum applies similarly to my Dad. Although he was a quiet man, he also had very many friends, especially his colleagues and neighbours. Most of the friends we have now, the people who helped us after the genocide, were my father's friends –

former schoolmates, colleagues. Usually the female parent is the one who is more familiar with the children, but our Dad showed us love as well.

Our parents used to give us everything we needed. They loved us so much and gave us everything they could. I remember we would always have new clothes and people in the neighbourhood would say our clothes were from Goma. Mum used to tell us she liked us to look smart. Relatives from both sides of the family were friendly with us. Sometimes they took us to their homes for holidays. Our parents would let us go; they didn't have any problem with that. We only started having problems after Mum and Dad were killed. They were wonderful parents throughout their lives. They helped and advised us and taught us how to be responsible. They told us what we should do and today we believe that our discipline comes from them. Patience, sociability, learning how to be responsible as a mature person, that's the training they gave us most of the time.

My sisters killed in the genocide were called Consolée, Angélique, Illuminée and Florence. But there was also an adopted child called Jeanne who was killed with them. We considered her our sister, as part of the family. My sisters were still young. There was quite a gap between us – it was a long time before my mother had any more children after we left Burundi. So the young ones were much younger than us. They were very obedient kids. They considered me like their aunt, someone more mature than them. We used to discipline them because Mum asked us to do that. She had forbidden us to fight. We used to teach the younger children good manners, tell them not to hurt each other. She used to say that calling someone stupid could make them grow up believing they actually were stupid. She would say she never wanted to hear them do that again. That's the discipline we taught our young sisters. Of course they were naughty just like other children and we would punish them. But they never called each other names because we told them not to.

Angélique was an extraordinary child. She was very bright. I remember she was good at playing draughts. She would play with people of 25 or 30. It's a game that requires thought, but she could beat them all, yet she was the youngest. She was only in Primary Two, but she was a very sharp child. She knew how to distinguish between different types of music at a very young age. She could listen to music and tell which one was funky, which was rock and which was zouk [a popular dance music of the French West Indies]. She also enjoyed dancing a lot. When she was still in nursery school, her teachers used to take her to the lake in Gisenyi or to Kibuye. She was such an interesting child that almost everybody liked her. She could sing and as young as she was, she knew how to make friends. She left us special memories and we'll always remember her. The other children had quieter characters, but she was different – noisier. It was easy to forget she was just a child – her ability to reason was like an adult's. But she was so young when she was killed; she was only ten years old.

The genocide

My most difficult memory of the genocide is seeing our parents killed by people who knew them, by their own neighbours, people who used to come and eat in our home, people our parents had taken to hospital. Some people who once lived at home with us were among those who came in the attack to kill them – and killed them with a painful death... That's the thing that hurts me the most – that they were killed by people my father never thought would kill him. He had been good to them – everyone used to say so – but when things changed, they all came to kill him. That's the thing I remember most and that hurts me so much. I was 14 years old, almost 15.

I saw it happen because we were all together when they took them. It was during the holidays... I remember I was with Mum coming from the market. She told me that horrible things were going to happen suddenly in Rwanda. Then she talked to her friend, Xavérine, who is still alive today. We went to the market and bought a few things, then went back home. She carried on telling me how bad the situation was. But we weren't prepared for anything like what happened.

Then on 7 April 1994, after Habyarimana's plane crashed, it began at night. We heard our parents talking in the bedroom, then they woke us up and said, "Wake up, things are not good." They turned on the foreign news and heard it in both French and English. We asked them what was happening and they told us not to worry, but bad things were likely to happen in Rwanda. In the morning, we heard that our neighbour had been killed. Then Mum sent us to tell a shopkeeper in our neighbourhood, also a Tutsi, to close his shop because things had deteriorated. He was running a bar. And as we went to tell him, we met people who were coming to kill others. We ran back home and never said anything. That was when the war really started and people started to kill.

They came to kill us at home on 12 April. At first some people were willing to protect us. "Nothing will happen to you," they promised. But people from different areas were saying that if our family was still alive, then the *Inyenzi* ['cockroaches', i.e. Tutsis] were still alive.

Later, we were attacked by groups from Gisenyi who had headed towards our home. They couldn't believe we were still alive. So they fought with those who were protecting us... The soldiers and *Interahamwe* [Hutu militia] who came to our house told us about other people they had killed and how they had killed them... Mum would comfort us constantly, saying, "Don't be scared. Even if you die, other people have died too, don't be afraid. It would just mean that all the Tutsis were meant to die. Maybe if you survived, you might suffer. So don't be afraid, all the people in this area have been killed; we're the only ones remaining..." Some people were protecting us and told us not to flee. They said we shouldn't go anywhere, we should just stay there.

They left us alive after the attack on 12 April, but they came to the house and said all the boys should go out. My older brother wasn't there; he was hiding in the roof of another house with some of our cousins. So the attackers didn't find any boys... they only found my parents, the young ones and me.

On 14 April, a group of attackers ran after us and searched for us in all the corners where we were hiding. We fled but they followed us and found us. I hid under the bed. They hit me in the ribs with a club when they were searching for me. Then I ran out from under the bed. They ran after my little sisters. They were young and they were screaming. The attackers took my parents and said, "Everyone is dead; you're the only ones remaining, yet you are the top *Inyenzi*." Then they killed them.

Mum said goodbye to us before they left. But they didn't let us say goodbye to Dad. Mum told us, "Be strong. Nothing will happen to you. You have several relatives in Burundi and Kigali. You will live with them, nothing will happen to you." The way she said that still surprises me today. The only thing she told us was to be strong. We said goodbye to her and then we left. The attackers said, "We won't kill you, we only want to kill old 'cockroaches'. The rest of you can go." My parents were clubbed to death and then the killers threw their bodies outside, cursing them. Later that evening, my brother went and covered them with some soil.

We were taken to a certain old man's house, but there were several other *Interahamwe* there. They told them to keep an eye on us, "These kids shouldn't leave this place. We'll kill them later!" The attackers were back on 15 April. The *Interahamwe* had spent the whole night watching us. They taunted us, bragging about how they had killed people, including some of our relatives. In the morning they came to get my sisters. They said, "You look older; killing you would require some energy." So they took my sisters and killed them. Poor kids, they left saying goodbye to us all the way, "Bye bye... we wish you a good life and may God help you..." It was surprising to hear them talk as if they knew we would actually survive. I really wonder why they said words like, "We wish you a long, good life." My sisters were beaten with clubs; they threw stones at Angélique because she was running away. Then they were thrown still alive into the septic tank. They were left to die there in agony.

Later, my brother Freddy and I left that place when we realized they wanted to separate us. They were planning to take me to Congo... We bribed someone and he helped us escape at night. We left and then walked so much that it seemed as if we had walked through the whole of Rwanda – Gitarama, Gikongoro and maybe in Cyangugu as well. Most of the time we walked at night. In order to survive, we went through many hardships. We were starving most of the time; we spent nights in the bush. I remember once in the forest, we had no idea where we were, not even which province it was. Suddenly, we heard hyenas squealing and heading towards us, wanting to attack us. We used to hide in the daytime and spend the night walking.

We witnessed the *Interahamwe* murdering many people. Some were shot and some beaten up with clubs; we saw it all happening. We sometimes had to jump over dead bodies as we were running away. Sometimes we reached a roadblock and they would tell us to go away in the hope we would be killed at the next one. In other cases we managed to escape somehow. I saw many of the *Interahamwe* killing people.

During the genocide, we spent two weeks feeling very frightened, terrified. But after we saw our parents, sisters and other people being killed, when we realized that all the people were being killed, all our fear disappeared. Our only remaining problem was wondering why we hadn't been killed with the rest.

I remember this man called Nyarusenge who came and told me he wanted to help me to flee. He said he was going to take my brother somewhere else. I was still very young, but I understood that he either wanted me to become his wife or he intended to rape me. He had a spiked club. He asked me to go into the house and wait for him. I replied very rudely, "I can't do that!" – which shows that all my fear had gone. I think that was why we left that place... when we realized that things were going so wrong. They were saying they would come to rape me.

When my brother heard about that, we decided to go and be killed elsewhere. I wasn't scared most of the time. I told that man, "If you feel like killing me, then just go ahead and kill me. My parents are dead; they were educated people, they had university degrees. You were among the attackers who came to kill them, yet once you lived together. They fed you; you were friends. And now you want to use me in any way you wish." I went on and said, "I'd rather be killed than become your wife or flee with you." He went into the house very angry, saying he had the right to kill me. Then I said, "Why don't you kill me?" He just kept quiet and left. But they were waiting for nightfall to kill us. It's even possible that they were thinking of other ways to mistreat me – or both of us, my brother and me. But God helped us and we left there in the morning. They never found us.

The one thing that still hurts very much is the way my sisters were killed. It's perhaps understandable that my parents were killed because they were Tutsis and were maybe even contributing to help out the *Inkotanyi* [RPF soldiers]. They were adults and responsible for the actions, but my sisters were just kids! I can still recall how they screamed, how the youngest was crying. They carried her and told her that my Mum had gone for a meeting, that that was where they were taking her. What hurts the most is the way children were murdered in the genocide. They didn't even know the meaning of *Inkotanyi* and they were accused of being *Inkotanyi*! They didn't even know whether they were Hutus or Tutsis. Sometimes I just don't understand it. Those people must have been extremely cruel to do such a thing. Killing an innocent child who doesn't belong to any political party, who knows nothing. Whenever I think of the children being killed, I feel so much pain.

After the genocide

In my immediate family, there were eight people and only two of us survived – my older brother and me. Personally, knowing that I'm a survivor makes me feel good because I realize that God helped us. I strongly believe there is a reason why God saved us. To me, being a survivor means having the responsibility to stand in the position of those who were killed. What do I mean? I have to be my Mum, my Dad and my sisters. I have to try and take their position. I have to do what I should do – go to school and finish my studies, then work. I wouldn't want to hear people saying that my parents left no one behind or that we are irresponsible. I don't want to let those who thought they had exterminated my family find us in a shameful position.

After the genocide, we tried looking for our family, but many of them had been killed. My mother's family was completely decimated. Only five out of more than sixty people survived. And in my father's family, all those who were in Rwanda during the genocide were killed; nobody was left. Our uncles were killed; only one aunt survived and a few very young cousins. Most of them were exhumed and reburied at Gisozi.

What helped us to live without them was the example of how our parents used to behave around other people. Everybody who saw us, would say, "These are so and so's children, they survived." And people were good to us; they helped us complete our school education. We didn't have anywhere to live, but we tried our best. Our parents had got on well with others, so we had to as well. There was a certain family who had remained in Burundi and when they came to Rwanda, we lived with them. Then we lived with a lady who adopted us. She had once lived with both my parents and we had known her a long time. Unfortunately, she recently passed away. Now we are living with the family she left behind.

Today and the future

In my opinion, the future is promising; it will be better than the past. When I think about today's leadership, I can say that their aim is to bring people together and stop divisions. They want to unite people. Therefore, the future will be good for many people. But I know that some people will still find the future disappointing because they are left with diseases; and some children never went to school.

Personally, I was lucky. I am educated; I completed my secondary school and have now completed university. Of course life is not totally based on education, but I've achieved a lot that I thought I would never be able to achieve. I guess the rest will go according to God's plan and personally, I want to emphasize that in many ways people's lives are dependent on the leadership. People lost their lives because of a bad Government. If the Government had done the right thing, people wouldn't have been killed. Thanks to today's Government's plans, many people have hope and this reassures me that the future will be good.

I'm not forgetting that some people will have a bad life in the future, or saying that it will be like milk and honey for everyone. I always think about people who were infected with HIV/AIDS during the genocide and the very young kids – two to three years old – who never experienced parental care. Today they are not well catered for in orphanages. Others live on the streets and are helped by passers-by. They move from house to house and that will obviously have a negative impact on their future lives. I guess I was lucky because I had the chance of having parents and they prepared me. I have a foundation.

Forgiving and forgetting? It is just not possible for us to forget our own families and people. Even wise men say that forgetting is a form of sickness. For example, there is no way I can forget that I have no parents. And just because I don't see them any more, it doesn't mean I can ever forget that I once had sisters. I often see children of their age who went to school with them and are now finishing secondary school. There's a lot that reminds me of them. We can never forget.

I think forgiving is possible. For example, I personally have forgiven. Although no one has ever come to ask me for forgiveness, I forgave all the killers. When I think about it, it goes beyond what I can comprehend. I always wonder if they really knew why they killed people, what they were thinking. Then I feel sorry for their hearts; they know they killed their own people. And sincerely, I believe they will die a terrible death with a guilty conscience. Deep in their hearts they must be wondering why they killed people – their relatives, their schoolmates, their colleagues, people they were brought up with, played football and other games with, kids who grew up together. Personally, I do believe forgiving is possible. Not holding any grudges against them is an extraordinary gift that God gave me. That's my personal conviction.

I would say that justice is necessary; it needs to take place. The victims of the genocide were innocent. Nothing can bring them back, that's impossible, but some Rwandans killed others while in reality, they were brothers and sisters! You can never find an appropriate punishment for them. Death is not a punishment. Nor is imprisonment. The law should determine the kind of punishment to be given, so that people learn that human rights have to be respected. Whether it's a child or an old man or woman, a Hutu or a Tutsi, a foreigner or anyone else, no innocent people should be killed. There needs to be justice, not only in Rwanda, but in the whole world. Innocent people shouldn't be killed.

I hope that genocide will never happen again in Rwanda. I think that with the ideology Rwanda has now and the lessons people learnt from killing one another, it won't ever happen again. We experienced it, but now we have the task of teaching people to respect each other. If everyone respects human rights, then there won't be a genocide again.

Rosette, 2004 © Aegis Trust

Anastase, 2006 © Aegis Trust

ANASTASE TWAGIRASHEMA

Nobody has asked me for forgiveness

Before the genocide

My name is Anastase and I was born in 1956 in Kirehe, in Gikongoro district. I was 38 at the time of the genocide.

I only discovered I was a Tutsi in 1963, when I was in Primary Three. The teacher would tell all the Tutsis to stand up, and at first no one did because we didn't know what tribe we were. Then the teachers started asking us to bring our parents' identity cards to school. In those days the cards had Hutu, Twa and Tutsi written on them. That's when I found out I was a Tutsi.

Before the genocide in 1994 I was a capable man, wealthy and living comfortably with others. I was young when there was genocide in 1963 and it only lasted three days. But in 1994 the genocide was really horrible. When they started that tribalism again, making Tutsis stand up in school and so on, I wished I had a way of leaving Rwanda.

Before the genocide really started, in the time of multiple political parties, I often heard incitement on the radio and there were meetings going on. I used to think that genocide couldn't happen – or if it did, that it would be like the events of 1963. I felt like an onlooker. I really believed that such a thing wouldn't happen in Rwanda, that the Government wouldn't just sit and watch it happen.

There were signs beforehand that something was going to happen – they used to call meetings and no Tutsis attended them. And if you applied for any governmental job, they first asked you your tribe. If you were a Tutsi, you wouldn't get the job. As an adult capable of analysing, I understood that all this was leading towards the genocide.

The genocide

On the night of 6 April 1994, I remember hearing on the radio that

President Habyarimana's plane had crashed. They said that because the plane had crashed a war was bound to happen. Our neighbours started saying that the end had come... there would be conflict between the Hutus and Tutsis...

The genocide started in my town on the night of 6 April when local leaders ordered everybody to stay in their houses. I stayed in the area where I was born until 10 April.

Then, on a Sunday, a man called François Gasana, alias Bihehe, called and asked me if I had a Hutu identity card. When I told him I didn't have one, he told me, "You're so foolish! You should have at least two by now." He offered to take me to get one and we went to town on his motorbike – to a commune called Nyamagabe. When we got there, we found Potien Semakwavu, the district mayor, meeting with some other officials, including Colonel Simba and Captain Sebuhura. Gasana went inside the house with the district mayor, then came to tell me I had to wait for the meeting to end to get my Hutu ID card.

That was how I knew about the meeting that took place at the commune, led by the mayor of the province. He asked the local councillors why he was seeing people moving up and down, escaping what was happening in their areas. He told the local councillors to go and tell their people, especially the Tutsis, to leave their villages and come and hide in the towns so they could protect them and ensure their safety. Then Colonel Simba asked Captain Sebuhura exactly how many Tutsi policemen were under his command. The Captain didn't remember the number, but said he would check and report back later. All this time I was still there waiting for the meeting to end.

In the end, some of the officials had a separate meeting, attended by the mayor of the province, Colonel Simba, Captain Sebuhura, the district mayor and the heads of some political parties. They went into the conference room and we waited outside. Meanwhile, Gasana came and told me to wait for him at another building. He said he would come and tell me if he managed to get the ID card. I waited there about 40 minutes before he finally came. He told me it wasn't possible to get the card. The district mayor had received orders not to give or renew any ID cards.

So we made our way back to Nzega. People were escaping by going into churches – the Catholics to the Catholic church, the Pentecostals to the Pentecostal church, the Protestants to their own church. People were running here and there. The *Interahamwe* [Hutu militia] had started slaughtering cattle, so we decided to hide as well.

I remember the roadblocks when I was trying to hide. At the first one, I paid out some money and also lied that I had no identity card. I claimed I wasn't a Tutsi. Some people would believe this and, after looking at my face, they would let me pass. Then I would just hide in the bushes till it got dark so I could dodge the other roadblocks.

At first I hid in my neighbour's house – by then I had the children with me. But because my wife was a Hutu, the kids went home with her, except for the eldest who stayed with me. But later the *Interahamwe* started to suspect where I was hiding because they knew my sister had married someone from the house where I was hiding. So after four days I left that place for another one – with a relative of the first person who hid me. I heard that people were slaughtering Tutsis' cows and burning their houses. And I saw it with my own eyes.

But then the attackers came and took me out of there. I tried to bribe them, but they wouldn't let me go. However, a group from the area where my Mum was born defended me. That's how I managed to survive until I was able to hide in the area called Mudasomwa in Kibirizi. So I lived there and patrols came to that house, but my son and I just remained inside.

The attack on Murambi was on 20 and 21 April. I knew what was going on because even the head of the family where I was hiding was among the *Interahamwe*. Our wives were sisters and we used to sit down and talk about what was happening. He came and told me how they had first attacked Murambi and the Tutsis fought back by throwing stones.

The attackers ended up calling Gasana and others to come to Murambi. Gasana asked everyone in the town and the suburbs to come. So they all came to Murambi [school] on the second day, 21 April, and killed with the help of the policemen. Even those who had grenades were defeated and killed. The people who managed to get out were killed right here, just where we are standing. [About 40,000 people were killed at Murambi school over those two days.]

Gasana told me what had happened about the Tutsi policemen. After Captain Sebuhura gave Colonel Simba the numbers, the Tutsi police were killed before anyone else so they couldn't save the people who had sought refuge here in Murambi.

Gasana again tried to save me because of our previous friendship. But he told me (and others hiding with us), "First of all, you're going to sign to say that you're giving me all your properties out of gratitude for what I'm doing for you." I saw him looting Tutsis' cars and properties – and yet he'd been appointed to look after and harvest Tutsis' millet plantations.

After some time, French troops came to Murambi – although to me it seemed as if they came to help the perpetrators. But the *Interahamwe* had already been defeated by the RPF troops [Rwandan Patriotic Front] and had started to flee. The French troops then started looking for Tutsis who had been in hiding. They gathered survivors from their hiding places after collecting all the dead bodies into a nearby mass grave.

Of the eight people in my close family, only two survived the genocide: the other six were all killed. My father was killed, but my mother survived. She is a Hutu and was protected by some of her relatives.

What were the worst times for me? Well, at first life was very hard because of the heavy rain while I was hiding in the bushes, waiting for darkness to fall. Then there was hearing how my relatives were being assassinated and being the only one still alive. And they also slaughtered our livestock and looted our property.

There were so many hardships. I had to give up my property so they would leave me alone. I lost my relatives. I was always afraid they would discover my hiding place. And people would refuse to give you refuge – my brother-in-law, for instance, refused to hide me.

I was very scared – especially after witnessing people being killed brutally. Some were hacked to death, others burnt and their property looted. I thought that if foreign nations intervened, maybe some of us would survive. We hoped the international community would come to our help once they knew what was happening in Rwanda, that they would save us and prevent further massacre. It didn't happen like that.

After the genocide

Before 1994, I was proud to be a Rwandan, but now that has lost its meaning for me – unless we can change and acquire a new way of thinking. Unfortunately, I think the Rwandans who killed still have the same mentality. For example, when *Gacaca* [traditional local courts] gave us the chance to testify about what we had seen, people started threatening us, saying that one day they would take their revenge. It's as though in Rwanda today, having killed someone is meaningless.

Can justice be done? The first justice I would suggest is punishing those who participated in the atrocities. I think they should be given the punishment they deserve. I personally think they should be killed as well, but unfortunately the present judiciary system doesn't accept this suggestion.

But the punishment should fit the crime committed. It has to be fair justice.

I think reconciliation might be possible if everybody tells the truth about what happened. Those who committed the crimes should plead guilty. Reconciliation is only possible after justice is really done. I think it's possible now because people have changed their understanding, but the judiciary system isn't doing its best yet.

Nobody has asked me for forgiveness. One of the people I gave money to, one of those who killed my father, has asked God for forgiveness in church. But he didn't ask me personally. I didn't forgive him because I had no forgiveness in me.

I feel a bit pessimistic about the future. I can't see any justice. If there were justice, people wouldn't carry on being killed. But people are still dying. And worst of all, survivors often feel very alone.

Anastase, 2006 © Aegis Trust

Marie Claire, 2006 © Aegis Trust

Marie Claire Umulisa

Your heart feels like stone

Before the genocide

My name is Marie Claire and I lived with my parents in Kamonyi district in Gitarama province, in a sector called Murehe. I was 11 years old and in Primary Four when the war began and my older sister, Grace, was 12. There were five children at home and I was the youngest. We never had any problems because both Mum and Dad were working and they looked after us.

The genocide

Just before the war, I didn't know very much about it, but I was aware that the political parties were in conflict. I remember we had a councillor called Emmanuel Iyakaremye. He came to our house and asked my Dad which political party he belonged to. My Dad replied that his political party was in his heart and that it wasn't necessary to tell him. A week later, some people from neighbouring sectors came to our district. They had come to kill the Tutsis and when they reached our house, they took Dad away. They asked him for money and he gave them 30,000 Rwandan francs. Then he was able to come back home.

Two days later, it was Sunday and we went to church. When we went back home, those people came again and called my Dad. We were all in the compound and they told Dad they were going to kill us all. They took all the cows and ate them, but they didn't kill us then. About a week, later, the war broke out.

I remember the attackers came one morning. They knocked on the front door. My Mum and all the kids who were at home jumped over the fence and only Dad remained. There was a millet plantation behind our house and we just hid there. We didn't recognize any of the people who came; we only managed to identify two of them later. One was called

Karamage and the other Minani. They came and took Dad to a local centre. They made him sit there and they beat him. I heard that they didn't kill him that day. We spent about two days in the millet plantation. Then they came back to the house again.

On the following day, I was with Mum and the rest of the family in the millet plantation, behind our home. We didn't know where Dad was. There were five children because by then the boys had left. I was there with my Mum and older sister. In the evening we went to a hill in our village and hid in a cave. We left there on the following evening and Mum took us to our neighbours. She asked them to hide me as I was the youngest. They told her they weren't allowed to keep *Inyenzi* ['cockroaches', meaning Tutsis]. We went back immediately to hide in a millet plantation. After about two days, Mum suggested we should go and hide in a church near there.

When we got to the church, it was around ten o'clock. We went inside and spent about three days there. Then the attackers came to get us and led us towards the river. When we reached a certain centre, we were stopped. They wanted Mum to stay, but told my sister and me to go back. We refused to leave our Mum. They started beating us and since we were young kids, we finally agreed and left Mum there.

My sister and I went to another neighbour's house. Our families were friends, so we decided to go there and we hid behind their house. When we were still hiding, we saw two members of the family, a girl and a boy and we called to them. We thought they would be merciful and hide us in their home.

When they came to us, they said, "How did our people [the Hutus] leave you behind?" They immediately took my sister and me to an *Interahamwe* [Hutu militia] called Byemayire who was a terrible killer, but fortunately he wasn't around. So they took us to a nearby centre, hoping to find some other cruel *Interahamwe* there who would kill us. But when we got there, the two men were hesitant, "We can't kill these two kids; their father was a very good man; he helped us out several times. Let them go and be killed elsewhere."

And so my sister and I left. But the boy and girl, Minani and Yansoneye, followed us, saying they were going to show us to other *Interahamwe*. We carried on walking, but when we got to Musenyi, I couldn't walk any more; I was very tired. Minani then hacked me on the leg and told me to hurry up.

I carried on walking even though I'd been hacked. I wasn't so weak that I had to stop. As we went down the hill, Minani and Yansoneye called to some people down at the river and told them to get ready because they had brought them some *Inkotanyi* [RPF soldiers; here Tutsis]. They carried on walking with us and when we got to the river, the people there made my sister carry a tree trunk and they made me carry two stones. Then they dumped us in the waters of the river Nyabarongo.

We spent two days in the water. I came out on this side in Kamuhanda and found myself among the sugar cane plants. My sister came out on the other side of the river, in a place called Nyagatovu. The waters took us into two different areas. So after two days, I was in the sugar cane plants but I didn't know where my sister was. The last time I saw her was when they threw us into the river.

I stayed in the sugar cane plantation. I was naked – I had come out of the water without any clothes. I thought of some of our relatives who were in Runda – there was an old lady who was my Mum's aunt. But I didn't know the place very well. They had dumped us in the river from a place called Iraro and we came out at a place called Kamuhada, at a bridge between Kigali and Gitarama. When night fell, I went to the hills of Kagina. It was the middle of the night, around one o'clock in the morning.

I walked and walked all night. It was almost morning, around four o'clock, when I reached that relative's home. I went and knocked on their door. They hadn't seen me for a long time. They opened the door for me – and I found my Mum already there. When she saw me, she was filled with sorrow. Then she asked me, "Where's your sister?" I told her that we were together when they threw us in the river, but I didn't know what had happened to her after that. Mum and I stayed there and two days later, my older sister also came there. Mum asked her how she had got there and she told us she had come from somewhere across the river, from a place called Nyagatovu. The three of us stayed there together. Mum's uncle was a Hutu and so wasn't being hunted or threatened. He hid us there – along with his wife who was also among those being hunted.

We all carried on hiding there, my Mum, my older sister and me. Then, in May, the man said, "I don't want to be accused of being an *Inkotanyi*. You'll have to go, all of you."

The following morning, Mum, my sister and I left. We went to Runda, then to a place called Gihinga. When we reached a roadblock, they stopped us. They asked Mum to give them her identity card, but she didn't have one. Then they asked her, "Whose are those kids?" And she told them we weren't her kids, we were just walking together. They made her

214

sit on a pit. We refused to leave her. We stayed there waiting for them to kill us, but they didn't. After some time, a group of *Interahamwe* came. One of them told the rest, "I know this old lady, she isn't a Tutsi." That's how we survived then and carried on our way.

I had a godmother in Ruzege and Mum took us there. But they told us they couldn't hide such a large number of people, that they would be killed as well. They told Mum and my sister to look for somewhere else to go, but let me stay with them. So Mum and my sister left and I stayed there.

We had other relatives in Nyamiyaga, in Musambira commune. When Mum and my sister got there, they found they had all been killed. Mum immediately left for Kabgayi and my sister stayed and hid there with some other kids. When Mum got to Kabgayi, we never knew what happened to her. I wonder if she was killed or if she's still alive? Most probably she was killed. We've never seen her since the war ended. We don't even know how she was killed or where.

So my sister was hiding with those other kids and I was at my godmother's. About two days later, my godmother came and told me, "I can't carry on hiding you because they might kill me as well. It's better for you to follow your Mum and sister." I asked her how I was going to do that because I didn't know where they were. I didn't know which way to go. She told me that was none of her business. "Whether you die or survive, that's your problem," those were her words.

I remember I was ill at the time; I had a terrible wound on my knee and couldn't walk properly. It was raining that morning. I sat alone on the road wondering what I was going to do. Then I thought of going to the place in Runda where we first hid when the war had just started. So I went back there. Although Mum's uncle was very motivated by genocide issues, his sons were good people. They interceded on my behalf, "She's a very young kid; they'll never ask her for identification papers, so why worry? Just keep her until the war is over." They managed to convince him by saying, "The *Interahamwe* don't know her; if they come, she can tell them she's your granddaughter."

I stayed there, not knowing where Mum and my sister were. The war went on and at one point they began shooting. The *Inkotanyi* came to Runda while I was there and we fled together during the shootings. I thought of staying alone in the house, but knew it would be hard. We went through Taba, my home village and carried on. We reached a place called Kanyinya where there was a roadblock. At the roadblocks they would normally stop people and look at the palms of kids who weren't yet old enough to have identity cards. When they looked at mine, they asked me, "Where are you from?" I lied and gave them false names of my parents. They let me go. We continued our journey through Nyabikenke and Bulinga. When we reached Gisenyi, we turned back because it seemed as if the war had calmed down.

A miracle

We went back to Runda where I had been during war. The war was over then. I found the old lady was still alive, but the man had died. Then we went to a camp in Ruyenzi. I thought that perhaps someone from my home might come to that camp, but no one did. I just stayed there.

Then, in August 1994, I remember I had gone to church one day. And when I came back, I found my sister there. It was like a great big miracle to me. Before I even greeted her, I said, "Are you still alive?" "Yes, I'm alive," she replied. Then I said, "You didn't die? Or am I just talking to a ghost?" She said, "No, it's me, I'm still alive."

"Where were you living?" I asked her. And she told me that she had been hiding in Musambira, where we had family. Later she went to Zaire [Congo], then came back. We waited to see if Mum or any other members of the family might come, but none turned up. We didn't know how or where our family had been killed – except for Dad. We knew he'd been killed at the centre where they had taken him.

After the genocide

Then the war was over. From August 1994 to January 1995, my sister and I carried on living there in the camp. But the people somehow wanted to make us their slaves... they stopped me from going back to school. My sister wasn't very old, but she was slightly wiser than me. She said, "How can we live this kind of life? They won't allow us to go to school. All they want us to do is collect grass for their cows, dig, fetch water and generally do all the domestic work. That's what they expect of us."

So my sister left me there and went to see the burgomaster of our home area, who was also a genocide survivor. She told him what was happening and he said, "What can I do for you? You're still young; you can't live alone in a house. And even if you did, what would you survive on? You have no one left in your family to protect you." My sister replied, "It would be better for us to live alone in a house. We don't care if that means dying."

By then there were some empty houses – the *Interahamwe* had fled from them. The burgomaster gave us a house and we started living there – that was in 1995. We both went to school for a short time, but later on, in 1996, the burgomaster got my sister a job as a tax collector. So when she started working, I was able to continue school. I started secondary school in 1997 and my sister carried on working until 2000 when the mayor was changed. I was in Secondary Four then. They appointed another mayor who wasn't aware of our situation. They stopped all employees who didn't have diplomas and my sister was among them. Fortunately, FARG [*Fonds d'Assistance aux Rescapés du Génocide*] was founded and they paid for my school fees. But as for domestic needs, we had a lot of problems then.

By then we were living in Gitarama at the farm. The farm was well looked after while my sister was working. She used to employ people to work on it and we lived on the harvest. Just after she left work, the harvests continued to feed us. But after a while, there was a new policy and we all had to give back everything that didn't belong to us. So we were asked to live in another house. Life became hard for us – it was as though life had stopped. But my sister managed to contact FARG and they gave us 20,000 Rwandan francs a month.

Then in 2001, I was in Secondary Five and we were still getting the FARG funding. My sister realised that her life was getting worse because she had never done any diplomas or certificates. The war began when she was in Secondary Two. So she told me, "You've reached Senior Five and you can see that FARG is helping us with school funds, transport and other school expenses. It's high time I went back to school as well." She found a school and then began studying.

FARG continued to help us until 2002 when they gave us a house in the Kimironko residences that had been specially constructed for orphans living on their own. We started living there. Later on, FARG was decentralised and they stopped helping people, but by then I had finished my studies. So I got a temporary job with Ibuka [Rwandan survivors' association] and the money was helpful. My sister was able to get some of the school materials she needed. Then that job stopped – and life stopped as well.

Life today

Life is really hard on us. Today my sister is in Senior Five. I was lucky enough to succeed and get a diploma. But life is currently very hard. I can't say that we are desperate; we always try to be serene and look for a way of living. Sometimes we meet good Samaritans who have pity on us and say, "I'll help those kids." Without that kind of help, life goes on but in such a miserable way. The hardest thing is finding food.

After the war, we met Minani, the boy who hacked my leg. We went to see our farm in the village and found him there. When he saw me, he was filled with fear. He said, "I know I betrayed you, I hacked you. What can I do to make up for what I did to you?" I just said, "There are laws that will punish you." We reported him to the district and he was arrested. Later on, he died in jail. His sister was also arrested and is still in Gitarama prison.

When someone comes to me asking for forgiveness because he killed my people, I think of how they killed intentionally with all their hearts. I think the law should punish them according to their crimes. Personally, as someone who lost everyone and is now living miserably, I believe that those who killed should be harshly punished in a way that affects them – so they feel that what they did was very wrong. It's not my place to say that they should be killed as well. That's the role of the law and I don't have the right to say that. But they should be given punishments according to the crimes they committed.

As a genocide survivor with many problems, there's a time when you think about all the things you went through and try to compare it with the life you're leading now. Then you come to realise that there's no difference between your past and your present. When things are like that, you just try to ignore it all. Because if you don't do that, you might end up on the streets – crazy. And that would only make your enemies happy. You just have to calm down and think about the future. We only know the past; we don't know the future. We can only wait for the future. It's important in life to wait for what's ahead of us.

My sister and I were the youngest, but all the others were killed. Even though the war ended, there were no other family members left and we have lots of problems now. For example, I can spend two days without eating, yet before the war, I never spent a single day or hour hungry. Whenever I felt like eating, I would eat. And there's no one I can share my problem with. Life after the war is very complicated. Mathematically, I would say it's not even a quarter of the life I was leading before the war.

My sister is young; she was born in 1981. But her life is horrible as well. She should have been able to do something at this time of her life. But because she didn't have anyone to push her to complete her studies, her life seems to have declined. When she realised that only the two of us had survived and she was the oldest, she had no alternative but to leave school herself so that I could go to school. She went back to school after FARG was founded, but before that, she sacrificed herself so that I would get my education. She hasn't completed her studies yet. Normally at her age, she wouldn't be still in secondary school but that's where she is now – in Senior Five. And whenever she comes back home from school, she finds problems. She finds nothing has improved because I have no job and no one to protect me, so I can't really help her. She comes from school and returns to the miserable life she left behind.

The advice I would give genocide orphans is this, "Never long for luxuries because they can turn out to be so dangerous." They should try to appreciate who they are, whether they are living in families or looking after themselves. All I can advise them is to look at everything positively – good or bad. It all contributes to building a better future.

We try our best to talk to genocide perpetrators, but however much you try, your heart isn't at ease. When someone has killed your parents, your entire family, there's no way you can remain indifferent like a tree. You're expected to talk to them nicely, but your heart feels like a stone. Genocide survivors shouldn't always carry that burden. They shouldn't let themselves be stressed by the killers. Instead they should try and ignore those feelings and in some way renew their hearts. They should try to ignore what happened to them. They should try to talk to those who hurt them and listen to their opinions. I believe that when someone hurts you, you shouldn't react with anger but talk to him or her instead. That person will never be at peace; they will always fear you.

And although the war happened, I would tell the children that in the future life will be new again. Because if you tell them the history of the war, all those bad stories, they may grow up not enjoying anything in life, believing that what happened in the past will continue in the future. I think we should reassure them that what happened will end. The future will be very good, unlike what they went through in the past.

Although I experienced a bad life in the past, I still have hope that things will change. I believe we have to work at the problems and, slowly but surely, they will be reduced until finally we'll forget about them. I know

you can never completely forget, but the burden will hopefully be lighter.
I believe in a better future.

Marie Claire, 2006 © Aegis Trust

Odette, 2006 © Aegis Trust

ODETTE UMULISA

It's still present in our lives

Before the genocide

My name is Odette, daughter of Matthias Kamuhanda and Yulida Nyiramatama. I am from Mabanza commune, from a place called Rubengera. At the time of the genocide, I was 18 years old. I had four brothers – Alfred, Edouard, Uwitonze and Shumbusho. Shumbusho is still alive today. I also had one little sister called Ngirabakunzi, but she didn't survive. From our family, only Shumbusho, my mother and I survived.

It all started when I was still very young. I remember how they used to ask us about our ethnicity in primary school. The first time they told us to stand up – first the Hutus, then the Tutsis – I was in Primary Three. I didn't know what tribe I was and so I remained seated. Our teacher was also a neighbour; she knew my tribe because she knew my father. She asked me, "Don't you know you're a Tutsi?" Then I stood up and I remember my friends started mocking me, saying, "So you're a Tutsi?" That's how I started learning things about ethnicity.

I remember meeting Dad on my way home. I was very sad and asked him why my friends had laughed at me. "What does being a Tutsi mean?" I asked him and he said he didn't know how to explain; it was just the way things were. At home, I asked my Mum and she told me, "In Rwanda, there are Twas, Hutus and Tutsis. It isn't something that should make you feel sad or cry. You're a Tutsi." She said that some people thought the Tutsis were bad, but told me it wasn't true, that we're all the same.

Then there was the multi-party system in 1990. Things went wrong in our area, but I wasn't there for long. I moved to Gisenyi, where I lived with some of mother's relatives. Things were worse there than in Kibuye. They used to say they'd kill us one day. I thought it was impossible. I didn't believe people could be killed just because they were Tutsis. But in 1990, things were so bad in Gisenyi that I saw where things were heading. I even realized it would probably reach me one day.

I went to see my father in 1992. I hadn't seen him for a long time because I'd been living with Mum's relatives. I was grown up then and we had a serious conversation. He told me things were going to be very bad soon. As I was leaving, he said, "Maybe I'll never see you again, my daughter."

I went back home five months later and talked with my brothers about what was happening. Edouard told me, "Odette, things are going to be really bad around here and I want to leave. Please help me find me a way of fleeing to Zaire." I promised to do what I could.

I went back to Gisenyi and a woman called Immaculée said she would help him. Edouard got ready and came to Gisenyi with his very good Hutu friend, Munyensanga. I remember how surprised I was when I saw Munyensanga, but he said that if Edouard was leaving, he was going with him. This was in 1993.

Immaculée told me everything was ready for them to leave. But in the end I didn't send Edouard. I was selfish and sent him back to Kibuye. I told him it would be too dangerous for me when they found out. So Edouard went back home and searched – without success – for a way to leave. That was the last time I saw him. He hid in Kavoye and that's where he was killed.

Later on, Munyensanga's family found out I had almost sent their son to the *Inkotanyi* [RPF soldiers]. I was taken to the police station and questioned. I told them I didn't know the *Inkotanyi* and, probably because I was only 17, they didn't keep me there for long – only three days. But I knew I would become a sort of outcast after being in jail. That's exactly what happened. I was no longer free to move around as I wanted. Gisenyi was full of roadblocks then because things were very tense; it was almost 1994. So I just stayed at home. I never even went back to see Dad. I was too scared that Munyensanga's family would harass me or I'd be imprisoned again.

The genocide

The tension continued in 1994. The genocide started when I was away from home in Rugunga, Kigali, staying with a family friend called Maria. Another lady called Melanie lived with us. I'd only been there three days when the war broke out. It was like a nightmare... Maria told me the President had died in a plane crash. She said I needed to leave her home next morning. When I asked why, she replied, "Don't you know that the Tutsis killed the President? That's why you need to get out of my house!" I begged her to let me stay because she was the only one who knew I was a Tutsi. But she refused because she would risk being killed as well.

There was nowhere to go and I didn't even know Kigali well. I went to hide in the toilets behind the house. That's where I met Mama Giramata. She was surprised to see me and said, "So, you're a Tutsi?" "Yes!" I replied. I asked her if she really thought they were going to kill us. She knew I had a white boyfriend and said I should start asking God for forgiveness. I told her I really wanted to see my Dad and Edouard. I wanted to ask Edouard's forgiveness because I should have risked being killed to save him.

I left Mama Giramata there and went back to Maria to beg her not to chase me away. She was just coming from Doctor Jean's house where the attackers had been killing. She sent Melanie and me to see if anyone had survived. When we went there, I understood it was over. For the first time, I saw people who'd been killed – everyone was dead, even the children.

We went inside the house looking for something to cover the bodies with, but everything had been looted. We left Jean's house... Mélanie was very scared and said she wasn't sure if we would survive. She wanted me to choose among her many clothes and said I could wear them if I survived. I laugh whenever I remember that. I chose some nice clothes and tied them into a shirt. Then we left Maria's house.

We went to a quarry in Rugunga. We used paths between houses and passed dead bodies everywhere. Mélanie was a lot more afraid than me. I felt strong. We went and sat in the quarry. Later, we went to Hélène's house – she was Maria's younger sister. We begged her to hide us, but she said she had nowhere. She took good care of us until evening, then told us to go back to Maria and beg her again. So we did that, but when we got to our neighbours' house, the killers had already caught other people. They took Mélanie and me with them.

They took us to Kigali Sports Club in Rugunga. When we got there, they started shooting; children and adults were begging for pity. Some children asked for forgiveness and even promised never to be Tutsis again. I was so frightened that I collapsed and a lot of people fell on top of me, including Mélanie.

About an hour later, when everyone was dead, I heard Mélanie's voice calling, "Odette! Odette! Are you still alive?" Then she helped me remove the bodies from on top of me. She'd been badly wounded. It was almost morning and Melanie suggested we should go back to Hélène's.

So that's what we did. We went into the kitchen and sat there. The house wasn't locked. Mélanie was bleeding a lot; she was so frightened that she was trembling. When Hélène came in the morning to make tea, she was surprised we were still alive. But she said if we stayed there, we'd still be killed. She tried to find someone to hide us, but without success. So we went back to hide at the quarry, even though Mélanie was so weak. While we were there, Mélanie told me that she wanted to go back home to Butare. She was going to pretend to be a Hutu because she had a Hutu identity card. She said goodbye and I never saw her again. I don't know what happened to her.

When Hélène came back, she took me to a lady called Thérèse in Rugunga who was going to hide me. She said I would be safe with her. Another child of about seven years old, Micheveux, was hiding there as well. By this time, about two weeks had passed since the war started.

I lived there for probably about three weeks. Micheveux's family lived nearby. One evening, she told me, "Odette, I'm going to die." I asked her why she said that and she said, "I can smell blood, I'm going to die." That evening, she went back to her home and the *Interahamwe* [Hutu militia] came and took them all.

I carried on hiding in the same house. It felt as if the war was never going to end. I was a risk to the people hiding me. Anyone found hiding a Tutsi would be tortured, if not killed. Thérèse finally said she couldn't hide me any longer because people in the neighbourhood knew I was still alive and were looking for me.

I remember leaving Thérèse's house. It was raining heavily and I went back to Hélène's. But she said it was too dangerous to hide me. She told me to go to the quarry where a man was giving out ID cards to those who'd lost theirs. She told me to say I was a Hutu and had lost my ID.

I walked towards the quarry. When I reached Kiyovu, there was a roadblock and it was raining heavily. They stopped me and asked me where I was from. I told them I lived at Maria's. They said I was lying and I was a Tutsi. I denied it. One of them had a gun. He said, "Listen! Tell me the truth. I promise not to kill you if you acknowledge you're a Tutsi. But if you say you're a Hutu and I find out you're not, I'll have no mercy on you!" He asked me for my ID and I gave it to him. Then I said, "I'm sorry I lied to you. I am a Tutsi, but please have mercy on me as you promised."

He looked at my ID, then told me to sit down next to some other men. I kept staring at him, hoping he'd ask them to have mercy on me. Then the man with the gun moved backwards and loaded his gun. I was so terrified. But his friend said, "Are you going to kill her here? We don't even have a hole to bury her. If you kill her here, she'll rot and smell bad. Just leave her; she can be taken with some others."

I sat there in the rain. At one point, a man passed by whom I'd never met before. He knew the *Interahamwe* and asked, "Why is that girl sitting there?" They said I was an *Inyenzi* ['cockroach', meaning Tutsi]. The man came back to me and asked, "Where are you from?" I told him, then he asked me where exactly in Kibuye and I replied, "In Rubengera." He asked me if I knew a Protestant pastor called Nzabahimana. When I said I knew the pastor, he went back to talk to the *Interahamwe* and asked them to let me go.

After that I went back to the quarry where I'd hidden with Melanie on the first day. I stayed in the bush till evening, then went back to Hélène's house to ask her to hide me again – or help me find another hiding place. Hélène had nowhere to send me. We tried Thérèse, but she couldn't help. Then I went to Mama Olivier's and she let me stay there three days. After that, she asked one of her neighbours to hide me. Mama Olivier was a Tutsi and was being hunted herself. I was about two days with that friend... Hélène kept on pleading with Thérèse and she finally agreed to take me in again.

Meanwhile the *Inkotanyi* kept on fighting. When they reached Imburabuturo, people had to leave their homes for some time. But when people came back to their homes, Thérèse told me she couldn't carry on risking her life for me. She'd already helped me a lot even though she didn't know me. That's when Hélène found an old lady from Kibuye who would hide me. She directed me to the place and told me to knock on the third gate. "She'll hide you because I've already talked to her about you."

So I went to the old lady, Mama Sania. I didn't know her and she asked me about myself and where I came from. But she said she could no longer hide me because things had got really bad. She said she was hiding a lot of people in her home – she wasn't sure they'd still be alive next day.

Despite all this, I remained convinced I was going to survive. Mama Sania told me to leave, but I begged her to have mercy on me. She again refused. Then I really felt as if it was over and I was going to die. I was mostly sad that I would die without saying goodbye to my father and asking Edouard to forgive me.

I was crying so much as I left that Mama Sania called me back. She told me she was a Muslim. She believed in God; she thought that if she let me go and I was killed, God would ask her to account for me. She took me to a room inside her house. I thought I was the only Tutsi still alive in Rwanda, but then I found all those people hiding there. There were so many!

Something happened there that really surprised me and made me wonder why people were so against the Tutsis. Mama Sania used to walk about a lot and one day she met a man called Minani who was dying of hunger. She brought him home and asked me to take care of him. He told me he was a Burundian refugee, that he and his family had been persecuted and he had fled the war in Burundi. A few days later, when he started to get back some strength, he asked me how I had got there. He asked me if I was a Tutsi and I said, "Yes". Then he told me he was a Hutu. He thought our meeting there was probably God's way of showing us that we had no reason to fight, that at the end of the day, we were all the same.

I stayed at Mama Sania's until the war was almost over. The *Inkotanyi* reached Kigali city and were not far from Rugunga. There were gunshots everywhere and we fled as soon as we could find a way out. They didn't ask for people's ID cards any more; you couldn't tell who was a Hutu and who was a Tutsi. Everyone was fleeing.

After the genocide

Later on, the *Inkotanyi* took us to St. André [a school in Kigali] where they protected us. After the war, they told us all to go back home. I stayed at Mama Sania's for a short time until the *Inkotanyi* captured Kibuye. I knew I would go back home one day because I believed there had to be some survivors. But when I got home, there was no one – not a single person, and all the houses had been destroyed.

So I came back to work in Kigali. Later on, I found out that my aunts who had married Hutus were still alive. They told me that some cousins and my little brother Shumbusho had survived, but they didn't know exactly where they were. Shumbusho had been beaten and left for dead. Someone had told them he was among the children picked up in the Turquoise zone.

I started looking for Shumbusho and my cousins, Violette and Claudette. I went to all the orphanages. Eventually, after about three months, the organization Concern in Gitarama told me they had a child called Shumbusho. It was a miracle. When Shumbusho saw me, he just stared at me and looked scared. "You're still alive?" he said. Then he ran away and refused to approach me again... His guardians told me to go back home and leave him; it was still hard for him to accept. So I went back home and started working again. Later, a neighbour told me that Violette and Claudette were still alive as well. I was very happy and felt it was a miracle.

I thanked Mama Sania for all she had done for me and told her I wanted to leave because I had found my younger brother and cousins. She helped me find a house and I had three mattresses ready, one for Shumbusho and the others for Violette and Claudette. But when I went to look for Violette and Claudette, I found out the truth. Aunt Chantal told me they had both been killed at the stadium.

I still look at their mattresses today... Some days it seems impossible that so many people could die at the same time. But I'm starting to accept it and I thank God that I have a good life today. I got married later on and now have two children. Whenever I remember my siblings who were killed, I feel very sad, but when I look at my children, it makes me want to go on living.

Mama Giramata also survived with her husband and children, but I never heard anything about Mélanie. Why did all those people help me? Hélène did it out of her good heart; I wasn't the only one she was helping. She used to take food to others in their hiding places, making sure her husband didn't see – he was a killer. But Mama Sania surpasses all the others because she was like a parent to me. Sometimes I was so discouraged that I asked her what crime we Tutsis had committed. I felt I was cursed... I didn't understand how God had created us and could allow us to die like animals. Mama Sania told me, "The things people say about the Tutsis and their wickedness aren't true."

Today

Shumbusho is still with me and I do my best to help him forget all the bad things he saw. Sometimes I get the impression that life is meaningless for him. But he's a source of joy to me. Even though our family was wiped out, I believe God will give it back to us one day through Shumbusho. The name Shumbusho means 'substitute'; it's almost as if Dad knew we would have a substitute family through him.

I turned 18 during the war, but I didn't think like an 18-year-old. All the hardships I had suffered made me feel mature. It was as though I became Shumbusho's mother. I started a new life and suddenly had all these responsibilities... I felt I needed to do all I could so that Shumbusho could study.

I no longer trust the people who were our neighbours because my Dad was killed by a Hutu man who was a very good friend... They were like brothers... I go home at times but there's so much fear in me even now. I feel as though they'd also kill me if they had the opportunity. Because if they were human beings, they wouldn't have killed children like my little sister Ngirabakunzi. She was killed by other children – the oldest in the group that took her must have been about 13. She told them, "Please forgive me! I'm sorry Dad committed the crime of being a Tutsi, but I promise I won't be a Tutsi any more!"

Most of the perpetrators still don't believe that what they did was wrong; they haven't come out in the open to tell the truth. I went home after the war and people told me how my family was killed and who killed them. But when killers started being arrested and the lawsuits started, people refused to testify. Some of those who killed my family or neighbours were never arrested, and those who were have been released. It would be so much better if they all accepted their crime and apologized. They should apologize from the heart, not because it reduces their sentence. We have to live together in order to build the country, but you can't tell me to be reconciled with them. That's asking the impossible!

I'm lucky to have a husband who gives me anything I want – but there's still nothing that gives me satisfaction here on earth. Nothing! Not the car I drive, the house I live in or travelling to the beautiful countries I always dreamt of visiting. It all feels meaningless without my family to share it with. Yet I know I am lucky. There are many who don't have a comfortable life, who are suffering from AIDS and have no source of revenue. But I never feel happy. I never go for more than a week without locking myself in a room to cry and asking God why my people were killed. And I wonder how things are for those who don't have anything to eat. It's all still present in our lives.

Odette, 2006 © Aegis Trust

Jean de Dieu, 2006 © Aegis Trust

JEAN DE DIEU UWAMUNGU

I didn't speak for six months

Before the genocide

My name is Jean de Dieu and I was only nine when the genocide happened. My father's name was Emmanuel Gatsimbanyi and my mother's Laurence Niragire. My Dad was born in Butamwa, which is currently in Kigali City but used to be in Kigali Rural province. There were seven of us in the family and I'm the only one who survived – except for my uncle who was living in exile. My Dad worked for SOMIRWA [an association that sold minerals] and Mum was a farmer. We lived in Butamwa and I was born there in 1985. I was the oldest child and there were four others younger than me.

Life before the war? I didn't like living with my parents. I only wanted to live with my grandfather because he was the person whose company I enjoyed the most. I reached the point of refusing to go to school because I wanted to stay with Grandpa. So eventually my parents let me move in with him. I was happy there because he had cattle and I would spend the whole day grazing the cows with him. Later, he started to tell me stories about the past. Sometimes he would give me examples of neighbours who were still alive. He told me how in 1959 they came and looted properties, took the cows and killed them. But in those days, they didn't kill people – it was rare.

I remember a time in 1991 or 1992 when I was coming back from grazing the cattle. I'd had a fight with Nshaka's kids who were also looking after cows. When Grandpa asked me why we'd been fighting, I told him they had hit a cow with a stick. They'd hurt the cow and I had to fight them. When I told Grandpa, he decided to tell me all about his past. He gave me another example of a time attackers had come to loot his house. I think it was in 1973, but that same Nshaka was leading the attackers.

When they reached our house, Grandpa told them he wasn't going to leave. "You'll have to burn me in it," he told them. So they took his cows and his harvest, but they didn't set the house on fire. They just left him there and took everything. From then onwards, I started developing a hatred towards them. I even started hating the people who looked after his cows. I wouldn't want to go near them. I loved my Grandpa so much, I can't explain it – maybe because he gave me total freedom. I liked my Grandpa's place and was happy there.

I didn't understand what it meant when I saw things happening, when the militia came. There were political parties such as MDR [*Mouvement Démocratique Républicain*], but at the time in Shyorongi commune, I only knew of MRND [*Mouvement Révolutionnaire National pour le Développement*] because I would hear them animated, singing loudly... It was only in 1993 that I understood they were political parties and why they were created. When I heard about the *Inkotanyi* [RPF soldiers], I thought of them in a negative way because I believed what was said about them. I wasn't aware of what was going to come next. In 1993 my grandfather told me he thought the attacks were going to start again, but he didn't think people would kill others. He thought it would be the same as usual – taking cows, looting properties, demolishing houses, and so on.

The genocide

When the war started in 1994, I personally liked soldiers a lot. I had an uncle, my Mum's brother, who had joined the *Inkotanyi* army. Many people used to say to us, "In your family, some people have joined the *Inkotanyi*." Whenever I heard about the *Inkotanyi*, I used to imagine they were very bad people. Mum's brother came home in February 1994. He didn't spend the night with us, but went back the same day. Then soldiers came to our house to look for him. They searched our house but didn't find him.

In April, I remember hearing on the radio that President Habyarimana was dead. After that, we heard shouts, people crying and shootings... the soldiers fired so many bullets. We didn't know what was happening and were so frightened. In the morning, they said on the radio that people shouldn't leave the houses, but I didn't obey that. I just went out.

There were some soldiers camping near there. When they were about to move to Ruhengeri, I went and stood near where they were packing their luggage. Then as they left, I went with them. They didn't go straight to Ruhengeri; they went first to Tare and camped there. I used to enjoy watching them using their guns. In the morning, some people came and said, "People are killing other people." But when the soldiers were about to go and help them, a higher-ranked soldier said, "Leave them!" And another soldier said, "You go and get to work as well."

But some of them didn't know what was happening and asked, "What work are you talking about?" The soldier replied, "The Tutsis have killed Habyarimana; the *Inkotanyi* killed him. So you have to kill all the Tutsis and wipe them out."

Then I remembered everything Grandpa used to tell me. I immediately went back home and found people were hiding during the day, then coming back to sleep at night. Whenever I asked what was happening, no one would answer me. One night, we came back and I asked Grandpa, "Why are we hiding all the time?" Then he told me, "You remember what I once told you. They've started again, but this time it's even worse." I understood immediately that the looting, killing cows and destruction of houses was going to happen.

Then I decided to go to my parents' home in Butamwa. I thought things were maybe safer back there. But when I got there, I was shocked. I didn't find a single person there and the house was wide open. It was around six o'clock in the evening. I looked for my family but couldn't find anybody. So I went to Grandma's house which wasn't far away. But when I got there, I couldn't find anyone either, so I went back home again. Grandma's house was on a hill and as I was going down, I heard a crowd of people across the hill... people who were perhaps coming back from an attack. They were running. It was getting dark and when I heard them making a lot of noise, I climbed up a mango tree and sat there. The people came, went round the house and inside, but they didn't find anybody. Then they started saying, "They've gone to hide, they'll come back at night. Or maybe someone else has already taken them."

From this, I knew my family were still alive. So I thought, "Maybe they're hiding somewhere." I was still in the tree at around 7:30 p.m. I got hungry and started eating mangoes. Suddenly I heard someone coming through the banana plantation. I waited to see who it was, then I saw it was my Grandma. So I climbed down the tree and greeted her. She was very surprised to see me alive.

She told me that the others were still alive as well and took me to the place where they were hiding – in a deep mine. They would spend the whole day in those mine holes and go back at night to sleep. We went home that night to sleep. The following day, when we were preparing to leave the house at three in the morning, a very big group of killers came. Some of those attackers were our neighbours from the area. They came and shouted. They surrounded the whole house. Dad slammed and locked the door. But they hit it hard and it fell in...

They ordered us all out and while Dad was still arguing with them, they beat him up. I was holding a mattress over my head. They started pushing us forward, saying they were taking us to be killed with the others. As they were still talking, I crouched down slightly. I was very small and it looked as if I was sleeping under the mattress. Then I sneaked away, leaving the mattress there. They thought I was still under it. I went and hid in the bushes nearby and when they checked under the mattress, there was no one there. But they didn't bother much; they just got confused and left. Still today, I don't know how my family was killed. But I'm sure they all died.

I was still hiding. I couldn't think of anything or feel anything. I sat and thought for a while. Around eleven o'clock in the morning, I left the bush because there were dogs passing all the time, trained to search for people during the day. I went back to the hole where we used to hide and in the evening, around seven o'clock, I left. Then I thought, "Maybe there's still someone at Grandpa's." So I went there, but again I found nobody; and the house had no doors left. I looked for people but couldn't find anyone.

I went to look for them on the road but couldn't find them. That's when I met some soldiers [Habyarimana's soldiers] walking around. There was a lady called Françoise who lived in Shyorongi. One soldier asked me, "Aren't you Françoise's brother?" "Yes," I said. Then he took me, saying that Françoise was his friend. So I went to live with the soldiers. Later on, all those soldiers were taken to Jari, where there's a radio antenna. I carried on living with the soldiers, but I'd never seen people being killed. I thought there was just chaos and things would change with time.

The following morning, the soldiers brought some other Tutsis. The first person I saw being murdered was a lady. They cut her neck open with a bayonet and blood spread all over. I was so scared. I'd never seen that lady before, but I can still remember her today.

The war went on and the soldiers I was with were fighting against the *Inkotanyi* in the hills. Meanwhile, the *Interahamwe* [Hutu militia] would take local people and kill them in the camp. One evening, some cooking oil had been brought for the soldiers, but they said there was no logic in eating good food when their father [President Habyarimana] had died.

Then they filled several drums with oil and set them on fire. They used to choose the shortest Tutsis, dump them into the oil and burn them alive. I was terrified.

I decided to move forward, towards where the war was taking place. But when I got there, I didn't know how to move on my stomach like the others did. I decided to go back when some of the people with me were shot dead. When I got back, I found so many kids who had come from their homes in the neighbourhood to join the army. Some *Interahamwe* came to investigate all those kids – including me. The soldier who had originally taken me there spoke on my behalf, saying I didn't come from that area. But some other people said I was born there, that they even knew me. I remember there was a certain *Interahamwe* who said he knew me and that I was Kayiranga's son – even though I didn't know who Kayiranga was. But my soldier friend told them that they'd got me from Byumba when the *Inkotanyi* had killed all my parents, and the refugees had taken me there. Then the *Interahamwe* immediately removed me from that group of kids – but they took the rest. One kid escaped, but unfortunately he ran off through a lot of landmines and was killed. All the rest of the kids were murdered.

So I stayed there with the soldiers. There was a small courtyard next to the camp before you reached the radio antenna. All the people who'd been caught were burnt there. They used to pour petrol on them as they stood there, then burn them. That was where they trained the *Interahamwe* to use guns. They ordered others to use pickaxes. They also made people dig holes. Once they'd dug a pit of their own height, they were forced to get into the hole. Then the killers would just put soil on top of the people while they were still alive.

Then some Hutu kids from Byumba accused me of being a Tutsi. I overheard them through the window saying they were going to tell the *Interahamwe* to kill me. I immediately ran away and when I got to where the *Inkotanyi* and soldiers were fighting, I sneaked into a house there. Inside, there were dead bodies all over the place; that's where they were keeping them.

I didn't have anywhere else to go, so I hid among the corpses. When the soldiers came, they couldn't see me. They closed the door and left. I spent about four hours lying with those corpses. Then I decided to leave the house when I realized it was calm outside. I stayed in the area where the soldiers were fighting. I used to hide at the front line.

There was an old woman they had refused to kill. I used to see her whenever we went to harvest fruit, maize and sugar cane. I would always take her some before I took the rest to the soldiers. They ended up killing her two days before we left that place.

The *Inkotanyi* had blocked the roads in that area that were used for taking food to the soldiers in the camp. When the soldiers realized they could no longer get food or delivery of bullets, they decided to leave. As we were leaving, the soldier who had taken me with him had a bag full of money. He said he was taking it to Françoise, the woman in Shyorongi. He had a gun, so he went in front and I followed him. Then we bumped into the *Inkotanyi* and he was the first to be shot dead. All the others were killed as well. I couldn't see a single living person. I didn't even know where I was.

One *Interahamwe* came from behind me and explained he had lost his gun; if he went back to camp without it, the soldiers might kill him. He asked me to go with him and look for it. I agreed as long as he went in front and I followed. When we moved forward, I heard some people talking. I quickly hid behind a tree trunk. The *Interahamwe* moved forward and I heard them firing a lot of bullets at him. He screamed just once and then died. I turned round and ran off.

When I'd gone far away from there, I saw two other soldiers and continued walking with them. We passed through the *Inkotanyi* camp while they were cooking. But they saw us running away, took their guns and ran after us. We went and lay in a trench covered by long grass. One of the soldiers with me had a grenade and said, "If we hear them coming, I'll explode this grenade and we'll all die together."

I had no alternative, so I agreed and we sat there. Fortunately they didn't see us and at night we left that place. Then we went to Mbogo, where we found some more of Habyarimana's soldiers. They took us to Muhondo and then at night to Shyorongi. We camped just in front of where my Grandpa used to live. I never thought they would have killed my family. I just kept thinking they ought to be there, so I decided to leave the camp and go to my Grandpa's house. But I found only ruins. All the houses had been demolished. I went back and spent the whole day thinking about the situation. I was so confused.

The soldiers sent me to buy some food at the station where refugees were camping. When I got there, I met all the other *Interahamwe* who used to be our neighbours. But no one recognised me because I was wearing the combat uniform shirt. I thought some of my family members would be there and went round expecting to see them. The soldiers had asked me to be quick, so I hurried back. But I found a roadblock set up by the *Interahamwe* with a man supervising it. He had a gun and asked me, "Aren't you ashamed of moving around still when we've killed all your family? You'll be the last to be killed." He made me sit down at the roadside. And then he hit my back with the butt of his gun. I had to go to hospital with that injury later on and I'm still suffering with it today.

While I was still sitting at the roadside, a military lorry came along, taking water to the camp. The soldiers saw me and asked why I was still sitting there. Then a soldier told me to get into the lorry. That's how I escaped that day. In the morning, that *Interahamwe* came and said my whole family had been killed and that I was a Tutsi as well. They were wondering why I had joined the army.

When the soldiers found out these details about me, I escaped from them and joined the refugees from Byumba. When they started asking me where I came from, I told them I was from Byumba and the *Inkotanyi* had clubbed both my parents to death. Some of the women liked me and treated me very well. Some time later, I met a man from Butamwa. He said he knew me, but I denied it. He insisted.

"Aren't you Gatsimbanyi's son?"

"Which Gatsimbanyi? I don't even know one!"

"Aren't you from Butamwa, in Ruriba?"

"No, not at all!"

I went on denying it. Then one of the women defended me and explained I was from Byumba and my parents had been killed by the *Inkotanyi*. They all believed it was true and treated me as their child.

After the genocide

We went on and reached the border together, but then I lost sight of them. They disappeared in the crowd. I carried on walking with people I didn't know. I didn't know where we were going. Then one day, I was sitting by the roadside and a lorry passed carrying water. I drank a bit of water, but it tasted too salty. I developed stomach aches and got diarrhoea. It was a Red Cross car, so when they noticed that I was seriously sick, they took me to their hospital. Later, a man came and asked me about my family. I told him that the *Inkotanyi* had killed them all.

He then added my name to the list of orphans and I was taken to the orphanage at Ndushu, in Goma-Congo DRC. I lived there, but left later on. Through the Red Cross, I sent a letter to my aunt who was a teacher here in Muhima. She replied and sent me a picture, then they took me there and I started studying. Through all this, I hadn't told anyone about my life or what I went through... And no one had ever told me that my family had been killed. So I disappeared again and went home to find out for myself. When I got there, it was hard even to find the way because almost everything had been covered by grass. I just sat there at home for a while.

My uncle was in exile and later I even saw my aunt [my father's sister] who was married to a Congolese. I lived with them until I'd completed primary school and joined secondary. I joined a Government school, Byimana in Gitarama. For the first time, I was living with people of my age.

Trauma

One day, one of the boys in my dormitory insulted my mother. At the time I just laughed, but at night I thought about it. It was as though my brain was expanding. I remembered the past. I thought about my current life and started asking myself why or what I was struggling for. I thought, "I have no sister, no brother, no father, no mother." I didn't see why I was studying! I remember I didn't sleep that night and I spent the whole day thinking about it. I was in class – but distracted.

When I went to bed that night, I couldn't sleep. I couldn't talk. They took me to Kabgayi hospital but it was all in vain. The hospital said I didn't have a problem and sent me back. Then I didn't speak for six months. I used to communicate in writing. That's when they took me to the Trauma Centre and I also started to work with Avega [Association of Genocide Widows].

In the months I didn't talk, I used to think about the way I was living. I was staying with my aunt [my mother's older sister] who had two children; one was abroad. Whenever I compared how they were studying with how I was studying, I found my schoolwork useless. I would go home for holidays and when the other children came back, they were received so warmly! It left me wondering who in my life would make me happy like that! There was no one and it really troubled me a lot. I had no one to talk to. I couldn't talk about things related to genocide because of being traumatized. I couldn't talk to members of my family – because they'd never seen a war. None of them had seen someone killed.

I started talking again at the Trauma Centre, but at first I used a pen. Then later, they told me to stop writing and started persuading me to try and talk. Basically, there were things I wouldn't feel like revealing and I could only answer what they asked. I would reply and keep the rest to myself.

I was able to talk again six months later and went back to school. But I moved from Byimana school to another secondary school called APACE. Things carried on like that until the Trauma Centre advised me to talk to my friends and tell them my story. They said that in order to overcome it, I must try and talk it out or even cry. But I have never cried in my whole life. That's how I started talking about my story this year; I recently told it for the first time. Even now as I'm talking, there's some information that I skip because there's so much that I forget some details.

I live with Dad's younger brother now. Recently I was wondering if my uncle understands the seriousness of genocide. Currently, I don't stress myself with studies because whenever I read a lot, I find myself not able to talk. Afterwards my uncle shouts at me, saying I should get 70%, not the 50% I manage to score. I've never told him what happened to me and how I survived. He only knows a little bit of my story. That's when I started to realize that keeping silent is stupid, so I decided to start writing. I tell the counsellors some things and it relieves me.

I think after completing my studies, I'd like to be self-employed. I want to do a project involving agriculture and cattle breeding. I can't study Agriculture at the moment because I'm doing Accounts, but I think I'll do Management at university. But if I had a chance to study Agriculture, I would do both.

Today and the future

It's very difficult for me to talk about my future. When I think about it, the first thing that comes to my mind is never to get married. But perhaps if I'm lucky, I'll come across a woman whose parents were killed in the genocide. I wouldn't want to marry someone who knows nothing about it. At times I do consider getting married so that I could have a child to replace those who were killed and restore the memories of those we lost.

If I do get married and have children, I'll teach them never to kill anyone. I'll tell them it's the worst thing ever! And I'll tell them about what happened, explaining how politics contributed to it all. Because when you try to analyse it, you find that not more than three people planned it – but more than a million participated. I'll tell my children that if they see someone inciting genocide, they should always try and stop them.

I have a problem with people saying that genocide survivors deserve justice. For example, Butamwa where I come from. I returned there when I needed my identity card. I got there when a *Gacaca* [traditional local court] trial was in progress. I attended even though I have little interest in court proceedings. I stood up and told them that I wanted to accuse some people as well. They all laughed and asked me if I'd come to seek compensation. I said that wasn't why I was there. Then one of them asked me to introduce myself. I told them my parents' names and after they heard them, they apologized.

Afterwards the judges told me to see the prosecutor and make a file. They told me to come back that Wednesday at 9:00 a.m. I went back on my bicycle, but on my way I was stoned by people I didn't know. When I looked back, I saw a group of people running after me. I got off the bicycle and started running. Luckily, I saw a vehicle and stopped it. I told them my story and we went back, but the people chasing me were nowhere to be seen. Since then I've never been back to follow up the case. Most of the killers are still free in Butamwa and one of them is a local leader.

Reconciliation? That's something I can't understand! I remember there was a time I joined vocational training organized by FARG [*Fonds d'Assistance aux Rescapés du Génocide*]. There was a lecture on reconciliation, but I couldn't attend it. In fact I almost got a trauma attack and had to walk out. There were other students who also rejected it and finally they decided to stop the lecture.

Personally, I don't believe in reconciliation and forgiveness because I think that first the perpetrator has to confess that he or she killed, and tell the whole story in detail without telling lies. Take the example of the old man, Nshaka. When I was young, I was told about his deeds back in 1973. Then recently I witnessed him doing the same things. How can you ever be reconciled with such a person? Because it's very clear that whenever he's with his children, he teaches them that Tutsis are bad. That's why I don't think about reconciliation.

To improve Rwanda's future, the coming generation should be educated. Because as they study, they understand better. Instead of only teaching people how to forgive, they should teach them the origins of everything –

and the cruelty of it all. Then everybody would want to stop such acts from happening again.

Jean de Dieu, 2006 © Aegis Trust

Beata, 2003 © Karen Kessi-Wiliams

BEATA UWAZANINKA

Treasure your mothers and fathers

Before the genocide

My name is Beata and I was born in Rwanda in 1980. At the time of the genocide, I was 14 years old. My father's name was Joseph Nemeye and my mother's Devotha Uwimana. My father was a farmer and my mother used to help him in the fields or looking after our cows. On the day I was born, our neighbour gave us a cow to celebrate. I was born at six o'clock behind our house and my father gave me the name 'Uwazaninka' – it means 'if you bring a cow, you'll get the bride' because in our culture when a man asks for a girl's hand in marriage, he has to give cows. So my father definitely wanted a cow from any man who married me! My mother told me that. My father had two boys by his first wife and he was very happy when I was born. He loved me so much. I cried every night when I was a baby and stopped my parents sleeping, so my Dad gave me the nickname 'Shobya'. Later on, my Grandma changed my nickname to 'Kiki' because I made her laugh.

My father died naturally when I was two years old, so my mother had to raise me on her own. We went to live with Grandma in Bugesera. Then my mother remarried when I was five. I was hurt, but my Grandma loved me so much and that was somehow enough for me. From then on, I stayed with her. She used to treat people who were ill; she was very good at using herbs. I wish I could remember all that knowledge now.

I started primary school in 1987. I didn't know anything was wrong in Rwanda because Grandma never told me anything – although she was always saying that wanted to go and live with her sons in Uganda. One of her sons, my uncle Gahima, lived in Mutara and used to buy her clothes. I can only remember seeing him twice because he lived a long way away.

I remember when Grandma came home one evening and a woman who lived nearby came and told her that a dead man had been found in the road. Grandma knew him – he was killed just because he was a Tutsi. My Grandma said, "*Mungu wanjye*," (That's awful) and from then on, she planned to move to Uganda. She sold the land and I was very happy at the thought of going to Uganda. I was looking forward to seeing people in other countries.

On New Year's Eve in 1987, Grandma was getting ready to go to church next day. I remember I went to pick a few green beans to put in the basket in church – that was our custom. Grandma asked me, "Shall we cook rice tomorrow for your mother?" And I said yes because it was my favourite food as well. Then she told me to make sure we came home straight after mass; I had to hurry her up if people started talking to her after the service and making her late.

Then we had our dinner and made a fire because it was the rainy season. That night, we climbed into our hammock bed and Grandma fell asleep soon after. Later, I heard some people push the door open and come into the house. They killed my Grandma with a hammer. It all happened so quickly. When the killers saw me, they said, "She's only little, leave her."

In the morning, I went to the neighbours. I told them I was very scared, but for some reason I didn't know where they had put Grandma. They had taken her outside, perhaps because they wanted to throw her in the river. But she was too heavy for them. That's when my dreams all went up in the air. We found Grandma in a ditch. It still gives me a headache when I think about it. It makes me angry because by that time I loved her more than anyone else.

Nobody was punished for doing that because it wasn't a sin if the person killed was a Tutsi. That was how I found out I am a Tutsi, but to be honest, I had no idea what it meant. I went to live with my mother and started a new life as an eight-year-old. In time I recovered, but my life had changed forever.

The genocide

The genocide in Rwanda that everyone knows about happened in 1994, but before that, there was another one that the world didn't hear about. That was in 1991 when all the Tutsis who lived in the north – the Abagogwe clan – were killed. I remember it very well. I was eleven years old then. We used to get water from the river Nyabarongo and at that time the river was full of Abagogwe bodies. And in 1992 many people were killed at Bugesera when Mugesera said, "We'll send the Tutsis back to Ethiopia via the short cut" – meaning via the river which flows to Lake Victoria in Uganda. All this was already happening to the Tutsis.

245

In March 1994, we were all getting ready to go home from school for the short break at Easter. I remember telling my mother that I didn't want to go home for such a short time. I hated the place anyway because they were killing people for no reason; I was scared. I asked my mother if she should have moved there after a woman had been killed. I can't remember the woman's name because it's a long time ago, but I can still picture her face in my mind. I remember her son was called Welarice; he was married to Nyiramasare and they had four kids. She was killed at midday in the sunlight. They said she was a witch – but it was only because she was a Tutsi.

My mother said in her letter that I could stay in Kigali if I wanted. She also said she was very concerned about me in Kigali because of the grenade that had gone off and the violence that was taking place... but it was better than being killed by people who knew me. There was a man called Nyarihanga, local area head of the *Interahamwe* [Hutu militia], who always used to say I had long fingers... and it bothered his mind. He used to call me *Muntu Kazi* (Tutsi female) and say I scared him to death.

I stayed in Kigali and things were tense: in the first week there was a grenade at the bus station. They said it was the 'cockroaches', meaning the Tutsis, but in reality it was *Interahamwe* who used to play around with grenades on the road. Some people were killed and all the Tutsis felt less secure. The week before the genocide began, they announced in Kinyarwanda on *Radio Mille Collines* that something big was going to happen the next week (*Mube maso rubanda nyamwishi kuko icyumwerugitaha hazaba akantu!*). That's what led to the genocide of 1994.

On 6 April when the President's aeroplane was shot down, I knew nothing until morning when we heard the news. They said the President had been killed – and the Tutsis did it. We were told to stay at home and roadblocks appeared all over the city. I was at my uncle's house with his four daughters, his son and his wife, and our house girl, Umutoni.

Nothing happened on 7 April, but you could hear people outside asking to be forgiven. I remember hearing on the news about a man whose body was found on the road. His face was smashed and his nose had been cut off. That terrified me. Everybody was so afraid.

The next day, I felt ill, as if I had a fever. When I woke up, I found everyone was drinking tea. I remember one girl saying that she didn't have to make her bed, she didn't know if she would ever sleep in it again. She told us she could feel something bad was going to happen. "Don't be foolish," her mother said. Then the girl said loudly, "Whatever happens, nobody's going to rape me." I think that was her real concern.

Uncle was just replying, "This will never happen," when we heard a loud bang at our gate. Suddenly, one of the killers came in and said, "If your daughters don't want to marry Hutus, we're going to have them for free now – and we'll kill them as well." They hacked my uncle and he collapsed. The girls ran outside but were caught near the gate and killed as well. The young boy and I ran through the gate at the back of the house that we shared with our neighbours. That's how I survived that day. From that moment, I never saw my cousin again – or anyone else. I went to stay with a family who were friends of my uncle's. They took me in and one of their daughters-in-law made lunch for me.

I was so tired and confused in my mind. I felt far away from everything. Then I became the family's housemaid and was sent out every morning to fetch water and food. It was very dangerous because of the roadblocks. I was nearly raped and sometimes had to hide among the corpses, pretending to be dead.

Yahaya and Aisha

Yahaya lived next door to the house where I was staying and was a very good Muslim. I can't remember how many children he had, but he was hiding a lot of people in his house – Desiree, Shududu, Antoine and his pregnant wife, Kdafi. They lived nearby and he used to take them in if the *Interahamwe* came – they would jump through the window into his house. I remember his wife always stayed at home. She was his second wife and around eight months pregnant; his first wife had died.

One day I didn't go to fetch water but to buy firewood instead. I remember I bought myself some sugar cane. When I got home, the woman who was head of the house told me to stay outside and see if anyone was coming. She said, "Don't say I'm here." Everyone was inside except me. I sat outside and started to eat my sugar cane. Suddenly, I looked up and saw a man with gun. He asked me where everyone was and – without thinking – I said they were in the house. He wanted the head of the household. He pulled my collar and said, "Come here, you rubbish, show me where she is." My heart was pounding hard as I knocked on the door. But I knocked with a kind of signal to tell them not to open the door.

All of a sudden I ran very quickly under the man's legs and took off. Then I knocked on the door between Yahaya's house and ours. Aisha, Yahaya's daughter, opened the door very quickly. She called her Dad because the killer was already there, telling her to open the door or he would kill everyone. The day before, that same killer had shot a man from the house called Innocent. Now he was going to shoot me.

Yahaya told his daughter to open the door and let the killer in. Yahaya came and took my hand. He said, "Come out, little girl." I thought he was going to give me away, but he said to the killer, "Yesterday you came and killed someone in my house and now you want to kill this little kid. Why? Don't you think God will punish you for this? You'll surely pay for it. I'm not going to give her to you. You'll have to kill us all." Then the killer left, but he said, "I'll make sure I clean up all this mess." By 'mess' he meant the Tutsis – that's how we were dehumanised, like little insects.

That's I how I survived that day. The rest is a long story: every one of those hundred days was dangerous – but some of them I will never forget.

A day I will never forget

On the morning of 15 April, they sent me to see one of their daughters who lived at Iryanyuma. I had to walk for about half an hour, but I passed through Nyamirambo market because I wanted to avoid the roadblock. It was terrible to see life going on as normal, people buying and selling, while other people were being raped and killed. I passed through the market with my head down, then I heard a woman's voice calling my nickname. "Kiki, did you know your mother was taken to the river with the others?" I looked at the woman; she was talking as if it was good news. There was a kind of mocking in her voice. I looked at her and said, "Oh, really."

I disappeared in the crowd and thought that maybe she wasn't telling the truth. But I went back home and cried. I couldn't think about anything but my own life at the time. I didn't know if I would survive. But I also felt a kind of guilt about my mother. How did she feel as she sank in the river? Why didn't I go home and be with her? I was going to be killed anyway and dumped in the road. If anybody was going to survive, I thought it would be my mother. I never thought they would kill her. I started imagining her on the way to the river. I wished someone would tell me what she had said with her last breath. I hadn't seen her for three months and now I would never see her again. I hated her for leaving me. I felt sadness mixed with anger.

A boy called Hassan was hiding in the same place as me. I remember him saying that he was going to take photos of us – but he was only pretending.

We posed for a shot and he said he would give us the photos after the war if we survived. But he was only trying to raise our spirits. Then he said, "If God put his legs down here on Rwandan soil, people would cut them off. How could he abandon us like this?" He started crying and then one of the girls said, "I've got a feeling you will survive, Hassan. Don't cry." Then he answered, "The Tutsis are a bad tribe..." but before he could finish the word, there was a loud knocking outside. We took our shoes off and ran away as fast as we could...

My finger

"Oh look, her finger's funny!" my school friends used to say. I would always tell them I'd cut it with a broken bottle when I was 12 – because I didn't want anyone to keep asking me about the genocide.

It happened when I went to look for water and came across an *Interahamwe*. "Oh, look at this one," he said. "That's what I wanted." He told me to sit down under a tree where another girl was waiting to be killed as well. We saw a lot of people killed as we sat there. It made me go numb. The girl next to me was wetting herself. After four hours, one of them came and said, "Look, she's wetting herself. You know what? We're going to finish all the Tutsis off. Does anyone want to taste a virgin Tutsi girl?"

Before anyone answered, he kicked the girl low in her stomach and she started screaming. To this day I can't remember how I stood up and ran away – but I suddenly found myself at the bottom of the hill near Nyiranuma medical centre. When I looked at my finger, it was bleeding... I ran home and they put on salt on the wound. It hurt, but it stopped the blood flowing...

After the genocide

On 3 July, three months after the genocide began, they wanted to make sure there were no Tutsis left in the city. On the road to Nyamirambo, someone was using a loudspeaker in a car, announcing that even people who looked like Tutsis, or Hutu women married to Tutsis, would be killed the next afternoon. He was saying "*Rubanda nyamwishi bavandimwe*, (Majority brothers and sisters), from tomorrow you have to wipe the city clean. Anyone who looks like a Tutsi has to be killed. Our Father will be buried tomorrow, so we'll make a bed and blanket for him" – meaning that the President's body would be buried and they would make a bed for him by wiping out the Tutsis.

Everyone was scared at this news. There was no hope of surviving. I'd seen how people were being killed and had no doubt that he meant it. I remembered three men I'd seen a few days before, digging their own grave at Gitega. They were looking around as they dug, hoping for someone to save them, but when one of them saw me, I worked very fast and didn't look at him. I felt guilty, then I thought to myself, "Anyway my mother is dead and I'll definitely be killed, so why am I angry with myself?"

We all waited to be killed next day. Many Tutsis were taken from their hiding places in Nyamirambo and killed. There was no hope from anywhere, but I said a short prayer. Two months earlier, I had started to follow Muslim ways because I wanted to be treated well in the house where I was staying. But I couldn't say my prayer in Arabic or really pray like the Muslims. So I said different prayers. I said, "God, if you save me this time, I'll love you and be good after the genocide." I remember vividly saying those words. I made lots and lots of promises to God…

That evening there were quite a lot of bullets being fired as the RPF [Rwandan Patriotic Front] fought with the *Interahamwe*. I still remember seeing the bullets going in a line from Mount Jali to Mount Kigali and back again. I thought the way they crossed over in the sky was rather nice…

Morning came and it was 4 July. No one was going to survive. One of the women, who was dying of HIV, told us she had dreamt that the RPF took us to the top of the hill and we were saved. She didn't know her dream would come true next morning.

I looked at the gate and suddenly, I saw this tall soldier with a hat. He looked different. He asked me if anyone else was there with me and I said no, because I didn't know if he was a killer or not. "Do you know who I am?" he asked. "I'm an *Inkotanyi*! [RPF soldier]." Then he told everyone in the house to get out because the war wasn't over yet.

Searching for my mother

The RPF took us all to St. André school. I remember that all you could see on Mount Kigali was people with mattresses on their heads, leaving to go to Congo. We got to the school and there were a lot of people, but I couldn't see anyone I knew. The next day, I saw two children from my village. Their mother was married to a Hutu and their young auntie was my godmother. I asked them if anybody from their mother's family had survived, but they told me there was nobody. When the killers went to get the family, the head *Interahamwe* in our village took them and made them work for him.

When I heard that, I couldn't think properly. I wish I had stayed with the children till they found their relatives, but I left them. I had nowhere to sleep myself, but I was thirteen – they were only seven and eight. I had nothing there. For lunch or dinner I would join any group that was having food and sit down to eat.

As I moved around in that crowd of people, I met a man called John. He had loved my cousin Goleta before the genocide, but she wasn't interested in him. He treated me like a brother or relative and asked me if I had anywhere to sleep. I told him I slept anywhere I could. I said I was fine; I was looking for my mother. Even though I'd heard how she was killed, I still couldn't believe it. John gave me a spare mattress, but I lost it after a while; someone else must have picked it up.

I went around, asking everyone if they'd seen my mother and met a man called Nyarihanga. "Have you seen my mother, please?" Of course I knew he was a killer, but I didn't have time to think. "She's behind," he said. I didn't see him again, but I carried on searching for her. She was nowhere to be found. Then, on 7 July, I went to Butamwa where my mother lived. Everybody told me there was still war there, but I went all the way just the same. There was no one on the road apart from soldiers – and dogs running with people's bones. I was scared of those big dogs, but none of them touched me.

I reached a place where you could see Gitarama. We used to pass that way going to my mother and father's relatives. Evode, my mother's brother-in-law, lived near the river, but when I looked for the house, there were only trees. I carried on, but the place was scary. When I reached where my mother lived, there was no one there. As I stood there, I looked over the valley between our house and my godmother's family. There was nothing standing. The houses had been demolished.

I couldn't think at all. My head and shoulders went heavy as tears started to roll down my face. I saw a lady coming towards me, although I didn't recognize her. I started wiping my eyes so I could see better. She was wearing my mother's skirt and sleeveless blouse. I felt so heavy; I could feel my weight. I was near to collapsing, but I put my arms on top of my head and walked away.

What was I going to do on my own? My mother had been everything to me. She loved me and wanted the best in life for me. She looked after me and raised me, but now it was my turn to look after myself. Suddenly, I heard her voice saying, "What will become of you without me?" She used to say that before, especially when I couldn't wake up to go to school. She would say, "I don't know what will become of you when I'm not there."

I thought about my mother in the river, probably in Uganda now or stacked up somewhere in the trees. I couldn't help thinking about it, perhaps because I'd seen so many bodies in the river in 1992 and could imagine it. I started to think how she must have swallowed water as they watched her drown. She must have been wearing that skirt. What did she say? How many killers had come to take her all the way from home to the river? The river where I washed and drank! It was the place where my mother had been killed. How could they do that to her? What on earth had she done to them?

How I see Rwanda today

Today Rwanda is rebuilding and for some, life is going on. There are night-clubs, bars, restaurants, swimming pools, basketball and volleyball grounds, tennis, golf, beautiful cars, lovely houses and so on. All these are in Rwanda. It's a beautiful green country, a wonderful place. I love it and have hope for my country. It's only 12 years since the genocide and Rwanda has been reborn.

But although life might seem good for some people, for survivors it's still hard. I can say this with all my heart. They live a different life with bad conditions – from a house of eight people, perhaps only one survived – or sometimes none. Many live with physical wounds and broken hearts. And they live alongside the people who killed their families...

Before the genocide, every Friday people would go to the villages to see their parents and relatives. School holidays were full of laughter as we all went home to our mothers, uncles and aunts... Today, some kids hate school break because they have nowhere to go. The weekends are not the same; the forest has taken over the villages and there are only trees where once there were houses. Where children used to play, there are no sounds; and where cows used to pass going to drink water, the roads have disappeared. And when survivors go back, there's the added sadness that their neighbours are still there and won't even tell them what happened. There's no time of happiness for survivors. When they finish school, there's no relative to attend their graduation. When they get married, there's no family to be with them. There's nothing left for survivors; it has all gone and our life has changed forever.

Justice

After the genocide, the UN established an international court, but to be honest, all it did was mock survivors. This was in 2000 when most survivors who were going to testify were mocked, especially by those talking about rape.

Then the Government introduced *Gacaca* courts (traditional local courts). But how on earth can we try in the local courts someone who killed one person, then another, then another...? This used to be for arguments between neighbours – cows trampling crops, kids fighting and so on. How can we talk about murder and rape there? Since the *Gacaca* trials started, 58 survivors have been killed. We are paying a high price to make Rwanda a better place, but I do think there's hope for the future.

Life today

For myself, yes, I'm rebuilding, but what about survivors who are still broken, emotionally and physically? Those who haven't got the means to get started again? I remember some times when I would only get food once in three days, when I had to mend my shoes five times. But still I kept my pride. The genocide was a very bad time for me, but afterwards my life was worse.

Today I'm fine, but I feel sad when I think of the children who have to grow up by themselves and the women who used to live with their husbands and children in nice houses. Now they're on their own in houses where they can't even buy a candle for light. I remember visiting one of the widows in the Avega [Association of Genocide Widows] village. When I got there, she was eating in the dark. She told me that she had no money for a candle or paraffin. And she went on, "I know where my lips are. Besides, I'm all alone here." She spoke as if there was no reason for light in her house now. That made me feel very angry. And many survivors live like that today.

Can I forgive?

I don't know what kind of forgiveness people mean. If you kill someone, you take his or her life away and it's impossible to mend it. It has gone forever. Those people have gone and cannot give forgiveness. Even if I forgive the man who killed my mother, she's no longer there to forgive him. I may forgive, but I won't ever forget. How can you forget that you once had parents? How can there be forgiveness when the impact of genocide is still with us?

But there is a new generation coming now and I hope there will be forgiveness among them. If we can teach them, there is hope. Our hope for a better future has to be with those being born today.

I feel sad that my mother never had the chance to see me grow up. To see me grow into a young woman and get married, to see her first grandchild. She missed so much in my life. But I'm always grateful that she gave me the foundations of life, taught me how to behave. I remember on my first day at secondary school, she took me into the room and told me never to drink, never to go to night-clubs (this wasn't part of our culture then), and so on. She told me I was there to study. After I left home, I could still hear her voice... then after the genocide she was no longer there. But I always remembered what she told me and followed her rules. That's why I feel so grateful to her – otherwise I wouldn't be here today.

All children should know how important parents are and be thankful to have them. They should treasure their mothers and fathers because they have something that others long to have – something they lost when they still needed them.

Left, Beata and her husband, James, 2003 © James M. Smith

Right, Ariella Aisha, born 2005, named after the girl who saved Beata © James M. Smith

254

Manzi, 2006 © Aegis Trust

MANZI GAUDENCE UWERA

Life no longer made sense

Before the genocide

My name is Manzi and I was born in 1983 in Cyahafi, a suburb of Kigali. My father's name was Emmanuel Ruzindaza and my mother's Immaculée Mukarubayizi. At the time of the genocide, I was 11 years old. I was the eldest of three children. I lived with my parents and younger brother, Rukundo J. Baptiste, and my sister, Uwitonze Clémentine. It was a happy home.

We didn't have lots of neighbours around, but members of our extended family occupied the whole hill. We had no problems with the few neighbours who lived nearby – except that sometimes people would throw stones on the roof and harass us like that... I don't remember any problems before the genocide, but perhaps that's because I was young then.

Our home was near school, so we used to walk along with other schoolfriends. There was no real problem, but sometimes people would stop us on our way to school – it used to happen when there was a demonstration. I remember one day when some people came to school and started asking pupils about their ethnic groups. That's when I found out about mine; I was in Primary Four then. Each group had to stand up and register in turn and the Hutus went first. People's hatred towards the Tutsis was obvious at school. You would only be spared if your teacher was a Tutsi.

The situation was really complicated in 1990 during the multi-party system. The most influential political parties were MRD [*Mouvement Démocratique Républicain*], MRND [*Mouvement Révolutionnaire National pour le Développement* and PL [*Parti Libéral*]. I remember that my father managed to get membership cards for all three parties. When MRND members came to ask him which party he belonged to, he showed them the MRND card in order to protect us. After 1990, life was really different from before. Children started being more involved in ethnic groups and division.

The genocide

When the genocide started, we were at home. It was evening and we heard some classical music on the radio. Then Dad said to Mum, "Something has probably happened." They sent us to bed and stayed talking in the sitting room. The following morning, we heard that President Habyarimana had been killed in a plane crash. Our parents were very upset about the situation.

That same day, an order went out, asking people to go to roadblocks with their identity cards. My father respected the order and went to the roadblock, but the rest of the family stayed at home. When it was Dad's turn to show his card, he showed a Hutu ID. He had changed his real one – a lot of people used to do that. But there was an Adventist man at the roadblock who knew my Dad. He said, "Hey, Emmanuel, we all know you're a Tutsi, so there's no point trying to hide among those people." I remember that on that day, people had been given the order to kill all the Tutsis. Another man helped my father escape from that roadblock and he managed to get back home.

It was about six o'clock in the evening and Dad really looked sad. He kept saying, "Masabo has turned me in." As things were getting worse, Mum suggested we should hide, but Dad said, "It's better for you to hide without me." There was a small bean plantation behind the house so that's where we went. We hid there until we fell asleep – we were just kids – I was only eleven, my sister was eight and my brother five. In the morning, we found ourselves back at home again.

Soon after that, the perpetrators started going to Tutsis' homes to kill them. I remember that one day, my uncle – my father's younger brother – was shot as he walked along the street. That was 14 April 1994. He didn't die immediately; he lay there in agony. When Paul, his older brother, heard about it, he went rushing to that place, but as soon as he got there, the perpetrators killed him.

The perpetrators kept on coming to our house, but Dad gave them money and they spared us. Then one day, they came again – not for money this time. They were really determined that day. They asked Dad, "What's your relationship to Paul?" My father was well prepared for that question – he'd persuaded my aunt always to say that he and Paul were stepbrothers. The theory was that Paul's father was a Tutsi, but Dad's father was a Hutu. The perpetrators weren't really convinced by that, so they kept coming back, over and over again.

One day as Dad tried to go out, he met an *Interahamwe* [member of the Hutu militia] called Magambo – his name means 'words' and applies to someone who talks a lot. Magambo told him, "We've been looking for you all the time, Emmanuel. We know you're a Tutsi – and all the Tutsis must die... If you don't want to be killed, just give me money and I'll find a way to hide you." But Dad replied, "Enough! If you want to kill me, just do it now. I'm tired." Then he came back into the house and Magambo ran to call some other *Interahamwe*. They came back to the house and started looking for Dad, but he had managed to escape. The *Interahamwe* searched everywhere, but couldn't find him.

Two days later, soldiers came to our house. I was in my bedroom and I heard them telling my parents to sit close to one another. When they cocked their guns, I knew they were going to kill them. I didn't want to see my parents dying, so I managed to get outside. But there was an *Interahamwe* standing right outside. He asked me, "Where are you going?" and I said I was going to the toilet. Then he stared at me... I was wearing a rosary. "Give me that rosary," he said, "so we can pray before we go and kill!" I took off the rosary and gave it to him.

In the meantime, my Mum was gesturing to me, telling me to go to a neighbour called Rutayisire. He was a Hutu; he used to go to the roadblocks, but I don't know whether he killed or not. But I didn't go to Rutayisire's house; instead I went straight to see my aunt, whose house was near ours. When I told her that my parents were about to be killed, she put down the baby twins she was holding in her arms and ran to our house. But when she got there, the *Interahamwe* said, "We've been looking for you. Sit close to your brother so we can kill you both together."

I don't know how Rutayisire got to hear about what was happening, but he went to look for François, the chief *Interahamwe* of the area. François soon sent some soldiers to our house to stop the perpetrators from killing my parents, but the soldiers refused to leave without getting some money. Dad had to give them all the money in the house before they were spared.

It was about six o'clock in the morning, but an hour later, the *Interahamwe* came back again. This time, they took just my father – to Kinihira, where they used to kill people. When they got there, they told him to dig his own grave. He dug and then they made him check if he fitted in the grave... Suddenly, a man came and said, "Why do you want to kill Kanyantekwe's son? Kanyantekwe is a very good man; he's never hurt anyone!" One of the *Interahamwe* replied, "This man's a Tutsi and all Tutsis must die." But the man insisted and said, "If you dare to kill him, we'll shoot you!" They talked some more, then released Dad about one o'clock in the afternoon.

Dad came home and spent a few days without going out. But the next time he went out, he came across a huge group of attackers who beat him till he couldn't walk. A man carried him home and Mum tried to massage him with warm water, but it didn't help much. Mum told me, "Go and sleep at Rutayisire's place. His wife was a Tutsi and maybe you will survive there."

The killers didn't come that night. The following day, Dad walked with great difficulty to see me at Rutayisire's. He came and said, "My dear, I feel as if tonight is my last night. Why don't you come and sleep at home?" But I said I couldn't go because Mum had told me to stay there at Rutayisire's.

Dad went home and as soon as he went into the house, the *Interahamwe* came again. People had heard these *Interahamwe* saying that they had exactly four bullets for four people. They knocked on the door and when Dad opened, they ordered him and Mum to sit down. They said, "This time there's no mercy. We're going to kill you." And Dad replied, "You've been tracking and torturing me all this time. I'm tired... Just do it now." They shot him in the head immediately, but he didn't die straight away. Then another *Interahamwe* stabbed him and shot him again. Mum saw all that happen, then she said, "Do me a favour, please. Let me show you where to shoot me... Shoot me in the ear." Fortunately, they did what she asked. They shot her twice and she died at once.

The following morning, Misigwa, another of Dad's brothers, came and told Rutayisire that my parents had been killed. I was asleep, but when I heard my father's name, I woke up and ran home. When I opened the door, I screamed as I saw their swollen corpses in the chairs... My scream was so loud that it alerted the *Interahamwe* who were nearby. They came with their knives and machetes and asked me, "What's going on?" but I never said a word. I just stood there in the rain... Musigwa had spread the news to all our family members; then they arranged the funerals and buried my parents. That was 15 May 1994.

My younger brother and sister and I stayed there the whole day, waiting for the killers to come – but they didn't. The following day, they attacked my aunt's home and killed her husband immediately. When she tried to complain, they shot her as well. Their children ran into the bedroom and hid underneath the bed, but the perpetrators tracked them down. They pulled one kid out and shot him without wasting any time. But when the killers heard people screaming, they took off.

After that, I went to live at my grandfather's with my younger brother, sister and Mum's younger sister. But the house was surrounded by *Interahamwe*. When they heard that the RPF troops [Tutsi-led Rwandan Patriotic Front] had come close, they made us walk at the front of their group, saying, "Your fellow Tutsis have attacked. They'll probably spare us if they see you with us."

We walked up to Mount Kigali. There were bombings happening here and there, but the *Interahamwe* didn't want to let us go. We kept on walking until we got separated because of the bombing – my brother and sister went with those *Interahamwe* and I went on my own.

My brother and my sister went to Ruhengeri, where fortunately a lady who knew our family managed to take them when the killers were distracted. She told them to get on a bus – people told me that life went on normally in Ruhengeri during the genocide. The bus travelled just a few metres, then it was stopped by some *Interahamwe* who lived in our sector. They immediately removed my brother and sister from the bus and went to kill them. They hacked them and stabbed them...

Separated from the others, I kept on walking and never saw any of my family until we heard people say that the war was over.

After the genocide

Very few people survived in my family. The only place I could seek refuge afterwards was at my Grandma's – although she wasn't really my Grandma, she was my father's stepmother. So I stayed there and went back to school. Life was very hard. Life seemed bitter every time I thought about my family and how I had been left alone. Life no longer made any sense to me. Later on, I went to live with my aunt – that's where I am today. I'm in my second year at university now.

The future

I feel that unity and reconciliation are things that we ought to achieve. But sometimes I feel like forgiving and sometimes not – especially when I think about how people had no mercy on you, and when I realize the kind of life I'm living now... Although forgiving and reconciliation are hard, we know they're important.

I don't know what to say about the hope for future. I can't predict the future... I just want to have a happy life, go to school and do the things I want to. On the other hand, I don't want my grandchildren to suffer the kind of things that we went through. I want them to love one another – because that's what was missing in our society.

Manzi, 2006 © Aegis Trust

Alice, 2006 © Aegis Trust

Alice Uwimpuhwe

Focus on what lies ahead

Before the genocide

My name is Alice and I am from Tambwe commune, in Tambwe sector, Nyamagana district. That's where I was with both my parents when the war broke out. There were four children in our family. I was ten years old when the genocide happened.

When the war started, I remember seeing people coming to Dad, talking to him, threatening him, saying they would kill him. They were mainly our neighbours. It seemed like some sort of conflict. They were not friends.

The genocide

As time passed, I saw the war really spreading and we fled. I was still with both my parents then. My Dad was killed two days later. A man called Kayishema came and took him away and he never came back. We don't know what happened to him.

We were all still together – my mother, my brothers and sisters and me. Someone suggested we should find a way to go to Burundi, but when we reached the border, they told us it was too late – no more crossing was allowed. So we turned back.

On our way back, we met a group of killers who wanted to kill me first. Fortunately, a man called Kayigamba implored them to let me go with him – I had the same name as his daughter. He wanted me to work as a housemaid and help his children. The man felt sorry for me and later on, took me to his home.

My Mum continued on her way towards Ruhango. She wasn't among those who came back. Perhaps she was killed by the roadside. Neither my Mum nor my brothers and sisters survived – only two cousins and I survived in my family. I am the eldest now.

The war continued and I stayed with that man, but I was never treated like family. I was just a housemaid. Every night I used to hide somewhere in the bush and then they picked me up in the mornings. At Kayigamba's home I would go and harvest coffee, then take it to the grinding machine. Sometimes I used to fetch water to wash the coffee. They used to give me a lot of work because I was vulnerable. We spent the whole day in the coffee plantations.

Then Kayigamba came and said, "I got you from your Mum and I don't want your blood on my hands, so please go away. It's up to you to find a way to Ruhango." I told him I didn't know where to go. But another child who lived with that family escorted me to a small road to help me find my way. Then I remembered my uncle's place that we'd once passed by with Mum. I decided to pass by there, expecting to find somebody. But I found no one. The grass had grown everywhere.

When I was walking, I just used to guess the way. I would look at a hill in front of me and guess that if I got to the top, perhaps I'd be in such and such area... I was simply looking for a way to survive. I didn't cross roadblocks; I used to avoid them. Whenever I met somebody, I asked for information about the situation. When someone told me it was dangerous, I went through bushes.

After a while, I decided not to go home. I thought that if I got there, they would kill me like they'd killed Dad and maybe even my Mum. So I made up my mind to look for a job. The first person I met was a lady, but she told me she couldn't give a job to someone who looked like me. Then I met a young lady gathering roses to decorate her home. I said hello and asked if she needed a housemaid. She told me I should ask her grandmother who lived with her. So we went to her home and by the time we got there, it was raining heavily. I was shown a place to dry myself and used that opportunity to dry my sarong. That was when her Grandma came to me and asked me openly where I came from. I told her that I came from Ruhango. "And how did you get here?" she asked. I tried to lie, saying that I came with my parents, but she automatically knew what had happened. She told me that she couldn't take a child like me among her own, that I should try something else.

Her granddaughter then took me to meet Benjamin, her father – because she had no Mum. Her Dad was living with another woman with sons of her own, but those boys wanted to kill me. Benjamin stopped them because he loved his firstborn daughter so much. He said, "You can't kill this girl here in front of me." That's how I came to live with Benjamin for a while, along with another girl called Gakecuru. Benjamin was her father's best friend and her father had taken her there to keep her safe.

But then one day Benjamin came and told us, "I'm taking you to be killed." I told him frankly that he couldn't take me. He said that if I didn't believe him, he would take Gakecuru first to show me he was serious. So he took Gakecuru and she was killed.

When he came back, he said I would be next. I told him he should kill me himself instead of delivering me to the perpetrators. He used to say that he would let the perpetrators kill us so he wouldn't be responsible. I convinced him to take me back to the grandmother's house – I would perhaps spend one night there. That's what I told him.

Benjamin told his son, Camakoma, to escort me across the river and back to the grandmother's. But when I arrived there, she told me I couldn't spend the night in her house. At sunset, she threw me out and told me to go and look for another shelter. I realised it wasn't safe to stay in a region that I didn't know. I didn't know where to hide. In fact the grandmother took me to a hiding place, but I didn't trust her. I thought she would send the perpetrators to kill me.

I was desperate and decided to commit suicide. I threw myself into the river – but the river refused to take me. I just swallowed some water and found myself on the other side. When I was young, I used to hear that if you try and commit suicide with money in your pocket, you'll never die. I had 1,000 Rwandan francs. "Maybe that's why I can't die," I thought. So I took the money out of my pocket and went back into the river. Still I didn't die. The river was full because it was the rainy season. It threw me back on the bank. When the river rejected me, it was near morning and day started dawning. I could hear birds singing.

I went back and knocked at the grandmother's house. She told me that they came looking for me and couldn't find me where she left me. "I was around," I said. I spent the night there. The following day, the granddaughter and I went gathering groundnuts in the grandmother's field. That night she asked her Grandma to let me sleep in the house instead of going back to the bushes. She promised to take me next day to Emmanuel, head of the attackers, so he could decide what to do with me.

When we got to Emmanuel's, she said, "This girl is from Ruhango. I caught her when she was passing by." The man asked me, "Aren't you a Tutsi?" and I denied it, "My God, I'm not a Tutsi!" He asked me again, "Aren't you a Tutsi?" This time I said, "No, the truth is I was living with my Grandma in Butare and my Mum re-married in Ruhango. But I'm not a Tutsi." But he replied, "It's obvious from your looks." And I denied it again, "No, I'm not a Tutsi at all."

Emmanuel didn't believe me, but decided to put me on hold before killing me. They didn't kill me that night. In the morning I went back to the grandmother's, but she refused to receive me – she said she didn't want to see me being killed.

Her granddaughter said we should look for alternatives and I asked her where I could go when her Dad had chased me away. By then, the attackers were holding meetings. People in Bugesera had started fleeing. One time, I was sitting in a place called Migina with the granddaughter and a man came and pulled me from the roadside. He asked me what my tribe was, but I kept quiet. I had nothing to say... But there was another man there called Biya. He knew me very well and defended me in the meeting; he said I was from his family. That's how I survived the attackers that day. Biya told me to go home and asked his father to take me because he had a motorbike.

Biya left and I walked away with the old man, his father. We walked for about one kilometre, but then the other attackers followed me because they wanted to kill me. Some of them said they'd be in trouble if they touched Kayigamba's child – meaning me – because Kayigamba was a strong and respected man at the time. They asked the old man, "Are you taking her to Kayigamba's or to your home?" And he replied, "She's Kayigamba's child; he asked me to take her to him." So I went back to Kayigamba's and spent another week there.

Another man called Emmanuel came there as well. He was looking for somewhere to hide and found a place in a sorghum field near Kayigamba's house. There was a big tree that looked like a guava. He climbed it, but unfortunately Kayigamba saw him and told him to come down. He killed Emmanuel later in the same sorghum field.

I thought I would also be killed at some point. I'd heard that the *Inkotanyi* [RPF soldiers] were in our home village, but I didn't know how to get there. I'd been hiding with some girls – Grace and Mugeni, both older than me. "You never know, maybe you'll find some of your family again," they said. By then the war was very bad and it was impossible to imagine you would ever see them again. I thought we would go together, but the girls left me behind. I didn't know where to go.

The people I was living with told me to flee with them. So I fled with the families of perpetrators running away from the *Inkotanyi*. But because I wasn't Kayigamba's real daughter, he made me carry a very hot pot on my head. Every time, after cooking, they would ask me to carry the pot so we could continue our journey. After walking some distance, they'd ask me to go and fetch water. I remember I walked up to Rusatira. I realised I wasn't going to cope with the situation for long because their family used to eat maize paste every day – maize flour mixed with water. That was the only food that satisfied them. I was in charge of grinding the maize and separating the fine flour from the big particles. So I would grind until my hands got swollen. But that never stopped me from having to carry the pot whenever it was time to move on. It was my job every day.

When we reached Rusatira, the *Inkotanyi* came. But on the way, the perpetrators would kill some of the people fleeing with them. They sometimes abused me. As I said, I used to fetch water. One day, as I was planning to get it, Abayi came and said to me, "Alice, I know you very well. I know you're a Tutsi. I'm suggesting we kill you and then we proceed on our journey without you." I knew there was no point lying because it was true, he knew me. So I simply kept quiet. But my hands were swollen and he asked me, "What happened to your hands?" I told him I'd been grinding maize grains and got corns in my hands. Then they turned into boils and burst.

Abayi told some men to take me and kill me. But there was a dispute among the men – they couldn't decide who would kill me. That was in Rusatira. So then I decided to leave them and go back to where we came from. I thought, "There's no difference. I might still die. Even if I keep going with these perpetrators, they might reach somewhere and kill me. I can't change my fate much."

So I left them and headed back. I avoided using the main road and went through the bush instead. As I was walking, I met some *Inkotanyi* who were collecting children. They took me to the orphanage in Butare and I lived there until I started to think, "Well, I'm here but how come none of my family is here? Does it mean no one survived to come and get me out of here?"

I lived there for some time, then later I found my cousins. They were younger than me and on their own, so I decided to join them. When I left the orphanage and started to look after them, I was 16 or 17. At first, there was a man called Esile Gahigi who told us that he used to know our family. He said, "I knew your parents, in fact your father was my good friend. Don't worry, come home and I'll take care of you like my own children."

The three of us went to his home and at first lived there with no problem. But later his wife became a problem to us. She told him, "I can't handle the kids you brought; they're disobedient." So we left there and that's how I started being in charge of the 'family'. I was the oldest and life was very hard for us.

After the genocide

We went to see a man called Papa Alisa and told him, "As you can see, our home has been destroyed." We asked him to do us a favour and get us a shelter. We told him we were the only survivors of our family and would never burden him for food or other needs.

That's how we got our house, but it was very tough. We used to sit endlessly in the house and sometimes even go to sleep without eating anything. Even today, despite all the time that has gone by, we still sleep hungry sometimes.

My cousins and I go to school, but when we come back on holiday, we rely on people feeling sorry for us and giving us beans or cassava flour... We normally find a way to survive on what we've got. We occasionally worry, thinking about when the time comes to leave school and where we will go. We dread going back to our so-called home. At my age, I would normally have finished high school. Sometimes I stay at home because I've no means of going to school.

In short, life's really hard. I didn't go to school last term because of similar problems. Up to a few days ago, I managed to attend this current term, but life is still too hard. It's difficult to get a job. Nobody can employ me yet. Of course I could never work as a housemaid because I can't stand that job – where everyone insults you and people treat you as they want.

Papa Alisa helped us with the house until 1997 when he told us he wanted to make some money from it. So I went to see another old man, a Hutu who was one of Dad's friends. I asked him to help us get a small house – and he did. It was his servants' house and had a single bedroom with a small living room.

After some time, that old man said we should give him at least 1,000 Rwandan francs for rent, but I told him I couldn't get the money. "You know the way we live, it's your wife who sometimes helps us." People would look at us and I would feel ashamed, but I never begged for food – even when we were starving. And I stopped going to school because there was no one in the world to help us.

Today and the future

I dropped out of school for a whole year – until a few days ago when I realised I risked stopping my studies altogether. So I went back to school near the end of term. But I still had a lot of problems and needs – things like soap, Colgate and so on. There was so much poverty then. Then there were the transport problems. It was all really difficult.

Then the headmaster told me I'd missed so much school that I wouldn't be able to sit my final exams. But I went to the exam council and explained my problems, and they allowed me to enter for the exams. At first going to school was very hard for me. I borrowed 1,500 Rwandan francs from a fellow student. I told her that if all went well, I would repay her very soon. I took the money because I needed bus fare. Like other students, I go to class now, but my heart is always wondering, "After school, how will we get home and what will we find there?"

In a word that's how my life is – I am half-alive, half-dead. Life goes on.

I try to assure my cousins that things will change for the better. I convince them that the future will be good and we're going to get a better life.

I believe God is with us and if we behave ourselves, the future will be brighter. That's how we keep our morale up – even when we haven't had dinner. But sometimes we feel discouraged. When you have to miss dinner simply because there's no food, it's very distressing. We get what we eat by luck, when someone gives us cassava flour and maybe beans. Sometimes it's not only a problem of food – finding firewood can be stressful as well because you need firewood or charcoal to cook. That's the situation we're in. Sometimes I just sit down and pray. I believe God knows us and He is watching.

My major problems? Well, at my age, I'm supposed to have someone to care for me. I shouldn't be worried with problems of salt, soap or anything else at home. Sometimes I can't sleep because I have so many problems. I spend the whole night awake and maybe fall asleep in the morning. Sometimes I wonder if people perhaps have two hearts because there's always a voice that consoles me, telling me do this instead of that.

Reconciliation? Well, if someone came and told me they had killed my Mum and Dad and the others, frankly speaking, I think I could forgive them. In fact, I've already forgiven those who killed them even though I don't know them. The perpetrator who killed my uncle – my cousins' father – came and said to me, "Alice! You're the oldest, can't you forgive me?" I told him that I wasn't the one to forgive him. That was for my uncle's children to do. He ended up talking to my oldest cousin, but she refused to forgive him. But if someone who committed a crime against me asked me to forgive him and was really sorry, I think I could forgive him.

The kind of advice I would give to orphans taking care of themselves after the genocide is that first of all they should be appreciative. They should be happy with the kind of life they are leading. I know it's not the best life, but they should have a positive attitude. They should focus on what lies ahead. For example, I am a student. I have to be happy with being a student – even though I had nothing to eat for dinner. If you're happy with the little you have and content with who you are, the rest will come slowly.

The main problem today is how to survive. We should be united and love one another. If all Rwandans were united, we could find a way to prevent genocide from happening again.

Alice, 2006 © Aegis Trust

Kigali Memorial Centre, 2004 © www.photographic-images.co.uk

Kigali Memorial Centre

The stories in this book are taken from the archive of the Kigali Memorial Centre, based at the burial site of some 250,000 victims of the genocide.

Back in 2002, the then Mayor of Kigali, Théoneste Mutsindashyaka, had a vision that the burial site at Gisozi in Kigali should become a place of dignified remembrance and learning. He invited Aegis Trust to work with the Kigali City Council to see that vision fulfilled.

The Kigali Memorial Centre is both a place of remembrance and a place of education. As such, when the past is remembered, one central aim is to learn from that memory to make a safer future.

The permanent exhibition of the Kigali Memorial Centre opened in April 2004 with the support of the William J. Clinton Foundation, the Belgian Government and the Swedish Government.

Before producing the exhibition, it was important to hear the stories of people who were there, who understand more than anyone the meaning of genocide. Their stories formed the beginning of the Genocide Documentation Centre at the Kigali Memorial Centre and this book is the first in a series of publications of testimonies about the genocide.

Aegis campaigns against genocide worldwide and is a membership organisation. It has its home in the Holocaust Centre in the UK and offices in Rwanda and London. It undertakes education and awareness programmes, with a view to influencing policy in relation to the prevention of genocide. It also runs a social programme to address the consequences for those still suffering in the aftermath of genocide.

www.kigalimemorialcentre.org
www.aegistrust.org

Visitors at the Centre, 2004 © www.photographic-images.co.uk

Sculptures in the permanent exhibition © www.photographic-images.co.uk

A section of the permanent exhibition © www.photographic-images.co.uk

Vedaste, a Guide at the Kigali Memorial Centre, 2004 © www.photographic-images.co.uk

Construction of mass graves, Kigali Memorial Centre, 2004 © Aegis Trust

Mass graves in the grounds of Kigali Memorial Centre, 2004 © www.photographic-images.co.uk